Popular Support for an Undemocratic Regime

The Changing Views of Russians

To survive, all forms of government require popular support, whether voluntary or involuntary. Following the collapse of the Soviet system, Russia's rulers took steps toward democracy, yet under Vladimir Putin Russia has become increasingly undemocratic. This book uses a unique source of evidence, eighteen surveys of Russian public opinion from the first month of the new regime in 1992 up to 2009, to track the changing views of Russians. Clearly presented and sophisticated figures and tables show how political support has increased because of a sense of resignation that is even stronger than the uncertain economic reliance on exporting oil and gas. Russia is not only an outstanding example of popular support increasing for a government that rejects democracy, but is also representative of a surprising number of regimes around the world that have been able to mobilize popular support for undemocratic regimes.

RICHARD ROSE is Director of the Centre for the Study of Public Policy and Sixth Century Professor of Politics at the University of Aberdeen.

WILLIAM MISHLER is Professor of Government and Public Policy at the University of Arizona, Visiting Professor of Political Science at the University of Aberdeen, and co-editor of the *Journal of Politics*.

NEIL MUNRO is currently a visiting lecturer in the Department of Asian Studies at the University of Edinburgh and was formerly a senior research fellow in the Centre for the Study of Public Policy at the University of Aberdeen.

Popular Support for an Undemocratic Regime

The *Changing* Views of Russians

Richard Rose, William Mishler
and Neil Munro

CAMBRIDGE
UNIVERSITY PRESS

CAMBRIDGE UNIVERSITY PRESS
Cambridge, New York, Melbourne, Madrid, Cape Town,
Singapore, São Paulo, Delhi, Mexico City

Cambridge University Press
The Edinburgh Building, Cambridge CB2 8RU, UK

Published in the United States of America by
Cambridge University Press, New York

www.cambridge.org
Information on this title: www.cambridge.org/9780521224185

First published 2011
Reprinted 2013

Printed and bound in the United Kingdom by the MPG Books Group

A catalogue record for this publication is available from the British Library

Library of Congress Cataloging-in-Publication Data
Rose, Richard, 1933–
   Popular support for an undemocratic regime : the changing views of Russians /
Richard Rose, William Mishler and Neil Munro.
      p.   cm.
   Includes bibliographical references and index.
   ISBN 978-1-107-00952-3 (Hardback) – ISBN 978-0-521-22418-5 (Paperback)
   1. Russia (Federation)–Politics and government–1991–   2. Russia (Federation)–
Economic conditions–1991–   3. Russia (Federation)–Social conditions–1991–
4. Democratization–Russia (Federation)   5. Democracy–Russia (Federation)
6. Political participation–Russia (Federation)   7. Post-communism–Russia
(Federation)   I. Mishler, William, 1947–   II. Munro, Neil, 1970–   III. Title.
   DK510.763.R662 2011
   947.086–dc22
                                                                        2011001820

ISBN 978-1-107-00952-3 Hardback
ISBN 978-0-521-22418-5 Paperback

Contents

Figures

Tables

Introduction: The need for popular support

The history of government is first of all a story of the state's capacity to mobilize support. Notwithstanding big differences between democratic and undemocratic political systems, they have one thing in common: All forms of government require political support to maintain their authority (Finer, 1997; Vu, 2010). Max Weber characterized authority as *Herrschaft*, a term connoting domination not democratization (1947: 152n). The pyramids of Egypt are a monument to the power of pharaohs to mobilize enough support to build a political system that lasted many centuries. North Korea is a striking contemporary example of a regime that has lasted more than half a century by using totalitarian methods to coerce citizens to be resigned to give it a show of support. However, the evolution of Anglo-American democracies shows that popular support can be achieved without coercion.

In the short term a regime may survive by coercion, for example, a puppet regime established by an occupation army; however, the long-term survival of a regime requires voluntary support or at least the resigned acceptance of the mass of its population. The history of the past century shows that many regimes have been assigned to the ash can of history because of a lack of support. For decades the Soviet Union appeared to be secure with the support of its citizens, and elsewhere in the Communist bloc regimes appeared to demonstrate that governments could rest on bayonets. The abrupt collapse of these regimes demonstrates the contingency of coercion as a source of support.

The eruption of competitive elections on many continents raised hopes of arriving at "the end of history" through the spread of democratic ideas and institutions (Fukuyama, 1992). National governments, with the United States in the lead, have funded many democracy assistance projects (see e.g. Carothers, 2004). Aspirations to democratize the world reached a climax with the introduction of competitive elections in Iraq and Afghanistan. The consequence has

been a rediscovery of the need to have a state as a pre-condition
of democratization (e.g. Weber, 1947; Almond and Coleman, 1960;
Rose, 2009a).

Failed hopes for democratization have now raised concerns about a
"democratic roll back" (Diamond, 2008) and even "the erosion of
political support in advanced industrial democracies" (Dalton, 2004: 1)
because of a decline in political trust and satisfaction with the way
that democracy is working (see e.g. Pharr and Putnam, 2000; Listhaug
et al., 2009). Some scholars of undemocratic regimes write about
"authoritarian resilience" and the "durability" of authoritarian
regimes (Brownlee, 2007), while others find evidence of "competitive
authoritarianism" creating openings for democratization (Levitsky
and Way, 2010a). Many studies have ambiguous implications (Gilley,
2010: 163). For example, Robert Putnam's (1993) theory of how social
capital contributed to *Making Democracy Work* in northern Italy also
shows that in southern Italy, where trust is harder to find, the consequence is *Making Democracy Fail*.

The regimes that rulers supply

What people are asked to support is determined by the character of the
regime that political elites supply. A government that does not rely on
elections to secure support is not failing to democratize; it is seeking
support for an undemocratic regime. There is a vast literature differentiating democratic regimes from each other and also differentiating
undemocratic regimes (see e.g. Linz, 2000; Haerpfer *et al.*, 2009). This
has led to a proliferation of adjectives qualifying the two terms. David
Collier and Steven Levitsky (1997) have identified more than 500
ways of describing "democracy with adjectives." Juan Linz has likewise been prolific in creating a typology of "authoritarian regimes
with adjectives." In particular, Linz emphasizes the difference between
undemocratic regimes that make totalitarian claims on their subjects
and those that limit their demands. Barbara Geddes (1999) and Axel
Hadenius and Jan Teorell (2007) emphasize subcategories of undemocratic rule in the form of military regimes, personal dictatorships,
party states, monarchies and theocracies.

Support reflects the interaction of political elites and the mass of their
citizens. Democratic governments are meant to do what the people
want. Governors claim the support of the governed because they hold

office by winning elections. The need to seek re-election makes elective officeholders willing to supply what voters want (Schumpeter, 1952). The ability to give direction to government at the ballot box makes those who vote for losing parties as well as those endorsing the winners prepared to support a regime that allows for a change in the government of the day. An election that changes those in charge of government does not signify the withdrawal of support from the regime. It shows that the system works by giving voters a chance to turn out of office governors who fail to do what they want.

To treat an undemocratic regime as the possession of a political elite is to see only half of what makes it effective, because it ignores how citizens respond to the demands of their leaders. Just as a democratic regime can mobilize support by its political and economic performance, so can an undemocratic regime. The first modern states, such as Prussia and the absolute monarchy of France, were "police states," because they created institutions effective in maintaining order and the rule of law (North *et al.*, 2009). This encouraged the development of voluntary support on the grounds that order was preferable to disorder. Today, Singapore is an example of an undemocratic regime that claims support by maintaining order through the rule of law. A nationalist or populist regime may rely on the "soft power" of ideological persuasion to rally support. However, this leaves open to question whether subjects believe what the regime promotes. Many undemocratic regimes employ arbitrary or repressive methods to mobilize a show of support. Coerced subjects may respond by using "weapons of the weak" in efforts to get around some of its demands (Scott, 1985; Havel *et al.*, 1985; Wedel, 1986), and harsh repression may lead subjects to combine their resources in a rebellion (Acemoglu and Robinson, 2006).

A regime that has indefinitely maintained support without challenge is often described as stable or consolidated. However, these terms imply an absence of change. It is more appropriate to describe such a regime as showing durability. A durable regime maintains support by adapting to changes that occur in its domestic and international environment. The United States Constitution, for example, has survived since 1787 because it has adapted to major changes in the scale, composition and demands of its citizens. Durability is not synonymous with democracy (cf. Chapter 9 and Przeworski *et al.*, 1996). The Kingdom of Saudi Arabia is an absolute Islamic monarchy that has maintained itself since 1932. This makes it much older than most regimes of the member states of the United Nations and of the European Union.

An undemocratic regime is most vulnerable to support being challenged by a split in its political elite (Bueno de Mesquita *et al.*, 2003). The importance of elite unity is illustrated by contrasting developments in the world's two largest and longest-lasting Communist regimes, the Soviet Union and the People's Republic of China. The Soviet regime fell not because of the withdrawal of support by the mass of its citizens. It fell because Mikhail Gorbachev's reform initiatives provoked a self-destructive split within the Central Committee of the Communist Party that led to the break-up of the party-state. In China, by contrast, after winning a civil war the leaders of the Chinese Communist Party have maintained both their unity and a show of popular support (Shi, 2008) notwithstanding substantial reversals of policy as well as changes in leadership. Since the break between Moscow and Beijing, China has carefully followed developments in Russia in order to learn lessons about how to avoid an elite split that would threaten the collective privileges of the leaders of the Chinese Communist Party (Marsh, 2005: 5ff.; Shambaugh, 2008).

When a regime does collapse, political elites must supply a new set of institutions with untested prospects for survival. The failure of the new regime's predecessor is a stark reminder that success cannot be taken for granted. However, there is no guarantee that the new regime will be democratic. A recurring feature of Middle Eastern politics is the replacement of one undemocratic regime by another (Posusney, 2004). Holding elections is no guarantee of support being forthcoming. Today, Iraq, Afghanistan and Pakistan each have an elected government, a major change from rule by a despotic Saddam Hussein, the Taliban or an army general. However, from Islamabad to Baghdad there is palpable evidence that elected governments are administering "failed states," because they lack the support needed to maintain order.

The Berlin Wall illustrates the capacity of an undemocratic regime to coerce a show of support indefinitely – but also its vulnerability. Before the Wall was built in 1961 Germans could voluntarily move between East and West Germany. Millions of subjects of the East German Communist regime "voted with their feet" and walked to West Berlin in order to become citizens of the democratic Federal

Republic of Germany. The Wall was put up by the East German regime to prevent its subjects escaping from its demands. The regime's security service, the Stasi, used hundreds of thousands of informers to intimidate subjects to give at least a passive show of support, and border guards were ready to shoot to kill the few who sought to escape its coercive system (Koehler, 1999). However, when Gorbachev announced as part of his reform program that the Soviet Union would no longer support the East German regime in coercing its subjects, massive street demonstrations showed its lack of support. Within a year the East German regime had disappeared.

Plan of the book

In order to address an issue of broad relevance to comparative politics, the persistence of undemocratic regimes, we first show the importance of popular support in maintaining undemocratic as well as democratic regimes. This is a counsel of realism rather than despair, for the majority of states in the United Nations today are not durable democracies. Secondly, the book explains why, with the passage of time, support for the Russian regime has grown, notwithstanding the fact that it has concurrently become more undemocratic. Since support is open to challenge at critical junctures (Capoccia and Keleman, 2007), the third object is to test the robustness of popular support in response to challenges. We examine the predictable challenge of dealing with succession to the presidency when Vladimir Putin stepped down as president after reaching the constitutional limit of two terms of office and the unexpected challenge of the 2008 economic crisis, which threatened the prosperity that has contributed substantially to developing support. The political inertia of the passage of time has consolidated a mixture of active and passive support for a regime that Russians now see, to use Juan Linz's (1990b) phrase, as "the only game in town."

This book takes a bottom-up approach to governance. It relates the regime supplied by the political elite to the support that is given or withheld by ordinary Russians through the analysis of a unique series of surveys, the New Russia Barometer (NRB). The critical time for tracking the development of or the failure to develop popular support is in its early years. It is not possible to do so in regimes established long before the development of public opinion surveys (for exceptions, see Weil, 1989; Noelle-Neumann, 1995). In recently established regimes, most surveys of public opinion have been undertaken soon after their launch, when citizens have not had enough time to judge them on the basis of their experience. This book is different, because the New Russia Barometer began interviewing Russians in the first month of the Russian Federation in January 1992. In all, eighteen nationwide NRB surveys have been conducted, in quiet times as well as when elections stirred up political interest. The latest survey included here was conducted a year after Dmitry Medvedev became president and the economic crisis hit the country (see www.abdn.ac.uk/cspp). The result is a data base beginning when Russians were hesitant or negative about the new regime and spanning the new consensus of support that has emerged. This dynamic is captured in the book's subtitle – *The Changing Views of Russians*.[1]

Because our study sets out to explain why some Russians support the regime and others do not, we avoid the mistake of assuming that the unitary nature of the state leads to a unity of public opinion (Katzenstein, 2009). Unlike the approach of area studies specialists, it avoids what Amartya Sen (2006: 45) calls the "illusion of singularity" by applying generic concepts to the experience of Russia. Since most regimes in the world are undemocratic or only partially democratic, the Russian system may today be more typical of how the world's peoples are governed than are Anglo-American democracies.

Chapter 1 sets out two contrasting stylized models of the generation of popular support: a democratic model in which support is a consequence of government doing what its citizens demand and an undemocratic model in which subjects indicate their support by responding to demands from government. A wide variety of theories offer reasons why individuals give support to or withhold support from their regime. These range from a belief that it is legitimate to the resigned acceptance of it as a lesser evil. In practice, every regime relies on a mixture of motivations. A review of World Values Survey data about endorsement of democracy as an ideal and of support for a regime finds that support, on average, is just as high in countries that are undemocratic as in countries with democratic regimes.

---

[1] Unless otherwise noted we use the word "Russians" to refer to all citizens of the Russian Federation, regardless of their ethnicity. The preamble of the country's 1993 constitution declares it is a compact of "We the multinational people of the Russian Federation."

During the political life of the median Russian adult, the country's leaders have brought about abrupt changes in the regime that they supplied. The earliest memories of such a person are of socialization into a totalitarian or post-totalitarian regime that had no hesitancy about coercing subjects. This regime was disrupted when Gorbachev's efforts to strengthen the Soviet regime through reform opened up a struggle between himself, hardline Communists opposed to change, and a renegade Communist, Boris Yeltsin. This led to the collapse of the Soviet Union and the creation of a Russian Federation confronted with the challenges of a transformed polity, economy and state. Initially, competitive elections offered Russians a choice between those more sympathetic to the old regime and supporters of the new regime under President Yeltsin. Chapter 2 charts the uneven and unexpected course of events that showed Yeltsin was better at disrupting Soviet institutions than at institutionalizing a new regime.

After becoming Russia's second president, Vladimir Putin made order his first priority, starting with enhancing the power of the Kremlin. Chapter 3 shows how the mass of the population was asked to show their support at elections in which competition had been closed down by alterations in election laws, intimidation of the media, and establishing United Russia as the "party of power." This has created what Putin's advocates describe as a "sovereign democracy," in which the sovereignty of the state takes precedence.

Chapter 4 draws on NRB surveys to track changes in the way in which Russians have evaluated what the leaders of the Russian Federation have supplied since the wreckage of the Soviet Union. It finds that a big majority of Russians regard democracy as ideal and that they think the new regime falls short of their ideal. Nonetheless, while the regime has been becoming less democratic, support for it has been growing and is now at the same or a higher level than support for Central and East European democracies that were once part of the Communist bloc. Since every NRB survey finds differences of opinion about the regime, four hypotheses are offered to explain variations: Political support varies with socialization, with political performance, with economic performance, and with the passage of time.

The breadth of topics covered in NRB surveys provides many indicators for testing hypotheses about the causes of support, such as social changes due to the turnover of generations, political performance in fighting corruption, fluctuations in the economy, the ineluctable passage of time, or a combination of multiple influences. Chapter 5 details the results of analyses that emphasize the importance of political performance for support, such as priceless political gains in freedom. It also shows that the economic influences that matter most are how people evaluate the national economy rather than their own household's circumstances.

Because political support for a new regime cannot be achieved overnight, it is an excellent example of Weber's dictum that politics is about the slow drilling of hard boards. With the passage of time performance makes evident how a new regime differs from its predecessor. The longer it remains in place the greater the likelihood that its subjects will abandon any expectation that it could be replaced. Chapter 6 sets out the results of an innovative statistical analysis showing that the passage of time has been of greatest importance in causing the great majority of Russians to support their regime.

Political shorthand often confuses political regimes with political personalities, for example, speaking of Putin's Russia, Bush's America or Blair's Britain. However, a regime is meant to be durable rather than expire with the passing of a leader. The 1993 Russian constitution imposed a two-term limit on the office of president. In a stable regime, such a limit presents no threat, since it is the office rather than the individual that is the object of support. In regimes in which support is problematic, leadership succession can threaten a struggle within the political elite that is resolved by a change in regime. If Putin had held on to the presidency by bending or breaking the constitution, this would have confirmed fears of the regime becoming a system of personal rule as in post-Soviet Central Asia. Chapter 7 shows how at this critical juncture Putin finessed the challenge by making himself prime minister and nominating his protege, Medvedev, as president. Although Western observers described the subsequent presidential election as unfair, Russians did not – and support for the regime remained high.

Since the national economy is one of the most important influences on political support, the 2008 global economic crisis was also a challenge to support. It abruptly produced a big fall in Russia's gross domestic product (GDP) and a rise in the number who were not paid regularly even though in work. Chapter 8 uses evidence from the NRB survey a year after the crisis began to determine to what extent support has been depressed by the reversal of the national economy.

While this lowered support, the effect was largely offset by the passage of time having created so big a cushion of support that a big majority of Russians continue to be positive about the regime.

The capacity of the Russian regime to maintain support when confronted with challenges confirms the potential for an undemocratic regime to become a durable regime. However, the transformation of Russia two decades ago is a reminder that undemocratic regimes are not proof against failure. The final chapter asks: What could disrupt the political equilibrium that has emerged in the Russian Federation? It compares the durability of Russia's regime with that of other post-Soviet regimes and marshals a global array of surveys to test the importance of political support for undemocratic as well as democratic regimes.

Because historical events and institutions provide "hard" data about the political context in which surveys ask people their opinions, this book offers a crosslevel account of the interaction between the performance of the regime that elites supply and the response of its subjects. It draws upon the work of institutionalists such as Archie Brown (2009), Richard Sakwa (e.g. 2008a) and Stephen White (2011) and of political sociologists such as Vladimir Shlapentokh (1989, 2001), and on Russian government sources too. Unlike studies of elections, this book is not concerned with why people support a particular party (see e.g. Colton and Hale, 2009) but with why people support a regime that international observers characterize as undemocratic in its conduct of elections and much else. Unlike James Gibson *et al.* (1992), we are less concerned with the cultural preferences of Russians than with how Russians slowly develop support for a regime that they see as incongruent with their preference for a complete democracy (Whitefield, 2009).

In the two decades since the New Russia Barometer was launched, the authors have accumulated many debts. Tens of thousands of Russians have given us their views about how their country is governed in interviews conducted by the Levada Center. Its staff has behaved with great professionalism and integrity, notwithstanding political and economic difficulties of maintaining a not-for-profit research institute originally founded in the final years of the Soviet Union as VCIOM, the All-Russian Center for Public Opinion. The complete set of surveys is now available from the United Kingdom Data Archive. Stephen White and Neil Robinson made helpful comments on a draft of this manuscript. The preparation of this book has been supported by a grant from the British Economic and Social Research Council (RES-062-23-0341) for Testing the Durability of Regime Support in Russia: The Challenge of Putin's Term Limits. Earlier New Russia Barometer surveys have been supported by grants from scientific, governmental and private foundations in Austria, Germany, Hungary, Sweden and the United States as well as the ESRC; from the program on the effects of relative deprivation on health led by Sir Michael Marmot at the University College London Medical School; and from the World Bank and UN agencies. At no point has any of these organizations sought to exert influence on the design or content of questionnaires or on the interpretation of survey results. This has always been the responsibility of social science authors.

Ideas in this book have been presented in academic seminars, conferences and public policy meetings in places ranging from Washington and Berkeley to Berlin, Vienna, Moscow and Tokyo. Articles from work in progress have been published in peer-reviewed academic journals devoted to political science; journals concerned with Russia and post-Communist countries; in social medicine journals; in the Studies in Public Policy series of the Centre for the Study of Public Policy (CSPP); and in shorter commentaries on public policy (for a list, see www.abdn.ac.uk/cspp). A number have been published in the Russian-language *Bulletin* of the Levada Center. A complementary book by the senior author, *Understanding Post-Communist Transformation: A Bottom Up Approach* (2009c), compares the experience of Russians with Central and East Europeans who are now citizens of democratic states of the European Union.

While this book builds on previous work, it is not nor could it be a repeat of what has previously been published. In the five years since our previous book (Rose, Mishler and Munro 2006), Russians have experienced a change of presidents and a reversal in economic fortunes, and their responses to these developments have been tracked in four nationwide New Russia Barometer surveys. Equally important, in keeping with the priorities of the Russian regime today, the emphasis of this book is not on democratic institutions such as elections, but on why a regime that is not beholden to the Western idea of electoral democracy has gained and maintained the political support of Russians.

1 | Democratic and undemocratic models of support

The concept of political support has been developed to answer a seemingly simple question: "How can any political system ever persist?" (Easton, 1965: 15). This shifts attention from a static analysis of institutions to the dynamic interaction between government and the governed. In David Easton's (1965: 159ff.) classic theoretical framework, political support is about "citizens orienting themselves favorably toward the regime." The lack of a favorable orientation toward the regime need not express endorsement of an alternative regime. Instead, it can reflect a lack of interest in politics or skepticism about whether the regime's performance will match its promises. Although these attitudes are not favorable, they are a second-best alternative, for people with no interest in politics or skeptical of whoever holds office are unlikely to be active opponents of the powers that be.

Compliance with core political laws is the behavioral manifestation of support. Whereas citizens want government to be responsive to their demands, governors want compliance with their demands. Core political laws are the "primary rules" that a regime uses to maintain its authority (Hart, 1961: ch. 5; Rose, 1969: 604ff.). Whether or not people approve core laws, there should be a high probability that the demands of governors will be obeyed by those whom they claim to govern (Weber, 1947: 152). What constitutes core political laws differs between cultures and context. In a theocratic Islamic regime a woman appearing in public with her head uncovered or face unveiled may be deemed to violate a core political law. By contrast, in Turkey a woman wearing a head scarf in a public office would be challenging a core law of that country's secular constitution.

In a democratic political system, core laws are a small portion of all laws on the statute books. They concern matters such as obeying decisions of the highest court in the land or accepting an obligation to perform military service. Most law violations are anti-social acts that disturb society but not the political order, for example, driving much faster than the speed limit or robbery at gunpoint. The motive in shooting a policeman illustrates this distinction. In a regime whose authority is unchallenged, killing a policeman is an anti-social act. However, the Irish Republican Army has shot hundreds of police in Northern Ireland as a political act intended to undermine a regime it refuses to support. The more a regime is inclined toward totalitarianism, an ideology justifying the state's claim to control all spheres of social life (Friedrich and Brzezinski, 1965), the greater the number of everyday activities classified as "crimes against the state." In the Soviet Union listening to a foreign radio station was classified as a subversive political act.

Individuals will give active support and voluntary compliance to a regime that they think is legitimate, that is, there is a congruence between how people think they ought to be governed and how the regime actually governs (Lipset, 1959: 77). As Easton (1965: 278) explains, if citizens see the regime as "conforming to their own moral principles and their own sense of what is right and proper," then they will "obey the authorities and abide by the requirements of the regime." It is ethnocentric for Western policymakers to assume that people will only support a political system that is just like ours. A fully legitimate regime does not have to be democratic. Subjects can be favorably oriented toward their regime for any number of reasons. For example, a theocratic regime may secure support if its subjects believe its religious values are right, and those who believe in national self-determination may support a regime that suppresses its minorities.

When individuals do not give active support to their regime, they may nonetheless comply with its core political laws on the grounds that it is a lesser evil than its predecessor; because there is no feasible alternative; or because they fear that failure to comply risks sanctions at work or at home. When this leads to resigned acceptance and passive support of the regime, as happened in the Soviet Union under Josef Stalin, then totalitarian pressures can be reduced, as occurred in post-Stalinist times. Extreme measures of coercion, involving surveillance of the private lives of individuals, arrest or terror, require the regime to invest substantial resources. Moreover, the more brutal the degree of repression, the greater the risk that this stimulates more dissent (see S. Carey, 2010).

The greater a regime's active support, the more effectively and efficiently it can govern (Gamson, 1968; Weatherford, 1987). The capacity to mobilize substantial support is important when a regime is at war. In World War II Winston Churchill mobilized a coalition of democratic parties to defend Britain and Stalin mobilized support to defend the totalitarian Soviet Union. Active support is also important when the national economy faces a major challenge that can be met only by policies that impose major costs on citizens.

The goal of governors is to maintain or achieve a consensus of support, that is, support so widespread in the population that opponents of the regime are relatively few and isolated. Where there is a consensus, support for a regime can be described as consolidated, and this is the case whether it is democratic or undemocratic. Where a consensus is lacking, as in a new regime, the trajectory of support is important. As long as a new regime is gaining popular support, this discourages doubters from challenging it and creates social pressures on doubters to comply with core political laws. However, if a new regime has little support, then any loss will encourage ambitious politicians to offer a replacement.

Mixing support and compliance

The relationship between governors and governed can be modeled in principal–agent terms. In a democratic political system, citizens are the principals and governors are the agents, complying with popular demands. By contrast, in an undemocratic system, governors are the principals and subjects are the agents, complying with what the government demands. In the ideal-type models outlined in Figure 1.1, the underlying political values are in conflict. In reality, the two models are complementary. Because all forms of regime require both support and compliance, regimes differ in the way in which they mix responsiveness to popular demands and pressures for subjects to respond to what the regime demands (see Almond and Verba, 1963: 17ff.).

In the "We the people" model, popular participation is the prime mover in the political process (Figure 1.1A). Citizens actively input demands to government at elections, by participation in civic organizations and vicariously through opinion polls. In a consolidated regime citizens positively input support, for they have been socialized to regard it as legitimate. This assures the governors of voluntary compliance with core political laws and a willingness to comply with

A. Support model

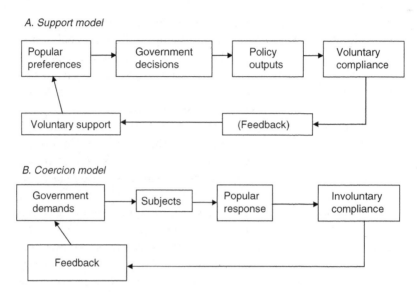

Source: Adapted and expanded by the authors from Easton (1965: 32).

Figure 1.1 Models of political support

government demands to pay the taxes needed to fund public policies. If the policy outputs of government are acceptable, this will generate feedback that reinforces popular support. If they are not, then in a democracy citizens can voice their dissatisfaction at the ballot box. Turning an unpopular government out of office can increase support for the regime because it shows "the system works."

Governors, as agents of the citizenry, are expected to have the technical and political skills to produce policy outputs that meet citizen demands. Insofar as this is done, the impact of policies feeds back to citizens who hold governors accountable for their performance. If governors are responsive to popular demands, feedback from their actions will maintain a high level of active support and compliance. The participant model of support and compliance has been developed in established Western democracies in which the same "rules of the game" are accepted by both politicians as players and by citizens who can enforce these rules at periodic elections.

In Figure 1.1B, individuals are not citizens but subjects; the model is supply-driven. The leaders of the regime decide what they want their subjects to do and people are expected to comply with these demands. Subjects are not encouraged to make demands on the regime. However, they are expected to pay careful attention to what governors demand. Whether or not the regime's demands are welcome, subjects are expected to comply with them. If the regime making demands is not regarded as legitimate, then compliance will be involuntary and the support coerced from subjects will be passive.

Methods used to coerce subjects vary from soft to hard. Soft measures involve intimidation such as threatening people with difficulties with government if they do not comply with the regime's demands. A military regime may appeal for support on the grounds that it delivers order, while also having weapons of coercion at hand. A personal dictator may, like a democratic populist, appeal for support on the grounds of "trust me." One-party regimes may invoke foreign threats or ideologies to justify their demands. Physical coercion can be soft, for example, preventing people from traveling abroad or controlling the ability to listen to foreign radio broadcasts, or it can be hard, enforced by omnipresent police or paramilitary groups. The occasional use of terror, the systematic use of arrest, imprisonment, torture and even execution, not only disposes of opponents but also creates fear among the surviving mass (Yakovlev, 2002: ch. 2). Totalitarian regimes are extreme in the methods used to coerce involuntary support from subjects.

Ideal-type models can clarify differences between theories of support and compliance, but they oversimplify, because in every political system the two are mixed. Popularly elected regimes will make some demands on subjects that they must comply with, like it or not, and a minority of citizens will give only passive support. Undemocratic regimes will make some demands that are popular with subjects and receive voluntary compliance. Gabriel A. Almond and Sidney Verba (1963: 17ff.) conclude that in a civic culture many citizens sometimes act as principals voicing demands while at other times acting as passive subjects of authority. In undemocratic regimes rulers can gain some active support and compliance by distributing benefits selectively to individuals or, in a multi-ethnic society, to one ethnic group. Oil-rich countries can use their petro-revenue to finance benefits that subjects gladly take up. Whether the chief component in the mix is contributed by popular demands or government pressure, the primary need in all types of regimes is for popular support and compliance.

Theories of support

Institutional theories of support emphasize the importance for political attitudes and behavior of the incentives, opportunities and sanctions that the choice of institutions offers. This is especially so in new regimes, when elites make choices between different combinations of democratic or undemocratic institutions and about what to do about those who served the old regime, whether in very visible political posts as low-level officials or as officials of its security forces (cf. Rustow, 1970; di Palma, 1990; Hall and Taylor, 1996). A combination of choices about how the new regime is to govern and who governs will determine whether there is a consensus among elites about maintaining the new regime or disagreements leading to competition between its adherents and those who support its overthrow.

There is still the need to secure popular support, whatever the institutions that elites supply. Long before democracy became the dominant frame of reference in political sociology, Max Weber (1947: 115ff., 328ff.) famously identified multiple grounds for supporting a regime as legitimate: tradition, values and charismatic appeal. He also distinguished between absolute values such as the rule of law and those based on instrumental rational calculations of the benefit of giving support and the costs of withholding it. With suitable adaptation, these categories remain relevant to theories of popular support for contemporary regimes.

Before the advent of mass literacy and mass telecommunications, *socialization into a tradition* could create durable support. A traditional political culture encouraged support for the existing regime as the only one we know by stressing values and beliefs drawn from the regime's history and excluding alternative forms of government as unacceptable because untraditional. This is most likely to be effective for those predisposed to take little interest in participating in politics. Neo-traditional support can be found today in regimes that have been maintained for so long that support is a matter of habit rather than reasoning or calculation. In the United States, England and Sweden, many citizens would literally find it impossible to imagine any system of government other than the current regime, because it is the only one they know.

Traditional support arises from a process of socialization that begins in early life, as children learn beliefs and norms of their political culture from parents, teachers and others in their community (for a classic statement, see Easton and Dennis, 1969; Jennings, 2007). They also learn what is expected of them as adults, whether it is to exercise the civic duty of voting or to avoid political discussions because this can lead to trouble with a repressive regime. Youthful socialization also creates emotional affect, for example, pride in one's country and its traditions. What one learns from socialization depends upon where one is socialized. The United States provides a striking example of traditional socialization, for history and civics courses in American schools not only provide information about the 1787 American Constitution but also encourage the view that it is the best of all possible forms of government. Similarly, the People's Republic of China socializes children to support it as the form of government best suited to Chinese traditions.

Socialization theories assume continuity in individual outlooks and political institutions. What is learned early in life affects adult experience of politics. Unexpected events can immediately affect both governors and governed, and journalists can treat such headline events as the only thing that matters for political support and much else. However, such a theory of "instant resocialization" implies that there will be many changes in popular attitudes each year and each headline event will have its effect washed away by the next event. If this were the case, then the influence of events would be transitory rather than lasting. By definition, an event with a lasting impact on regime support is likely to occur only once in a decade or generation or longer.

When a regime sanctified by tradition disappears, the result is a discontinuity that requires resocialization in keeping with the character of the new regime. New leaders must find the means to mobilize support for their new regime and citizens or subjects must adapt to what it demands. Both governors and governed are likely to be influenced in evaluating the new regime by how they evaluated what went before. If the old regime was disliked as an alien imposition, then the new regime, whether democratic or not, can start with a substantial amount of popular support because it is different from what went before. Postcolonial regimes established in the wake of a country achieving independence from an imperial ruler have frequently enjoyed a honeymoon of support. However, with the passage of time this advantage may be dissipated as people learn that the new regime, although different from its predecessors, is not noticeably better, and people may even become nostalgic for an old regime whose failures have become dimmed.

By contrast with the emphasis of socialization theories on continuity, the concept of *charismatic* leadership describes a leader able to supplant an existing regime with a new regime by drawing support from his followers (Weber, 1947: 64ff.). Charismatic leaders may justify their claim to support by prowess in war, skill in oratory or the manipulation of ideological symbols, by doing God's will, or by displaying a character that citizens admire. Vladimir Lenin, Benito Mussolini, Adolf Hitler, Charles de Gaulle and Fidel Castro are twentieth-century examples of charismatic leaders. Political journalism often uses the term "charismatic" to refer to politicians who have a high opinion poll rating and are electorally successful. However, this usage confuses support for durable institutions of the regime with the personal appeal of politicians holding high office within it.

Charismatic leaders have difficulty institutionalizing their appeal; the usual pattern is that when he (it is hardly ever a she) leaves office, there is a change in regime. For example, when the Spanish dictator Francisco Franco died, the regime was transformed into a democracy. General Charles de Gaulle was exceptional in not only using his personal appeal to bring about the downfall of the French Fourth Republic in 1958 but also in establishing a constitution for the Fifth Republic that has maintained popular support long after he left office in 1969. Boris Yeltsin was a textbook example of a charismatic leader mobilizing support to destroy the Soviet regime. However, he could not mobilize much positive support for the new Russian regime; the task of doing so was left to his successor, Vladimir Putin. In efforts to do so, Putin has sought to attract personal popularity by presenting himself not only as a personable, athletic Russian but also as one who has pride in its multiple traditions, including respect for the Russian Orthodox Church, the Soviet industrialization of Russia and victory in World War II.

Fundamental *values* about how a country ought to be governed can generate support provided that there is congruence between the values of citizens and those of the regime (Eckstein, 1966; Eckstein *et al.*, 1998). Theories of democratic political culture postulate that the best foundation for political support is the widespread distribution of democratic values within a society and the regime's conformity to these values in its behavior. The values used to assess what is "right and proper" or "most appropriate" need not be democratic. A government and its citizenry may believe in the racial superiority of one portion of the society, thus justifying the repression or worse of other members of society, as in the white supremacy regime of South Africa; or a regime and subjects committed to Islamic values may restrict the rights of women and nonbelievers.

Compliance with core political laws is an absolute value in the Anglo-American idea of a government of laws, not men, and in the German doctrine of the *Rechtsstaat*. Justifying a claim to support of a statute on the grounds that it is the law of the land is consistent with Weber's emphasis on the importance of laws in modern bureaucratic political systems. However, it does not take into account the content of laws. The test of legality as an absolute value is if people will comply with laws that they do not approve of or that are made by a government that they did not vote for. An appeal to support the law of the land was the grounds for asking officials in the American Deep South to implement Supreme Court decisions on racial desegregation that went against their own traditional values and the demands of their white electorates. However, a constitution can be so drafted that it fails to protect basic human rights. In the absence of such rights, a government can enact laws that lead to the "banality of evil" (Arendt, 1951).

The Soviet doctrine of socialist "legality" made judicial institutions subordinate to the Communist Party. Decisions about imprisoning or executing people accused of crimes against the state followed the party line. Thus, the legal status of the regime's core political laws was irrelevant to the party's commands. The willingness of the courts to do what governors wanted made Russians averse to entanglement with the law. In the words of a folk saying, "The law is like a door in the middle of the field. You can go through it if you want, but you don't have to."

An *instrumental calculation* of support involves rational analysis of the costs and benefits of going along with a regime. If material economic benefits are deemed important, then a payoff can be calculated in cash terms, and rational choice theories hypothesize that a booming economy will "buy" support for a regime. However, statements about the importance of economic conditions for politics leave open the answer to the question: Which economy? (see Kinder and Kiewiet, 1981). Egocentric theories postulate that what counts is an individual's personal economic circumstances. At its crudest this implies that those in the bottom of a country's economic pyramid ought to support a regime favoring income redistribution, and Marxist regimes have claimed support on the grounds they favored redistributing wealth from a minority of capitalists to the masses, for whom the party-state acted as the trustee of wealth.

Sociotropic theories emphasize collective concerns such as the ability of a regime to maintain economic growth. The fruits of growth can then finance both rising wages and popular welfare state public policies in education, health and social security. A regime does not have to be democratic to buy support. In late nineteenth-century Prussia Otto von Bismarck pioneered "welfare state authoritarianism," that is, the state providing free education and social benefits as part of a strategy of maintaining support for an undemocratic regime (Flora and Alber, 1981). In the Soviet Union in the 1970s Leonid Brezhnev adopted a similar policy of expanding the supply of consumer goods in the planned economy, albeit with far fewer resources (Breslauer, 1978; Cook, 1993).

A strict materialist justification of support implies that if there is an economic recession, then a regime will lose support because of the presumed "populist myopia" that wants to see benefits appear promptly (Stokes, 2001: 9ff.). When the transformation of Communist command economies into market economies in the early 1990s led to the contraction of official GDP, this was sometimes invoked to forecast the repudiation of post-Communist regimes, because of the costs that were initially imposed (see e.g. Przeworski, 1991). The ability of post-Communist regimes to survive notwithstanding big contractions in national economies highlights the fact that calculations about the economy need not be myopic and that political benefits, such as a new regime abandoning repressive actions and giving citizens greater freedom, may offset short-term economic costs.

Clientelism can mobilize support by offering individuals the modern equivalent of bread and circuses, e.g. subsidized housing, assistance in getting a job or a municipal swimming pool or road improvement (Stokes, 2007). This can most readily be done in a regime in which elected and party officials dispense patronage rather than ideology to benefit individuals and communities seeking particularistic advantages. In return, the recipients of benefits are expected to support their patrons. In the absence of clientelistic institutions, a regime may tolerate petty corruption as a means of maintaining grudging support by allowing individuals to "work the system," that is, to get what they want by bribing a pliable official or using *blat*, a Russian term meaning "connections" (Rose, 2000a; Ledeneva, 2006). To maintain elite support, governors can co-opt potential opponents into supporters by offering them public offices. In a democracy, this gives the recipients a stake in the re-election of the government of the day; in an undemocratic system it gives them a stake in maintaining the regime (Smith, 2005; Magaloni, 2006). Vladimir Putin has used Russia's security apparatus and the tax police to remind multimillionaires that to maintain their stake in enterprises that make them rich they should show support for a regime prepared to use selective law enforcement to punish its critics.

The logic of rational choice can justify supporting an unsatisfactory regime when the alternative is perceived as a greater evil. The lesser evil approach was very relevant in the Soviet Union when the German army invaded in 1941. Soviet subjects who did not support the Stalinist regime nonetheless fought to defend it when the alternative was Nazi rule. Winston Churchill (1947) defended democracy as "the worst form of government except all those other forms that have been tried from time to time." The Republic of Italy is a contemporary example of a regime riddled with corruption and dubious associations that has maintained support for itself as a lesser evil compared to a return to fascist rule or a Communist regime.

The worse the present situation, the stronger the incentive for the regime to seek support by promising that the future will be better. However, this tactic cannot be sustained indefinitely. If foreign aid offered to improve living conditions is wasted or skimmed off by corrupt officials, if roads and schools are not built and if repressive behavior is maintained, then expectations can lead to resentment and encourage calls for a change of regime. At this point an undemocratic regime requires repressive institutions to make it clear to disaffected subjects that there is no alternative to the current regime. When subjects see little or no chance of changing regimes, they can avoid frustration by giving resigned acceptance to the powers that be.

Fear is the ultimate inducement that a regime can use to compel individuals to comply with its demands and thus give a public show of support (Shlapentokh, 2006). Undemocratic regimes engage in tacit negotiations with their subjects about how much or how little criticism can be voiced and how much "soft" or "hard" repression the regime will use to punish critics. A regime does not need to make a continuing show of force in order to instill fear in its subjects.

Intermittent and exemplary punishments demonstrate that sanctions for stepping out of line politically are at the ready (www.amnesty. org). Uncertainty about whether sanctions will be invoked encourages caution among would-be political dissidents. For much of its history, the Soviet regime used "hard" repression to silence anyone suspected of not supporting the regime. The denunciation of Stalin's reign of terror was followed slowly by a shift to "soft" repression in which individuals were allowed more scope for expressing dissatisfactions in private conversations. This did not erase the knowledge of what could happen to those who did not show support for the regime (Yakovlev, 2002).

If a regime falls because it is alien and repressive, then for a limited period an unknown new regime may enjoy temporary support if only because it replaces a regime regarded as a known evil with one that is an unknown quantity. However, with the *passage of time* a new regime is no longer a set of untested institutions. Subjects learn, for better and for worse, how it performs in the face of the challenges of governing. Subjects can measure its actions against their own values to see the extent to which they are congruent and people can make rational calculations about the benefits of supporting the regime and the costs and opportunities offered by a possible alternative regime.

Cumulatively, the passage of time can encourage support through a process of individual resocialization and institutional inertia (see Weil, 1987, 1989; Morlino and Montero, 1995). At the start of a new regime, everyone will have been socialized under the previous regime and many will have given it passive or active support. The longer the new regime is in place, the more pressure it puts on adults to be resocialized, whether because of its positive achievements or on the pragmatic calculation that it is better to join than to fight the system. Moreover, the longer a regime persists, the lower the expectation that regime change is possible. Even if undemocratic regimes are disliked, the more durable they become, the more this encourages at least passive support.

Worldwide support for regimes of all kinds

Two important theoretical hypotheses are embedded in the democratic model of political support in Figure 1.1A. The weight given to popular demands predicts:

- Hypothesis 1: If popular endorsement of the desirability of democracy is high, then a regime is more likely to supply democratic institutions.

The feedback loop suggests as a corollary:

- Hypothesis 2: If leaders of the regime supply democratic institutions, then support for the regime should be higher than in undemocratic systems.

In order to test these hypotheses we need evidence of public opinion that is not confined exclusively to democratic regimes, but comes from undemocratic political systems too. The global spread of social science technology and the worldwide recognition of the importance of assessing public opinion has led to multinational sample surveys being conducted not only in established democracies but also where there are undemocratic regimes.

The multicontinental World Values Survey has asked respondents in sixty-nine countries to say whether in principle they think a democratic political system would be good or bad for governing their country. This question invites people to anchor their evaluation within a national context which may not meet all the theoretical conditions deemed suitable for democracy. In addition, it avoids the mistake of asking people how satisfied they are with the way democracy is working in their country when the national regime is undemocratic (see Canache *et al.*, 2001). Throughout the world there is overwhelming popular endorsement of democracy as a good way of governing one's country. Nine in ten World Values Survey respondents are positive about democracy as an ideal, and in every country surveyed an absolute majority is positive. Moreover, only 8 percent reply don't know when asked to evaluate democracy.

Freedom House, an international nongovernmental organization, provides the best-known evaluation of the political status of regimes. It rates each country on a seven-point scale according to the extent to which its regime respects political and civil rights (www.freedomhouse.org). Given that such numerical ratings are approximate, country scores are then grouped into three categories: free, partly free and unfree. Partly free countries are defined as those having "more limited political rights and civil liberties, often in a context of corruption, weak rule of law, and ethnic strife"; countries such as Armenia, Tanzania and Indonesia were classified as partly free

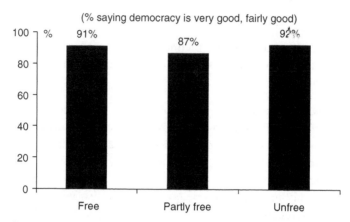

Q. Would you say having a democratic political system is a very good, fairly good, fairly bad or very bad way of governing this country?

Source: World Values Survey, waves 3 and 4, 68 countries, 1995–2003, Q. E117, Political status: Freedom House rating as reported for year of survey (www.freedomhouse.org).

Figure 1.2 Democracy endorsed in both undemocratic and democratic countries

when their citizens were interviewed. The unfree category includes countries such as Saudi Arabia, Belarus and Iran.

The fact that democracy is universally viewed as a positive symbol is encouraging but it also means that the first hypothesis must be rejected, because there is a disconnection between what citizens want and the regimes that political elites supply (Figure 1.2). The endorsement of democracy as a good form of government is just as high in unfree and partly free regimes as in countries where the demand for democracy is met. The statistical correlation between what most citizens of a country want, democracy as an ideal, and how Freedom House evaluates their regime is insignificant, 0.02. Even if citizens would like their regime to be democratic, it is the preferences of the political elites that determine what type of regime is supplied. In undemocratic regimes popular demands are not inputs that give direction to government; they are preferences that can be voiced to a public opinion survey but ignored by the regime's rulers.

The World Values Survey has also asked about support for a country's system of government in undemocratic as well as democratic countries. The vagueness of the term "system of government" is intentional. It avoids making the mistake of assuming that everyone on all continents of the world lives in a democracy. The use of a

Q. People have different views about the system for governing this country. Here is a scale for rating how well things are going: 1 means very bad and 10 means very good. Where on this scale would you put the political system as it is today?

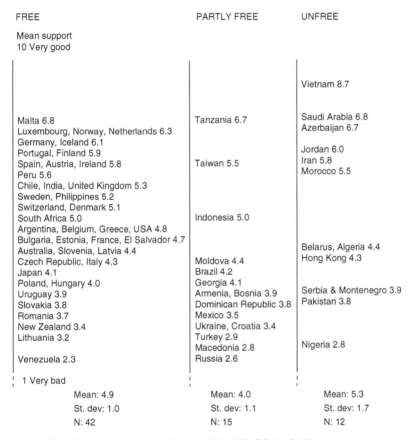

FREE   PARTLY FREE   UNFREE

Mean support
10 Very good

	Vietnam 8.7

Malta 6.8   Tanzania 6.7   Saudi Arabia 6.8
Luxembourg, Norway, Netherlands 6.3   Azerbaijan 6.7
Germany, Iceland 6.1
Portugal, Finland 5.9   Jordan 6.0
Spain, Austria, Ireland 5.8   Taiwan 5.5   Iran 5.8
Peru 5.6   Morocco 5.5
Chile, India, United Kingdom 5.3
Sweden, Philippines 5.2
Switzerland, Denmark 5.1
South Africa 5.0   Indonesia 5.0
Argentina, Belgium, Greece, USA 4.8
Bulgaria, Estonia, France, El Salvador 4.7
Australia, Slovenia, Latvia 4.4   Belarus, Algeria 4.4
Czech Republic, Italy 4.3   Moldova 4.4   Hong Kong 4.3
Japan 4.1   Brazil 4.2
Poland, Hungary 4.0   Georgia 4.1
Uruguay 3.9   Armenia, Bosnia 3.9   Serbia & Montenegro 3.9
Slovakia 3.8   Dominican Republic 3.8   Pakistan 3.8
Romania 3.7   Mexico 3.5
New Zealand 3.4   Ukraine, Croatia 3.4
Lithuania 3.2   Turkey 2.9
    Macedonia 2.8   Nigeria 2.8
Venezuela 2.3   Russia 2.6

1 Very bad

	Mean: 4.9	Mean: 4.0	Mean: 5.3
	St. dev: 1.0	St. dev: 1.1	St. dev: 1.7
	N: 42	N: 15	N: 12

Source: World Values Survey, waves 3 and 4, 1995–2003, Q.E111, Political status: Freedom House rating as reported for year of survey (www.freedomhouse.org).

Figure 1.3 Support for democratic and undemocratic regimes

ten-point scale to record replies allows citizens to qualify their support or rejection of their regime.

There is a wide variation between countries in popular endorsements of political system. In total, 37 percent of respondents gave their regime a positive endorsement; 20 percent rated it at the psychological midpoint of 5.0; and 43 percent gave a negative assessment. However, whether a regime is democratic or not has no influence on how it is evaluated by its population (Figure 1.3; see also Rose and

Mishler, 2002). The correlation between political support and a country's Freedom House rating, 0.05, fails to achieve significance. There are free, partly free and unfree countries where support is high and where support is low. Vietnam and Saudi Arabia, two of the three countries with the highest level of support according to the World Values Survey, have undemocratic regimes. Sweden, democratic on every rating of regimes, reports a mean support score of 5.2, while unfree Azerbaijan has a mean support score of 6.7.

Given great variations in support within each type of regime, the second hypothesis must also be rejected. Instead of support being lower in countries that Freedom House describes as unfree, the mean rating is actually higher, 5.3, than in countries that Freedom House describes as partly free, 4.0, or free, 4.9. The very wide range of scores within each category emphasizes the lack of a meaningful association between how people rate their regime and how it is rated by independent nongovernmental organizations. Moreover, political support for a given regime varies between individuals within a country (Mishler and Rose, 2001). The ability of undemocratic as well as democratic regimes to secure much the same level of support shows that democratic institutions are neither a necessary nor a sufficient condition for achieving political support.

2 | Changing the supply of regimes

The governors of a regime do not have the freedom to make intellectual comparisons of different types of regime. The governing elite must take as given the regime that their predecessors have supplied. For governors to debate whether a different regime would be better would question the support on which it rests. In a democratic regime reforms can be openly debated and advocating change is accepted as a legitimate role of the loyal opposition (Dahl, 1971). In an undemocratic regime, challenges to the institutions that confer power on governors can be viewed as a sign of disloyalty and end up in a split in the political elite between advocates of competing regimes.

Comparative politics supplies a great variety of regimes to those who refuse to support their current system, but national history offers many intellectual constraints on choice. The shortcomings of the current regime impose limitations on institutions and leadership as well as material resources. This is evident in the three regimes that have ruled Russians in the past century. World War I showed that the tsarist empire lacked the resources to defend the country against an invader; its pre-1914 history showed that it had neither the resources nor the will to introduce reforms that would turn an arbitrary regime into a constitutional monarchy. The Bolsheviks supplied a new type of regime, a one-party dictatorship, and the Communist Party supplied the cadres necessary to mobilize support from subjects.

The break-up of the Communist bloc created a political void. In Central and Eastern Europe political elites had a clear goal, supplying a democratic regime. In the extreme case of Latvia the new national assembly reinstated its 1922 democratic constitution. By contrast, in successor states of the Soviet Union, the past did not supply any model that could be invoked, for tsarist institutions had disappeared and the monopoly power of the Communist Party of the Soviet Union had been shattered. The change happened so abruptly that any attempt at democratization meant supplying "democracy from scratch" (Fish, 1995, 2005). The "democracy Bolsheviks" were clear about their negative goals, the dismantling of the repressive apparatus of the Soviet regime, but not about how to turn Moscow-based cliques into political parties mobilizing mass support (Lukin, 2000). Advocates of the rapid introduction of institutions of a Western economy were described as "market Bolsheviks," because Russia lacked the institutional infrastructure on which markets depend. The tactics that the founder president, Boris Yeltsin, used to maintain his personal position were obstacles to institutionalizing a new regime, whether democratic, authoritarian or a hybrid of the two.

Hard and soft coercion

Ideology and fear: the Stalinist approach

The Soviet regime was not distinctive in wanting its citizens to comply with its core political laws, for this is a condition of survival for every regime. Nor was it distinctive in being prepared to compel citizens to comply. Most regimes use some compulsion to make their subjects toe the line on issues that matter to it. The Soviet regime was distinctive in where it drew the line between what was and was not of central political importance. Instead of limiting core political laws, the Communist party-state used a mixture of ideological exhortations and fear to pursue the totalitarian aspiration of controlling the whole of the lives of its subjects (Arendt, 1951; Friedrich and Brzezinski, 1965).

The Communist Party of the Soviet Union was the organizational weapon used to mobilize subjects to show support through ritual repetition of party slogans in everything from compulsory youth groups and workplace meetings to Ph.D. theses (see Jowitt, 1992; Shlapentokh, 2001; Yakovlev, 2002; Figes, 2007). With one fulltime proponent of the party line for every sixteen households in the Soviet Union, the penetration of the system's ideology and apparatchiks was great (cf. White, 1979: 75ff.). State security agents prevented organized public expressions of disagreement with the party line and informers were planted to report on classmates, workmates and even family members. The party-state controlled all formal organizations of civil society, such as the radio, the press, theatres, cinemas and universities. The Russian text of Boris Pasternak's

Doctor Zhivago was first published in Italy in 1957; it could not be published in Russia until three decades later.

The Soviet regime refused to recognize a distinction between public and private life (Linz, 2000; Shlapentokh, 2001). Margaret Thatcher's assertion that there was no such thing as society was inverted to claim that there was no such thing as individuals. People were simply productive units that could be used or sacrificed to build a new society by making subjects conform to the party's image of the "new Soviet man" (Heller, 1988). Public opinion was not an expression of what people were thinking in private; it was an expression of what the party-state would allow to be said in public (cf. Noelle-Neumann, 1993).

The totalitarian aspirations of the state meant that any form of criticism could be classified as "anti-state" behavior. When peasants refused in large numbers to comply with the regime's policy of collectivizing agriculture in the early 1930s, repressive measures included imprisonment, deportation to Siberian prison camps, induced famine and execution. This caused millions of deaths (Wädekin, 1994; see also Conquest, 1990; Shearer, 2009). In the late 1930s Stalin purged the Communist Party of people he imagined to be plotting against him in show trials that demonstrated the capacity of the regime to force people to comply with its demands. Whereas Western commentators referred to coercion by a "secret police" (McCauley, 1998: 208), for ordinary Russian subjects there was nothing secret about the methods the regime used to compel a show of support.

Critics of describing the Soviet regime as totalitarian emphasize that its achievements fell short of this ideal type, because no set of political institutions could monitor everything that was done and said in a society of hundreds of millions of people. There was an hourglass society in which political elites competed for power, wealth and prestige at the top, while those at the bottom relied on family and very close friends to insulate themselves from the intrusive influence of the party-state (Rose, 2009c: 23ff.). The spaces in which people could say and do what they thought were limited. To the extent that the Stalinist system fell short of achieving the totalitarian ideal, this was a problem for party stalwarts. Insofar as it came closer to doing so, that was a problem for ordinary Russians.

Evidence of evading totalitarian controls can justify characterizing the Stalinist system as quasi-totalitarian, that is, trying to be totalitarian but falling short of achieving all that the term implies. Such gaps are common to many types of regime. The premier contemporary theorist of democracy, Robert Dahl (1971), refers to regimes that aspire to but fall short of achieving democratic ideals as polyarchies rather than as "quasi-democratic."

Promoting positive support

The rise of Nazi Germany presented a serious ideological and military challenge to the Soviet regime. In August 1939 a pact between Stalin and Hitler turned the party's ideological enemy into a partner in the military occupation of territories between them. The Soviet Union invaded parts of Poland, Finland and the Baltic states. Less than two years later Germany invaded the Soviet Union; this confronted subjects with the alternatives of fighting for a Stalinist regime or siding with Nazi Germany. Although some groups harshly repressed under Soviet rule sided with Germany (Reitlinger, 1960), the great majority supported a regime invoking traditional symbols, and the brutal Nazi treatment of occupied territories further strengthened support. While the costs in human life of what was called the Great Patriotic War were very great, the consequences were politically very positive. That the Soviet regime could defeat an army as great as that of the German *Reich* made clear that there was no basis to expect it to give way to any other.

The death of Stalin in 1953 was followed by the denunciation of his "cult of the personality" by his successor, Nikita Khrushchev, and a reduction in the use of terror. In the post-Stalin era the regime reduced the political demands with which its subjects were expected to comply. Fewer activities were evaluated in terms of their ideological correctness. The party-state's aim was to confine expressions of dissent to small informal groups of individuals. At international social science congresses where Westerners were present, the party-state controlled who was allowed to attend and what was and what was not said. By the 1970s it was tolerating the public display of typical symbols of Western society such as blue jeans. Rock concerts could be held, as long as entertainers refrained from singing lyrics that might rock support for the regime. Censorship prevented the public statement of anything that might be even remotely regarded as inconsistent with the party line. For example, the senior author's book, *Politics in England*, could not be published in the 1970s;

it was circulated in *samizdat*, that is, typed with multiple carbon copies and passed from hand to hand among professionals in institutes of the Academy of Sciences.

By conventional sociological criteria, in half a century the Soviet regime succeeded in modernizing a society that had been rural, uneducated and often illiterate (Boutenko and Razlogov, 1997). More than two-thirds of Russians lived in cities; a large majority of women as well as men were employed in industry or the service sector rather than subsistence agriculture; and free secondary education was available throughout the country. Some Western scholars interpreted these indicators of socioeconomic modernization as promising that sooner or later the Soviet Union would become a normal society by Western standards (see e.g. Parsons, 1964; Hough, 1977; cf. Hollander, 1981; Engerman, 2009). However, while making progress by comparison with the past, Russians were falling behind rising living standards in Western Europe, a fact that was hidden from the great majority of Russians by restricting direct contact with Westerners (Rose, 2009c: ch. 3). In the extreme case of health, between 1965 and 1981 the so-called golden years of peace and prosperity under Leonid Brezhnev, official statistics recorded that the life expectancy of Russian men actually fell by 2.3 years while it was rising by 3.1 years in major member states of the Organization for Economic Cooperation and Development (OECD) (Rose and Bobak, 2010: Figure 1).

The regime's maintenance of quasi-totalitarian practices meant that there was an "anti-modern" polity and economy (Rose, 2009c: ch. 2). Instead of being responsive to popular demands to secure political support, the Soviet regime conformed to the prototypical model of a totalitarian regime. At election time the regime mobilized people to show nominal support or, as Bertolt Brecht sardonically commented, the people faced the prospect of being dissolved by the state. In the 1984 Soviet election official records reported a turnout of 99.9 percent and Communist candidates received 99.9 percent of the vote.

The readiness of Russians to comply with the many political demands of their regime leaves open the determination of causes of popular compliance and support. The absence of overt signs of dissent was consistent with the theory that obedience to authority was part of political culture in tsarist times that the Soviet regime had not created but was quick to take advantage of (cf. Keenan, 1986; White, 1979; cf. McAuley, 1984).

The party-state rejected surveying public opinion on principle. The Communist Party knew what people ought to think and anyone with a contrary opinion was guilty of false consciousness or worse (Reddaway and Glinski, 2001). Insofar as sociology was a subject of academic study, it was meant to be practiced within a Marxist framework (Shlapentokh, 1987). The desire of the party-state to understand the world of work and of youth made it possible for Boris Grushin to undertake controlled surveys in the city of Taganrog between 1967 and 1981. However, Soviet publishing houses refused to publish his results. After the fall of the Soviet regime, Grushin published a retrospective analysis in which a majority of subjects were characterized as conformists with whatever the regime wanted; the second-largest group were active supporters of the regime; and only a small minority were nonconformists (as discussed in Levada, 2001; Shlapentokh, 2001: ch. 10).

Social science surveys of Russians were first undertaken with people who no longer lived in the Soviet Union. World War II resulted in masses of Soviet subjects becoming displaced as prisoners of war, deportees to German labor camps or refugees fleeing westward from an advancing Red Army. The Harvard Interview Project made use of this accident of history to interview hundreds of Russians, all of whom had lived through the Stalinist terror and some of whom had first-hand knowledge of life under the tsar. Since the collection of respondents almost certainly overrepresented people who were anti-Soviet, it is all the more striking that many expressed opinions consistent with Communist ideology. For example, four-fifths or more endorsed state control of the economy and two-thirds or more hailed its promotion of social welfare through education and health services (Inkeles and Bauer, 1959).

Three decades later an exodus of Soviet Jews enabled the Soviet Interview Project to interview a sample of emigres who arrived in the United States between 1979 and 1982 (Millar, 1987). During their last normal period of life in the Soviet Union, that is, before they sought official permission to emigrate, only 10 percent reported engaging in any kind of nonconformist activity such as meeting in private with a group of friends to discuss current affairs or a book and no more than one in five were characterized as showing any signs of activities inconsistent with Soviet norms. Furthermore, more educated people were more likely to participate in activities that helped make the system work, such as trade union work or activities of the Communist youth group Komsomol (Bahry, 1987: 63ff.; Silver, 1987: 114). Respondents endorsed the Soviet economic system and the state provision of social welfare. American researchers interpreted such social democratic views about welfare as showing "support for the established political order" of an undemocratic regime (Silver, 1987: 109). When Russians did have to deal with public officials, the Project found that the great majority acted like a resigned New Yorker wanting to get something from City Hall. They were trying to work the system for their own benefit rather than fight it.

The passage of time resulted in the regime's fear of anti-state activities subsiding as Russians complied with its demands and popular behavior appeared to give overt evidence of support. This was consistent with Emile Durkheim's (1952) theory that any social organism that survives for decades becomes accepted, actively or passively, by members of that society. It is also consistent with the retrospective nostalgia about the regime after it collapsed at the end of 1991 (Munro, 2006). Vladimir Putin, born in 1952, reflected this outlook when explaining his youthful ambition to become a member of the state security organization, the KGB: "I didn't think about the Stalin-era purges. I was a pure and utterly successful product of Soviet patriotic education" (Putin, 2000: 41).

Competition for support

In a regime in equilibrium there is a consensus of support for its core institutions. In an undemocratic regime, it is sufficient for the political elite to be in agreement; the role of the mass of subjects is to comply with rather than challenge the political system that elites supply. Because an equilibrium reflects a tension between competing pressures from the larger national and international environment as well as from within the political system, it is never entirely static. In the 1980s the consensus of the Soviet elite cracked. Initially, there was a discussion about whether major reforms in the regime were necessary and, if so, what changes would be appropriate. Differing views were wrapped in the Marxist-Leninist ideology of building socialism in order to make clear that proposals for change were intended to strengthen rather than challenge the regime.

Although Mikhail Gorbachev was a loyal party member, he belonged to a different generation than predecessors who had risen under Stalin (Brown, 1996; Breslauer, 2002). After he became general secretary of the party in 1985, his response to pressure for change inadvertently opened up a divide in the elite that led to competition between those who supported reform, those who opposed it and those who wanted a new regime. The pressures did not come from the ballot box or the media, which the party continued to control. Instead, they came from the economy, which the party-state commanded with limited success. Whatever official statistics showed, the production of consumer goods for Soviet citizens did not match that in Western Europe. The failure of collective agriculture reduced many Soviet subjects to urban peasants, growing some food for home consumption (Rose and Tikhomirov, 1993). Even though the military-industrial sector of the economy was favored by the regime, it was visibly lagging behind costly high-technology developments of the United States under President Ronald Reagan. Furthermore, world oil prices were at a cyclical low, thus facing the Soviet Union with a shortage of foreign currency that could be used to import food.

The *perestroika* (restructuring) initiative that Gorbachev launched in 1986 was intended to make the economy more productive while retaining the socialist emphasis on state ownership. The initiative created a debate within the party high command about the extent to which it should accept market mechanisms such as prices set by supply and demand rather than by ministry planners. Gorbachev's endorsement of *glasnost* (openness) meant that the debate could be carried out in public. This violated a cardinal rule of democratic centralism; the party no longer spoke with a single public voice. Not only were the specifics of economic restructuring contested but also there was vocal opposition to the principle of reform by those whose power and interests it threatened.

In pursuit of popular support for his reform policies, at the 1988 Party Congress Gorbachev secured endorsement of multicandidate elections for the Congress of People's Deputies. The first semi-competitive elections in Soviet history were held in March 1989. Two or more candidates were on the ballot for five-sixths of the seats. Elections showed that the Communist Party was divided about what line party members should take: Some of its candidates favored *perestroika* and *glasnost* while others were strong defenders of the regime as it had been. Boris Yeltsin, who had been removed from his official party post because he wanted reforms going further than those of Gorbachev, was elected by a Moscow district with 89 percent of the vote. Given a choice of candidates, the electorate split its votes. While some veteran party officials received electoral endorsement, others were rejected by voters now able to express publicly views they had harbored privately (see White *et al.*, 1997: ch. 2).

Gorbachev stretched reform further by calling for a constitutional amendment to fill the office of president of the Soviet Union by a competitive election. However, he was unwilling to call an immediate presidential election in which he could campaign for a mandate to change how Russia was ruled. Instead, Gorbachev stipulated that the new office would initially be filled by a vote in the Congress of People's Deputies. When this happened in March 1990, even though his was the only name on the ballot, only 71 percent of deputies positively endorsed Gorbachev as president.

Efforts to reform the regime came under attack from two sides; there were hardliners against change and radicals who increasingly saw the regime as meriting repudiation rather than reform. Disagreement on this scale was over the heads of ordinary Russians, who became preoccupied with problems of coping with increasing shortages of goods in the shops as the economy deteriorated. In Gorbachev's final year in office, instead of showing slow growth or stagnation the official economy contracted by 5 percent (Marer *et al.*, 1992).

Gorbachev's initiative to reform the Soviet regime had a very different meaning in Central and East European states subject to Moscow. *Glasnost* released Central and East Europeans from the pressure to endorse a regime that they did not positively support. *Perestroika* created an opening for a fundamental change in relations with Moscow. After Gorbachev announced an end to the Brezhnev doctrine of Soviet military protection of Communist regimes, demonstrations in East German cities led to the nonviolent fall of the Berlin Wall in November 1989. The first free elections in new Central and East European regimes showed the difference between the authoritarian mobilization of support and a popular expression of demands that tells politicians how much or how little support they have (Rose and Munro, 2009: chs. 6–16). Even though Communist parties had registered up to 99 percent of the vote in previous elections, they were disbanded. The exception was Russia, where the Communist Party of the Russian Federation correctly claimed to be the heir of the Communist Party of the Soviet Union.

Contested elections in the fifteen Soviet republics in 1990 created new sources of destabilization. The winners did not owe their position to Moscow but to political allegiances formed within a particular Soviet republic. Yeltsin was elected president of the Russian Republic in June 1991, with more than three times the vote of the conservative Communist candidate (White *et al.*, 1997: 30ff.). Newly elected leaders in the republics began to question the continued existence of the Soviet Union itself and to entrench their positions in moves that made independence an attractive option (see e.g. Solnick, 1998; Hale, 2008).

The collapse of the Soviet regime was not due to massive demonstrations of the regime's lack of popular support, as had occurred in East Germany, the Baltic states and elsewhere in the Communist bloc. Instead, it was due to divisions within the Soviet elite. Hardline defenders of the Soviet regime placed Gorbachev under house arrest in August 1991. Lacking the support of the military, the attempted putsch failed. Within a week Gorbachev was free, but he had now become eclipsed in political significance by Yeltsin, president of the Russian Republic. The Communist Party of the Soviet Union ceased to function as a party and Soviet republics began to declare independence. By Christmas 1991, the Soviet Union was dissolved. Its place

Q. Which statements do you think apply to our system of governing under present conditions?

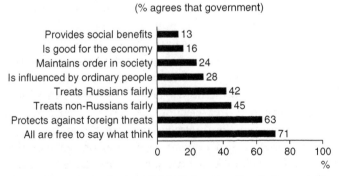

Source: Centre for the Study of Public Policy, New Russia Barometer I (January–February 1992).

Figure 2.1 Consequences of *perestroika* evaluated

was taken by fifteen post-Soviet states. Each was then faced by the need to create a new regime and mobilize popular support.

When the New Russia Barometer asked about the consequences of *perestroika* at the beginning of 1992, judgments were mixed (Figure 2.1). On the one hand, more than two-thirds thought it gave people the freedom to say what they thought, a big change from the Soviet era. However, less than one in four thought it had had a positive impact on the primary activities of government: managing the economy, delivering social benefits and maintaining order.

Yeltsin struggles to fill the void

The treble transformation of state, polity and economy disrupted the regime that the subjects of the new Federation had been socialized to support since birth. In place of a party line to which everyone was expected to give outward assent, there was a continuing flow of differing opinions about how Russia ought to be governed.

Yeltsin became president of the new Russian Federation because he had been successful in his fight against the old regime. However, his charismatic character was unsuited to the task of institutionalizing a new regime. In terms of Beatrice Webb's division of the politically powerful into a's and b's (that is, anarchists and bureaucrats), Yeltsin was an anarchist. Building institutions requires the skills of a bureaucratic politician, which Yeltsin conspicuously lacked. Having been elected as an anti-party candidate, he could not rely for support on party loyalties. Nor did he wish to rely on Soviet-era bureaucrats who populated the ministries that were transferred wholesale from the former to the new regime. Instead, he relied on a coterie of personal advisors to protect and advance his political interests and on *vlast*, a Russian term connoting raw power (McFaul, 2001: 17).

Legacies from the old regime created competition for control of the new. It inherited the 1978 constitution of the Russian Socialist Federal Soviet Republic, adopted a year after the Soviet Union's constitution, which stated that the Communist Party was the guiding force in society. The Russian Congress elected in March 1990 contained a mixture of hardline, reform, confused and opportunistic Communists. In April 1992 the Congress called for the Yeltsin administration to reduce the market-oriented measures that it had introduced. In December 1992 it ousted the acting prime minister, Yegor

Gaidar. President Yeltsin nominated in Gaidar's place an experienced Soviet-era minister, Viktor Chernomyrdin.

Competition between the president and the Congress of Deputies was "a matter of political struggle rather than constitutional law" (Sakwa, 1996: 118). Although both Yeltsin and the Congress agreed about the need for a new constitution, there was a basic conflict about which should have the most power. In April 1993 Yeltsin called an extra-constitutional "referendum" with public opinion poll-type questions asking whether people had confidence in him and whether there should be early election of deputies or of the president. The official results showed the population split: 59 percent said they had confidence in Yeltsin, 39 percent said they did not and 2 percent spoiled their ballot. Similarly, 53 percent endorsed the administration's policies while three in seven did not (White *et al.*, 1997: Table 4.2).

The dispute about who governs came to a violent head in September 1993 when President Yeltsin dissolved the Congress and called a December election for a new parliament. The Constitutional Court ruled that this violated the constitution and gave grounds for impeachment. The Congress voted to depose Yeltsin as president and named Vice President Alexander Rutskoi to act in his stead. Rutskoi called for a new election of both president and parliament. When Yeltsin ordered deputies to vacate the White House, which he had defended against Soviet tanks two years earlier, deputies barricaded themselves inside. The president marshaled loyal troops to surround the building. More than 145 people were killed in the bloodiest street-fighting in Moscow since the Revolution.

Once the gun smoke cleared, a constitution was drafted for the new regime under the watchful eye of President Yeltsin. In the words of a Russian political commentator, "It is a constitution for presidents in general and for President Yeltsin in particular" (quoted in Sakwa, 2002: 62). It created the office of a directly elected president. By comparison with the United States Congress, the popularly elected chamber of the new parliament, the Duma, had limited powers to check the president's actions. Nor was the prime minister's position vis-à-vis the president as strong as in France. South America offered a more appropriate source of comparisons for a presidentialist regime loosely constrained by institutions (Riggs, 1988; Linz, 1990a; O'Donnell, 1994). Although the constitution was what the president

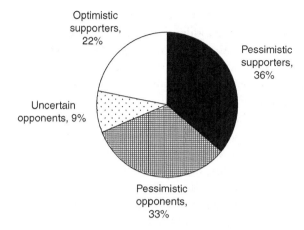

Optimistic
supporters,
22%

Pessimistic
supporters,
36%

Uncertain
opponents, 9%

Pessimistic
opponents,
33%

Source: Centre for the Study of Public Policy, New Russia Barometer III
(March–April 1994). For details of the questions, see White *et al.*, 1997: 98ff.

Figure 2.2 New constitution gets pessimistic support

wanted, it was not what most Russians wanted. In a New Russia
Barometer survey a few months before the constitution was prepared,
only 30 percent endorsed giving the president final authority and an
equal percentage endorsed giving the Duma the final say. Two-fifths
wanted a system of checks and balances between the president and the
Duma or disliked giving a lot of power to either.

A referendum seeking popular approval of the constitution was held
in December 1993. Given a straight yes/no choice, 58.4 percent of the
reported votes endorsed it while two in five were against. However,
when the New Russia Barometer probed the degree of support for the
new constitution, replies showed widespread pessimism (Figure 2.2).
Most who said they voted for the constitution did not believe that it
would create a lawful and democratic state. These doubts were also
held by a big majority of those who voted against the constitution. In
all, less than one in four Russians were optimistic about the new
constitution ensuring a lawful and democratic state.

The limits of the regime's ability to secure compliance were spectacularly demonstrated when the popularly elected president of
Chechnya, a national republic of the Federation, sought independence. The Russian army went into the region in December 1994 to
impose its authority, but met with heavily armed resistance. A truce
was negotiated in June 1996. This ended what subsequently became

known as the First Chechen War (Lieven, 1998). In dealing with leaders in Russia's eighty-seven regions, the Kremlin did not invoke force but engaged in political bargaining from which local politicians gained substantial freedom of action in return for delivering votes and other resources that the Kremlin wanted (Gel'man *et al.*, 2003).

Organized crime demonstrated the weakness of the new regime's capacity to supply order. Gangs that had operated illegally in the interstices of the Soviet regime came out in the open (Frisby, 1998; McCauley, 2001). A so-called *Mafiya* took protection money from shopkeepers and new small firms and carried out assassinations to order of those involved in disputes about the riches that the market promised. When asked to characterize the political situation in 1995, 51 percent of Russians thought it tended toward anarchy as against 11 percent seeing it as developing in the direction of democracy. When asked "What is more needed for our society now: order or democracy?," more than three-quarters gave priority to order and only 10 percent to democracy (Levada, 1995: Figure 3).

As a legacy of its predecessor, the new regime initially controlled all economic enterprises. This was a mixed blessing, because these enterprises were not run in accordance with conventional principles of a market economy but according to Marxist principles as adapted by Lenin and Stalin. Major decisions about the economy were in the hands of powerful party and ministry officials whose commands made up the five-year plans (Winiecki, 1988; Kornai, 1992).

The economic policy of the Yeltsin administration weakened the power of the state by privatizing major assets. This was seen not only as a means of making major industries efficient economically but also as a way of destroying the power of Communist-era bureaucrats still in many ministries and of creating new holders of wealth who would support Yeltsin. Acting prime minister Yegor Gaidar launched what he described as a "kamikaze" attack to destroy bureaucratic controls over the economy (1999). The strategy introduced market forces and ended shortages. However, it also led to treble-digit annual inflation and disrupted the payment of wages by state-owned firms that could no longer rely on ministries to fund their budgets. Privatization in the absence of a private sector proceeded very differently than in Thatcher's Britain or Reagan's America. There was neither a functioning stock market nor banks and investment funds with the capital to buy state-owned assets. The outcome was that the privatization

of the country's natural resources was too private. Ambitious entrepreneurs with political connections in the new regime and with the
old bureaucracy were able to strip the state of assets through opaque
procedures that made them multimillionaires or billionaires (Blasi
et al., 1997; Klebnikov, 2000).

Politically, the new regime offered Russians competitive elections in
which the parties most closely associated with President Yeltsin did
badly. In the December 1993 contest, Russia's Choice won only 14.5
percent of the list vote. In the December 1995 Duma election, the
biggest share of the vote was won by the Communist Party. The party
favored by the Kremlin, Our Home Is Russia, came third with only
10.1 percent of the vote. The June 1996 presidential election was the
Stalingrad of the new regime. The alternative to Yeltsin was the leader
of the Communist Party, Gennady Zyuganov. Notwithstanding the
advantages of incumbency, in the first-round ballot President Yeltsin
was able to gain only 35.3 percent of the vote, less than half what he
had gained when challenging the Soviet system six years earlier. The
vote for his opponents was split; Zyuganov came second with 32.0
percent of the vote. In the second-round runoff ballot, which the
Yeltsin campaign portrayed as a choice between the new and the old
regimes, Yeltsin appealed as the lesser evil to those whose candidates
were no longer on the ballot. He was re-elected with just over half the
vote. The election marked an end to the Communist Party as a
substantial electoral threat. Never again has it won enough votes in
the first round of a presidential election to force the contest to a
second ballot.

The presidential election was won at the price of confirming the
billions of dollars of Russian entrepreneurs who had benefited from a
"loans for shares" agreement that transferred from the state to their
hands the ownership of energy and other natural resources at heavily
discounted prices. The problem with the deal was not that Russian
businessmen were avaricious in pursuit of wealth, but that "the state
allowed them to get away with it" (Freeland, 2000: 180).

The continuing weakness of the regime was made evident to every
Russian household by the collapse of the ruble in August 1998.
Politically connected Russian speculators had been able to take advan-
tage of billions of dollars of International Monetary Fund (IMF) loans
to profit by exchanging their rubles for dollars before the roof fell in
(Lopez-Claros and Zadornov, 2002). However, ordinary Russians

could not escape the effect of prices inflating by 86 percent in a single year and of a major contraction in the economy. Reviewing the economic achievements of his years in office, President Yeltsin declared, "We are stuck halfway between a planned, command economy and a normal, market one" (quoted in Gaddy and Ickes, 2001: 103). This position was described as stable but undesirable, a "partial reform equilibrium trap" in which those who had gained great benefits from lawless privatization now had a vested interest in maintaining the status quo (Hellman, 1998: 205).

Although victory at the presidential election was enough to give Boris Yeltsin a second term, it was not a positive endorsement of his behavior as president. When Yeltsin first burst upon the public in 1989 as a radical candidate for the USSR Congress of People's Deputies, he won massive majorities from the electorate. In the summer of 1990 Yeltsin's mean rating of 8 on VCIOM's one-to-ten approval scale was substantially higher than the mean rating of Gorbachev, 5 (White *et al.*, 1997: 166ff.). By January 1992, Yeltsin's rating was below the midpoint. Thereafter, instead of fluctuating his assessment drifted downward. It fell below 3 for the first time in January 1995 (Figure 2.3).

During President Yeltsin's second term of office, his public appearances were demoralizing. When he appeared unsteady or unwell,

Q. What marks on a scale of 1 (lowest) to 10 (highest) do you give to the performance of Boris Yeltsin?

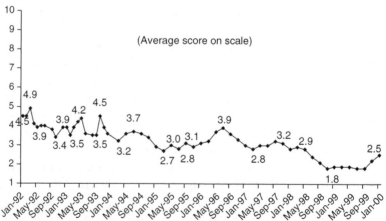

Source: VCIOM nationwide monthly surveys.

Figure 2.3 Decline of confidence in President Yeltsin

opponents attacked him as a drunkard or a "painted mummy." When the president avoided public appearances, it encouraged rumors that he was too ill to perform official duties. From time to time, Yeltsin showed that such rumors were exaggerated, appearing healthy on television to announce decrees or unexpectedly sacking his prime minister. However, the bad days and the bad polls outnumbered the good. His mean rating was as low as 1.8 in November 1998; this meant that a majority of VCIOM respondents gave Yeltsin the worst possible rating. He remained near the bottom for the rest of his term of office (Mishler and Willerton, 2003).

A peaceful succession

The circumstances in which the Federation's regime was created inevitably identified it with Boris Yeltsin personally rather than with institutions. Since the constitution imposed a limit of two consecutive terms on being president, as the date for the 2000 presidential election came closer this raised a question about what would happen to the regime. Would the succession be peaceful or create yet more political turbulence?

President Yeltsin had three broad options. The first was to stretch or break the constitution and remain in office after his term was due to expire in June 2000. A second alternative was to let politicians ambitious to succeed him compete for the favor of the electorate. Trial-heat presidential polls consistently showed that the front runner in the competition for votes was the Communist leader (Rose and Munro, 2002: fig. 4.3). While the name of Zyuganov's most likely challenger varied from one month to the next, the sure loser appeared to be any name that Yeltsin had floated as a successor. The ideal alternative was to identify a candidate who could be elected and maintain the regime, giving the Yeltsin family continued access to power. The nightmare prospect was that both candidates in the runoff ballot would campaign as opponents of Boris Yeltsin and his family.

Less than a year before the presidential election was due, both metaphorical and real bombshells were thrown. President Yeltsin sacked a prime minister who could gain only 3 percent of the vote in trial-heat opinion polls and appointed a hitherto unknown staff official, Vladimir Putin, in his place. Concurrently, two Moscow apartment buildings were destroyed by bombs and there were additional explosions in southern Russia, killing more than 200 people. The attacks were officially attributed to Chechen terrorists (Sakwa, 2008a: 20ff.). Prime Minister Putin described the bombs as threatening "the Yugoslavization of Russia." In an effort to show control of the whole of the territory of the Russian Federation, the Kremlin launched a major military attack in Chechnya.

In retrospect Vladimir Putin appears a natural leader of Russia, but this was hardly the case when Yeltsin named him as prime minister. In the first VCIOM trial-heat presidential poll held after his appointment, only 2 percent named Putin as their favorite for the presidency. However, his service in the shadows of the Yeltsin administration meant that he was not tarred with its failures. As prime minister, Putin gained name recognition and popularity in leading the fight against Chechens. By November 1999 Putin was ahead of Zyuganov in opinion polls (Rose and Munro, 2002: 94ff.). The Duma election of 19 December 1999 confirmed popular support for Unity, a party newly formed to support Putin's presidential candidacy. This encouraged Boris Yeltsin to believe that opinion poll results were not a mirage. On 31 December 1999 he resigned as president. In accordance with the constitution, Prime Minister Putin became acting president.

Although the charismatic Yeltsin had destroyed the Communist regime, he had not succeeded in mobilizing positive support for the new regime (see Chapter 4). At best, the corruption and disorder that accompanied transformation and the weakness of the new regime produced passive support in keeping with the Russian principle of *pust' oni budut* (let them be). In the words of a Russian focus group participant:

So what should we do: Rebel? I think our history is packed with evidence that rebellions never improve the situation but only make it worse . . . Anything is better than civil war and that's what will happen if people get militant. (Shevchenko, 2001: 86)

Given the disruptive effects of the transformation of a Communist into a post-Communist regime, it was no small achievement for Boris Yeltsin to survive in office and hand over the keys to the Kremlin in a peaceful manner. In his farewell television address (31 December 1999), Yeltsin claimed that he had achieved "the main job of my life: Russia will never return to the past."

3 | *Putin consolidates a new regime*

The ambiguous legacy that Vladimir Putin received from his predecessor at the start of the millennium was summed up in the subtitle of a book, *Stability or Disorder?* (Bonnell and Breslauer, 2001). In an address on taking office, the new president made his choice clear: political stability:

Russia has reached its limit for political and socio-economic upheavals, cataclysms and radical reforms. Only fanatics or political forces which are absolutely apathetic and indifferent to Russia and its people can make calls for a new revolution. Be it under Communist, national-patriotic or radical-liberal slogans, our country and our people will not withstand a new radical break up. The nation's patience and its ability to survive as well as its capacity to work constructively have reached the limit. (Putin, 2000: 212)

In striving toward this goal, Putin benefited from the popular desire for the consolidation of order after the turbulence of transformation (Carnaghan, 2007).

To introduce order in place of the existing disorder required institutionalizing a regime, whether democratic or undemocratic, that in one way or another could gain the support of its population (cf. Huntington, 1968; Figure 1.1). The Yeltsin administration's strategy had been to dismantle institutions central to the power of the Soviet party-state. Putin saw this as the Federation's powers being "highjacked." His political strategy has been to repatriate to the state powers that had been appropriated by the regions and billionaire businessmen.

Mobilizing political support required institution-building too, for Boris Yeltsin had succeeded in weakening the Communist Party but had not created an alternative to it. The result was a floating system of parties in which politicians formed and abandoned parties at will, leaving a plethora of short-lived organizations that could not provide stable popular support for those in power (see e.g. Lentini, 1995;

Rose and Munro, 2009: ch. 17). In reaction against this floating party system, Putin declared in a press conference on 18 July 2001:

> If there are de facto two-, three- and four-party systems in developed, civilised countries, why do there have to be 350 or 5,000 parties in Russia? This is a kind of Bacchanalia, not democracy. This leads to a situation in which the population cannot determine their political sympathies.
>
> (translated in Sakwa, 2008a: 320)

To help Russians determine their political sympathies, Putin promoted laws reducing the number of parties in the Duma and creating United Russia, which subjects could support as what Russians call "the party of power" (*partiya vlasti*; Oversloot and Verheul, 2000). These steps consolidated popular support by removing what Adam Przeworski *et al.* (1996: 51) have described as a defining characteristic of democracy, some uncertainty about whether the governing party would lose an election.

Repatriating power to the Kremlin

Although Putin and Yeltsin had originally made their careers in the Soviet party-state, the consequences of this for their behavior were very different. Yeltsin was an anti-state politician who saw bureaucratic institutions as an obstacle to exercising his will. By contrast, Putin was a bureaucratic politician who saw the state's institutions as the means of exercising power. Given the weakness of the regime that was Yeltsin's legacy, Putin (2000: 214) gave precedence to strengthening it:

> Our state and its institutions and structures have always played an exceptionally important role in the life of the country and its people. For Russians, a strong state is not an anomaly to be got rid of. Quite the contrary, it is a source of order and the main driving force of any change.

While many Western experts agreed with Putin's diagnosis of the desirability of strengthening the regime's institutions (see e.g. Holmes, 2006), their prescriptions differed. In the words of OECD economist William Tompson (2004: 115): "Russia does not need a strong state; it needs a state different in kind to that which it inherited from the Soviet Union."

To get rid of what Putin (2005: 1) denounced as the "degradation of state and public institutions," he cumulatively strengthened the central institutions of the regime (Sakwa, 2008a). Having had his own career disrupted by Gorbachev's reforms spinning out of control, Putin preferred making changes gradually. Whereas the Soviet regime had used party commissars to keep an eye on state officials, Putin called on former members of the KGB and other security services of the state (Kryshtonovskaya and White, 2003; Kryshtonovskaya, 2008). These *siloviki* were not Bolshevik or democratic idealists but men experienced in how an authoritarian Soviet regime had achieved support for the party-state without regard to the rule of law.

To strengthen the *vertikal*, that is, the relationship between Moscow and its regional governors, Putin created seven federal districts, each headed by a Kremlin appointee responsible for supervising regional activities. Five of the seven district governors were generals. Ex officio seats in the upper house of parliament were abolished, thus depriving governors and chairs of regional legislatures of immunity from prosecution. In his second term of office, the president claimed the power to appoint all regional governors, and they were recruited to support Putin's party, United Russia (Reuter, 2010). Within central government the president exerted influence through patronage, appointing ministers and the prime minister. Tax laws were altered to increase the flow of revenue to central government.

To reduce the risk of billionaires with financial and media resources challenging his position, Putin sought to "liquidate the oligarchs as a class." He did this by using the power of the state to deprive of their assets billionaires who had *"failed the loyalty test,"* that is, used their media to criticize the Putin administration (Sakwa, 2008a: 143; Brown, 2001: 38). Taking advantage of the fact that no one could have amassed great wealth in Yeltsin's Russia without breaking laws, civil and criminal actions were selectively filed against oligarchs such as Boris Berezovsky, Vladimir Gusinsky and Mikhail Khodorkovsky. The first two went into exile; Khodorkovsky went to prison. A substantial number of Russian entrepreneurs remained billionaires, but they were no longer a class with independent power. Instead, they had become subjects of a regime with the will to deprive them of their wealth if they stepped out of line politically.

The free-floating discussion of ideas that had been encouraged by *glasnost* and the development of competing media were inconsistent with Putin's idea of order. The first target was independent television, the main source of information for the vast majority of Russians. Boris Berezovsky, the owner of a major stake in the main national television station, ORT, and in TV6, fled abroad to escape prosecution. Vladimir Gusinsky, founder of Russia's first privately owned TV station, NTV, came into conflict with the Kremlin over coverage of the Second Chechen War and broadcasting a satirical political puppet show modeled on the British program *Spitting Image*. He was placed under house arrest and, he alleges, forced to sign over control of his companies before fleeing abroad. Opinion polls found Russians ambivalent about such actions. While there was no sympathy for media billionaires, there tended to be a preference for media being free to voice different political opinions.

Print publications have remained relatively free from being taken over, since the Kremlin has succeeded in creating an atmosphere in which journalists understand the need to be careful about offering critics of the regime a platform (Lipman and McFaul, 2005; Linan, 2009: 143ff.). More than a dozen journalists conducting investigations of corruption and worse were murdered during President Putin's two terms; no one has been convicted of these murders.

The political significance of nongovernmental organizations (NGOs) grew as political parties voicing democratic values have been eliminated from the Duma. This has made NGOs targets for state-supported measures to curtail their independence. For example, in September 2003, the leading independent not-for-profit survey organization, VCIOM, which had undertaken New Russia Barometer surveys since 1992, was taken over through a legal technicality and a director dependent on the Kremlin appointed. Its staff and co-founder, Professor Yuri Levada, who had been deprived of his chair at Moscow State University under Brezhnev, left to carry on independent research as the Levada Center. NGOs independent of the Kremlin's network have few sources of domestic support and have received funds from foreign foundations such as George Soros's Open Society Institute (A. Evans *et al.*, 2006; Robertson, 2009). A 2006 law on the registration of foreign NGOs gives the state powers to monitor and, if it chooses, close down such bodies.

To co-opt civil society organizations, the Kremlin has created a Public Chamber to comment on public measures (A. Evans, 2008). One-third of its members are nominated by the president; that group chooses another third of the members; and the two groups together choose the remaining members. Putin's administration has also sponsored youth groups such as Nashi (Our Own) to promote patriotism and support the regime.

Internationally, Putin has sought to re-establish Russia as a major player in foreign affairs (cf. Lynch, 2005; Linan, 2009). The war on terrorism following al-Qaeda attacks on the United States in 2001 enabled him to claim that fighting in Chechnya was justified as an anti-terrorist measure. When Chechen terrorists took hostages at a theater in Moscow in 2002 and at a school in Beslan in 2004, the regime's method of rescuing hostages had a high cost in human life. Putin secured Russia's admission as a member of what thereby became the G-8, a club of leaders of major rich and democratic countries. However, an application to join the World Trade Organization has not been accepted, and the Kremlin objected without effect to intervention by NATO in Kosovo and continuing NATO expansion eastward. However, events on its border with Georgia in August 2008 gave Russia the opportunity to demonstrate its readiness to use military force against a neighbor that NATO would not rescue.

In seeking international influence, President Putin was greatly helped by the fivefold increase in dollar-denominated oil prices after the 1998 ruble collapse (Figure 3.1). When he became acting president in January 2000, oil was selling at $28 a barrel, and during his first term of office the price fluctuated around that figure. However, during Putin's second term of office, which followed the Iraq War, he gained a massive fiscal dividend from the great, even if unsteady, rise in oil prices. The lowest price of oil in his second term was greater than the highest price in his first term. Just before Putin left the presidency the price of oil reached $135 a barrel.

The massive inflow of petro-dollars has brought with it many of the textbook characteristics of a petro-state. Oil revenue has been used to pay off foreign debts, boost domestic consumption and create vast foreign exchange reserves. It has also fueled political corruption and disputes about the ownership of assets in which the regime was judge in its own interest (Goldman, 2008; Karl, 1999). The regime's power over joint ventures with major international oil companies such as Shell has created anxieties about expropriation among foreign investors. Following the Putin administration's abrupt suspension of gas shipments to Ukraine, concerns about dependence on Russian energy rose in European Union countries.

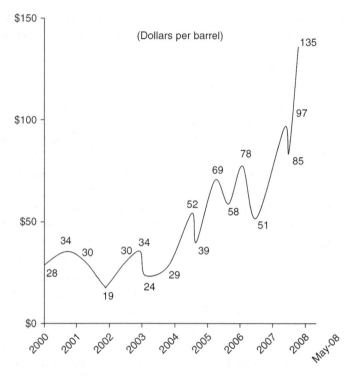

Source: Financial Times Online, http://markets.ft.com/tearsheets/performance.asp
?s=1054972&ss=WSODIssue (accessed 15 June 2010). Price shown is the highest
and lowest price each year for ICE Brent crude.

Figure 3.1 Oil price boom during Putin's presidency

Putin's recurring denunciations of corruption in the public sector
are a tacit admission of the limits of his power over public officials of
the regime. Officials have failed to act as bureaucrats applying rules
and laws and have gone into business for themselves in order to
enhance their income, prestige and power (Ryavec, 2003; Sachs and
Pistor, 1997). Large numbers of regulations, some left over from the
Soviet era, give officials the power to extract "rents" (that is, bribes)
for doing promptly what they ought to do and to extract even more
money for doing what they are not supposed to do. The Kremlin's use
of selective law enforcement against its enemies weakened its efforts to
promote the rule of law (Hendley, 2007; Kurkchiyan, 2003). In 2008
the Perception of Corruption Index of Transparency International
gave the Russian regime a score of 2.1 on its ten-point scale. This

placed it in the bottom quarter of countries globally, below Egypt, Nigeria and Ukraine. It was also deemed worse than the People's Republic of China, where the Communist party-state has been better able to control who could and could not benefit from corruption than the post-Communist Russian regime (see www.transparency.org).

The strategy followed by Vladimir Putin, acting within the formal framework of the constitution, has strengthened institutions of the regime (Remington, 2005: 31; Herspring, 2007). Moreover, his gradual changes have avoided a split in the political elite, thus differing from Gorbachev's destructive alterations in the Soviet regime. Nor have changes followed a dramatic gun battle between the Kremlin and elected representatives, as happened before the introduction of the 1993 constitution. The physical scale of Russia nonetheless sets limits on the reach of a Kremlin that has neither the political will nor the organizational resources to attempt a totalitarian takeover of society as in Stalin's time. As Tsar Nicholas II complained, "Do you think I rule Russia? Thirty thousand officials do."

The outcome of Putin's reforms has been described as a "sovereign democracy" by Vladislav Surkov, deputy head of the Kremlin's administration. This term rejects the assumption that definitions of democracy in international use are appropriate to apply to sovereign states. It appeals to national pride and a tendency to view Western ideas as alien to Russian society. It also emphasizes the sovereignty of the state over the country's billionaire businessmen. Political power is more important for acquiring money than money is the means to power (see White, 2010: 275ff.).

Putin's strengthening of the regime against his opponents has not produced popular protest, since it has been about the redistribution of power within the political elite. However, reform measures that do affect masses of subjects have occasionally provoked public protest. At the start of his second term as president, Putin attempted to reform social welfare benefits that had, like those in Western counterparts, grown in cost and had not always taken into account the reduction of the social welfare services provided by enterprises (cf. Rose, 1996a; Cook, 2006). The proposals stimulated protest demonstrations in a number of Russian cities. While these were small by West European standards, their unexpectedness caused President Putin to back off promoting welfare reform.

When the New Russia Barometer asked for evaluations of what Putin had achieved, the popular verdict was mixed (Figure 3.2).

*Q. Since Vladimir Putin became president of Russia how much has
the situation of this country changed in the following areas?*

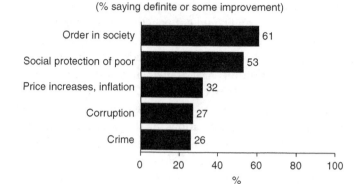

(% saying definite or some improvement)

Source: Centre for the Study of Public Policy, New Russia Barometer XV
(April, 2007).

Figure 3.2 Impact of the Putin administration

A total of 61 percent endorsed his efforts to promote order. In
addition, a majority also thought that the government had
improved the social protection of the poor. However, there was also
widespread awareness of what it had not achieved. Two-thirds
thought that not enough had been done to control inflation, and
only one-quarter were positive about the impact that the Putin
administration had had on corruption within government and on
crime in society as a whole.

A floating system of parties

In established democracies, competition between parties at free elections is the means by which citizens can hold governors to account,
whereas in regimes that practice electoral authoritarianism the government supplies the party which subjects are expected to support
(Schumpeter, 1952; Schedler, 2006). The parties in a party system
must be institutionalized in order for citizens to hold governors to
account from one election to the next (Mainwaring and Torcal,
2006; Meleshevich, 2007: ch. 1). If there is supply-side volatility,
voters cannot re-affirm or withdraw their support from governors.
A high level of supply-side volatility creates a "floating system of
parties" (Rose, 2000b).

The legacy of Boris Yeltsin, a nonparty president, was a floating system of parties that appeared and disappeared from the ballot quickly. In promulgating by decree the law for the first Duma election in 1993, the Kremlin chose a mixed-member electoral system to deal with "competing goals, uncertainty over future electoral outcomes and compromise between competing institutions" (Moser and Thames, 2001: 255; see also McFaul, 2001: 217ff.). It stipulated that half the 450 Duma seats would be filled by first-past-the-post contests in single-member districts (SMDs) and half by proportional representation (PR) from party lists. In single-member districts candidates could be party nominees or independent. When parties had to be supplied from scratch, as in Russia, there are strong political incentives for candidates to make a personal appeal as independents (J. M. Carey and Shugart, 1995: 419) or for local interests to use independent candidates as "party substitutes" (Hale, 2007: 20–21).

In most single-member districts, parties refrained from nominating candidates, thus preventing the institutionalization of accountable parties in 225 Duma seats. In the first Duma election, none of the eight successful list parties had candidates in half the districts; only two parties did so at the second election and one at the third contest. Even if a party nominated many candidates, there was no assurance of electoral success. For example, in 1995 the Liberal Democratic Party put up 184 candidates but won only one single-member seat. Selective targeting of seats could avoid such a disaster. In 2003 United Russia took 103 of the 136 seats it contested while conceding 89 by not nominating candidates. In all four SMD elections, independents were collectively the largest "party" in terms of their share of the vote.[1] In the first three Duma elections independents won the most SMD seats and they came second in the 2003 contest (Rose and Mishler, 2010a: Table 1).

In theory, independent representatives could be more accountable to their electorate, because they represent well-defined geographical constituencies and interests (Hale, 2007). However, most nominal independents quickly abandoned that label. Between the December 1995

---

[1] In accordance with Russian practice, the total vote is calculated with the inclusion of invalid votes and votes registered against all, a ballot option removed by legislation before the 2007 election. Calculations of votes and parties are based on data in Russian-language sources of the Central Electoral Commission, as reported in Rose and Munro 2009: ch. 16.

election and the seating of Duma members a month later, more than two-thirds of independents were quick-change artists, joining a party in the Duma rather than remaining unaligned. Following the 1999 election more than five-sixths of independents joined Duma parties (Rose and Munro, 2002: 106–107) and after the 2003 election two-thirds of nominal independents affiliated with a Duma party.

Proportional representation forces voters to endorse a party, since seats are distributed among parties according to their share of the PR vote and then awarded to candidates in accordance with their position on the party list. Thus, it is the decision of party leaders to give an individual a high or low place on the list that decides whether he (or occasionally she) receives a Duma seat. The 1993 election law stipulated that a party must win at least 5 percent of the list vote to qualify for a share of PR seats. Since political parties were organized from scratch, there was initially a high degree of uncertainty about how much electoral appeal they would have and a lot of optimism. In the extreme case of the 1995 Duma election, four parties that collectively won 50.5 percent of the list vote took 100 percent of the PR seats because none of the thirty-nine parties that took the other half of the vote gained enough support to clear the 5 percent threshold to qualify for seats.

Electing a president is different, because the presidency cannot be divided between parties by proportional representation and it is visibly a contest between high-profile rather than local politicians. As is common in continental Europe, the law stipulates that an absolute majority of votes is required to be elected Russia's president. If no candidate achieves this in the first-round ballot, there is a second round in which the choice is reduced to the top two contestants in the first round in order to make sure that the leader has an absolute majority of the popular vote. The likelihood of no candidate receiving a first-round majority is a function of the number of candidates nominated and of the appeal of the front runner. The law allows a candidate to run as an independent or as the nominee of a party. A party nominee could expect to receive the votes of those who had supported his party at the preceding Duma election. However, in the first three Duma elections no party won as much as one-quarter of the list vote, implying a low ceiling on the presidential vote it could deliver. While an independent lacks a floor of support, there is no ceiling on what might be won by appealing across party lines.

Initially, Boris Yeltsin had no choice but to run as an independent candidate, since the Communist Party of the Soviet Union was the only party when he successfully won office in the Russian Republic. The weakness of pro-Kremlin parties in the first two Duma elections meant that there was no party at hand that he could rely on for re-election as president. By winning without a commitment to any party, there was no way in which party members in the Duma or in a party Congress could hold Yeltsin accountable. The result was consistent with models of "delegative democracy" or "populist authoritarianism" (O'Donnell, 1994; Wigell, 2008: 244).

Three different systems of electoral competition – single-member districts, proportional representation, and a two-ballot presidential contest – are major obstacles to the formation and institutionalization of a unified party system. Nonetheless, this has been achieved in the United States, where competition for the presidency, the Senate and House of Representatives, and state governorships is between the Democratic and Republican parties.

In Russia politicians have viewed parties instrumentally and without long-term commitment. They have preferred to float free of any commitment to a party. Only 3 of more than 125 parties that have contested list seats have appeared on the ballot at all five Duma elections. Of the eighty-five parties that have appeared on the list ballot and won at least 1 percent of the vote, sixty-nine have done so at only a single election. When the party that voters have endorsed at the last election is not on the ballot at the next election, they are forced to change their party preference (Rose and Mishler, forthcoming: Figure 2). Thus, the swing in votes between parties from one election to the next is primarily due to supply-side volatility. A high level of supply-side volatility creates a floating system of parties in which the condition that "representation entails accountability" is not met (O'Donnell, 1994: 61).

Emergence of a party of power

The upshot of the abrupt transformation of a one-party system into a system of floating parties was the disorientation of the Russian electorate. The Communist Party on the ballot was no longer the party of power but a party that had been banished to opposition. Old ideological cleavages had little meaning when the Communist Party stood for conserving central features of the Soviet past and its opponents were not radicals of the left but anti-statist and pro-market. The two-ballot Duma system offered a confusion of independents and floating

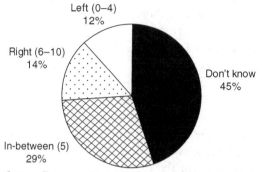

Q. In politics people sometimes talk of "left" and "right." Using this card, where would you place yourself on this scale, where 0 means the left and 10 means the right?

Left (0–4)
12%

Right (6–10)
14%

Don't know
45%

In-between (5)
29%

Source: European Social Survey conducted in Russia by CESSI (Institute for Comparative Social Research), interviewing a sample of 2,437 nationwide between 18 September 2006 and 9 January 2007.

Figure 3.3 Russians puzzled about what's left, right

parties. Instead of dividing along familiar European lines, the Russian electorate has had trouble, in multiple senses, in identifying what was left and what was right (Figure 3.3).

When the European Social Survey asked Russians to place themselves on a scale designed to measure left/right political orientations, almost half said they did not know where to place themselves and an additional 29 percent put themselves in between these two alternatives. By contrast, when the same question was asked in surveys in the first fifteen member states of the European Union, only ten percent could not place themselves on the scale. About one-quarter of Russians place themselves on the left or on the right, and most who do so are closer to the neutral midpoint than to the opposing ends. In the confused ideological space of Russia, a big majority of Russians have no understanding of what the terms "left" and "right" refer to (Colton, 2000: 148). For example, the right can refer to pro-market liberals or to conservatives who may favor either the Soviet regime or reactionary nationalists (cf. Shenfield, 2001).

Institutionalizing a noncompetitive party system

Political scientists are ambivalent about the number of parties that a competitive party system ought to have. An election with only one

Table 3.1 *Hurdles to getting on the Duma ballot*

Requirement	1993	1995	1999	2003	2007
	(Number of parties passing hurdles)				
Prior registration	130	273	139	44	15
Certified candidate lists	35	69	34	26	14
Submit candidate list	21	51	31	23	14
Lists disallowed	*(8)*	*(8)*	*(5)*	*(0)*	*(3)*
Parties on the ballot	13	43	26	23	11

Source: See Rose and Munro 2009: 255–256.

party on the ballot, as was the case in the Soviet Union, is not a competitive election. However, a system with 111 parties competing and 29 winning seats in the parliament, as in Poland in 1991, has too many parties. The Poles dealt with that problem by amending the electoral law to make it harder for small parties to compete. Tightening the law worked: In 1995 only four of the thirty-five Polish parties on the ballot won any seats (Rose and Munro, 2009: 193).

The number of parties on the ballot reflects the law of the land and the resources and calculations of politicians. Russian laws set out the conditions a group of politicians must meet in order to have a party appear on the ballot (for details, see Rose and Munro, 2009: ch. 17). At each stage of the process, some groups usually fail to clear a hurdle (Table 3.1). First of all, a group must register as a political party with the Ministry of Justice. Before the 1995 Duma election, 273 groups registered as parties. The enthusiasm of most groups is not matched by their political resources, for many have not presented names of potential candidates for the commission to certify as eligible to be placed on the ballot. The field is further reduced by some groups not following through and actually nominating a slate of candidates. At this point, the Central Election Commission can disallow a party's list, thus ruling it off the ballot. The effort and resources required to clear each hurdle meant that during the Yeltsin administration the number of parties on the ballot was always far fewer than those that initially registered as a party.

During the presidency of Vladimir Putin, new electoral legislation drastically reduced the number of parties competing for Duma votes (for details, see Bacon, 2004; Wilson, 2006, 2009; Moraski, 2007). Before the 2007 election the mixed-member Duma electoral system was replaced by a system in which all Duma members are elected by proportional representation. This eliminated the opportunity for politicians to gain a Duma seat independent of a party machine. With all Duma seats allocated by the list system of proportional representation, each member now depends on the party's elite for a place on the party list that is likely to guarantee a seat in the Duma. As intended, the law has got rid of "too many" parties. The number of parties on the ballot fell by more than half compared to the previous election.

The threshold to qualify for proportional representation seats was raised from 5 to 7 percent and small parties are no longer allowed to form an electoral bloc in order to clear the threshold. This was a particular threat to two parties identified as democratic opponents, Yabloko and the Union of Right Forces, which between them had won 7.6 percent of the list vote at the previous election.

Creating United Russia

To institutionalize support for the regime that he headed, Vladimir Putin slowly crafted a party of power, that is, the dominant party of the regime. This has three advantages: It controls access to the ballot, it cues the electorate about how to show their support for the regime and it commands a disciplined majority of votes in the Duma. This goal has been achieved by the revision of election laws, structuring a party organization that centralizes authority in the hands of a nonaccountable leader, and winning elections by margins that make opposition parties irrelevant.

Unity was the impeccably consensual name of the party created in September 1999 to provide a platform for Yeltsin associates in the Duma election three months later. It was endorsed by thirty-nine regional governors. Vladimir Putin, who had earlier in the decade been a member of three failed parties of power, the Communist Party of the Soviet Union, Russia's Choice and Our Home Is Russia, gave Unity his endorsement. It could thus draw on the political and financial resources of the government nationwide. Unity had no clear partisan orientation, beyond strong support for the war in Chechnya (see Colton and McFaul, 2000). Its main competitor for votes was Fatherland–All Russia, formed earlier in 1999 by Yury Luzhkov, the mayor of Moscow; Yevgeny Primakov, a veteran Soviet official and foreign and prime minister to Boris Yeltsin; and various regional politicians.

Unity won 23.3 percent of the list vote at the 1999 Duma election, placing it a close second to the Communist Party. It also finished ahead of Fatherland–All Russia, which took 13.3 percent of the vote. However, the regional base of the latter was stronger, enabling Fatherland to win more single-member districts and end up with almost as many Duma seats as Unity. In the absence of any ideological difference, Putin made Fatherland–All Russia an offer it could not refuse, namely, to merge with Unity. United Russia, created by this merger in 2001, had more Duma members than the Communist Party and better prospects for future electoral success.

At the 2003 Duma election United Russia gained the first victory for a Kremlin-backed party. It won 38 percent of the list vote and took almost half the list seats, because one-quarter of the PR vote was wasted on parties that failed to cross the PR threshold to qualify for seats. United Russia's links with governors of regions helped win seats in single-member districts. Once the Duma met in January 2004, an additional seventy-eight members joined United Russia, giving it the two-thirds majority important for amending the constitution.

Prior to the 2004 presidential election, changes in election law made it more burdensome to nominate candidates, for example, requiring two million signatures on an election petition. This reduced the total number of candidates on the ballot to three party nominees and three independents. The two major opposition parties demonstrated their rejection of the Kremlin's electoral practices by nominating token candidates. The Communist candidate was a former Agrarian Party member and the Liberal Democratic candidate was the former bodyguard of its leader, Vladimir Zhirinovsky. The two candidates together won only 7.9 percent of the first-round vote; running as an independent, Putin won 71.3 percent of the vote. So large a share of the vote is without equal in free and fair elections.

In the first all-PR election in 2007, most party lists named three of their leaders on the ballot. United Russia gave only one name, Vladimir Putin. It won 70 percent of the Duma seats. When the New Russia Barometer asked about motives for voting for United Russia, 69 percent said they did so because Putin headed the party's list, as against 31 percent saying they did so because they liked the party. Statistical analysis confirms that the stronger a voter's endorsement of Putin, the greater the likelihood of voting for United Russia. Since President Putin's approval rating was high long before

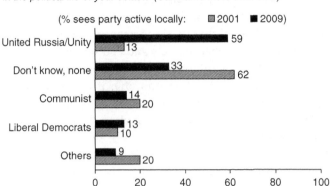

Q. Which of the parties and fractions in the Duma participate actively in the political life of your oblast? (Can name more than one.)

Source: Centre for the Study of Public Policy, New Russia Barometer X (June – July 2001) and XVIII (June 2009).

Figure 3.4 Nationwide recognition of United Russia's dominance

United Russia was founded, the direction of causation is clear: Putin's appeal carried the day for a party that he created to strengthen his hand in the Duma (Rose and Mishler, 2010a: Table 3).

To test whether parties are visible to electors where they live and not just "brands" publicized by national television, the New Russia Barometer asks respondents about parties present in their region (*oblast*). Even though single-member district elections ought to have encouraged local party activity, in 2001 three-fifths could not identify any party that was active in their locality (Figure 3.4). The Communist Party was the most visible party; however, it was named by only one in five Russians, a great decline from its presence during the Soviet era. Unity, the fledgling party of power of the Kremlin, was named by only one in eight respondents. The lack of a party presence where most voters lived reflected a decade of elite competition in a floating system of parties.

Eight years of Kremlin efforts to promote United Russia as the dominant party has made it a party that is dominant nationwide (Gel'man, 2008). The 2009 NRB survey found that three-fifths saw United Russia as active in their city and the proportion seeing no party active locally had almost halved (Figure 3.4). Communist Party activity had fallen and the activity of other parties has been slight too. As a result, United Russia is the only party active in two-fifths of localities; in one in five localities it has competition; and in one-third no party is seen as active. In the absence of visible local party competition, Russians must rely for news about competing parties on Kremlin-dominated television presenting "a world apart from viewers" (Mickiewicz, 2006; see also Oates, 2006).

A hegemonic party system

On the face of it, the Russian party system today appears to be institutionalized. In the 2007 Duma election, the list PR system ensured that party candidates won 100 percent of the Duma vote; party nominees also won 99 percent of the presidential vote. There is also competition, with a double-digit choice of parties on the ballot at each election and at least four parties winning seats in the Duma. If elections are the only criterion for democracy, then Russia may be considered an electoral democracy of a distinctive type (Oversloot and Verheul, 2006).

Russia today has a hegemonic party system, because the position of United Russia goes far beyond the position of a party that usually comes first in votes in a parliamentary election but lacks an absolute majority of seats enabling it to govern on its own (as the Swedish Social Democrats have done.) Giovanni Sartori (1976: 230) characterizes a hegemon party as follows:

The hegemonic party neither allows for a formal nor a de facto competition for power. Other parties are permitted to exist, but as second class, licensed parties, for they are not permitted to compete with the hegemonic party in antagonistic terms and on an equal basis.

Opposition parties divide the vote and lack the collective strength to challenge United Russia (Laverty, 2008; March, 2009). To use a Leninist term, opposition parties are "useful idiots" giving the appearance of competition but not threatening the hegemony of United Russia. The Communist Party can be portrayed as out-of-touch relics of the past and the Liberal Democratic Party's leader, Vladimir Zhirinovsky, as making irresponsible appeals inconsistent with holding presidential office. The current fourth party, Fair Russia, endorsed Putin's presidential successor, Dmitry Medvedev. The dominance of United Russia is consistent with Russia being described as an electoral authoritarian regime (Schedler, 2006).

Whereas the Communist Party of the Soviet Union used ideology to justify its hegemony, Putin rejects such rhetoric. Like third-way prime minister Tony Blair, Putin promises to do "what works" when mobilizing support from the electorate. In the words of Andrei Illarionov, a former Putin economic advisor:

A guiding principle of Russia's new economic and legal model is selectivity... It does not look communist, or liberal, or nationalistic, or imperial. Instead, it is an ideology of "*nash*-ism" or in English, "ours-ism," in which subsidies, credits and powers are handed out to those who are "nashy" . . . The point of the new model is to redistribute resources to "our own." (quoted in Burger, 2009: 47)

In institutionalizing a party system to support his power, Vladimir Putin has adapted the Communist Party's practice of democratic centralism, a doctrine "in which centralism always won the day" (McCauley, 1998: 150). This contrasts with dominant party systems such as Japan under the Liberal Democrats and Italy in the time of Christian Democratic dominance, because these parties were divided into factions which effectively competed against each other (Pempel, 1990). In United Russia power is centralized in the hands of Putin as chair of its ruling council. Putin can deprive dissident Duma deputies of their seat at any time, since Duma rules stipulate that members who are expelled from their party thereby lose their seat. In the words of United Russia's general secretary, its Duma members are "not there for political discussion but for technical issues" (quoted in Jack, 2004).

Officeholders are beholden to the United Russia leadership for their positions. In creating his cabinet as prime minister, Vladimir Putin has favored handpicked nonparty appointees for four-fifths of the ministerial posts. They must be personally loyal to him to retain office. The fifth who are United Russia members are also accountable to him as their patron. After United Russia won 70 percent of Duma seats at the 2007 election, 105 of its members resigned their places, thus removing any vestige of those running for election being personally accountable to the electorate. Their Duma seats were taken by United Russia placemen who are immediately accountable to the party leader for their seat. Technology means that United Russia's Duma members do not even need to attend for their votes to be counted in support of the Putin administration. Votes are cast by pressing electronic buttons at the assigned desk of each Duma member. In a May 2010 ballot on drinking and driving, less than one-fifth of Duma members were present. Nonetheless, the measure carried by a vote of 448 to 0. The explanation was caught on CCTV cameras: Dozens of United Russia members ran around the chamber pressing the yes button on behalf of absent colleagues. They also voted for the government measure in the name of absent opposition members.

The response of Russian subjects has been pragmatic too. Although most Russians do vote, more than five-sixths think that they have little or no influence on what government does (Figure 3.5). Even among those who voted for United Russia only one in five thinks that their views are inputs that influence government, while four-fifths who show support for the party of power tend to be subjects, aware that while government can make demands on them, they have little or no influence on what government does.

Q. *How much influence do you think people like yourself can have on government?*
Q. *Did you vote in the election for the president? If so, how did you vote?*

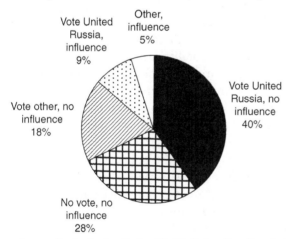

Source: Centre for the Study of Public Policy, New Russia Barometer XVII (March 2008). Influence: replies a lot or some.

Figure 3.5 Subjects support United Russia

4 | *Increasing support for an undemocratic regime*

To describe regime change as a political transition is correct but vague; it raises the critical question: In what direction is the regime heading? The simultaneous collapse of undemocratic regimes stimulated a vast literature about change in a single direction, democratization. Samuel P. Huntington (1991) proclaimed a third wave of democracy and Francis Fukuyama (1992), invoking a Hegelian metaphor, described the collapse of the Communist system as "the end of history." Many quantitative ratings of regime change make democracy their end point (e.g. Vanhanen, 2003; Przeworski *et al.*, 2000). Countries at the other end of the scale are simply treated as "not democracies," when in fact they may be successfully consolidating undemocratic regimes.

In a totalitarian regime change can go in only one direction: a reduction in the intrusive claims of the state over the lives of its subjects. The abandonment of totalitarian aspirations does not imply a commitment to democratization. Changes within the Soviet Union and its satellites simply made Communist regimes govern in a post-totalitarian manner through institutions that had been created in pursuit of totalitarian goals. Post-Communist transformation was something very different: It involved the simultaneous alteration of the economy and of society as well as the political regime, and the creation of more than a dozen new states (Rose, 2009c). The maelstrom of transformation gave confusing signals about the direction of change. Political and economic imperatives led to reversals in direction and rhetoric in a trial-and-error search for support. It thus took time for subjects to learn whether their new leaders were trying to consolidate support for a democratic or for an undemocratic regime.

The result of transformation in Russia has led one Western scholar to describe the Russian regime as having "failed to advance to democracy" (Fish, 2005: 1). However, this imputes American values and aspirations to Russia's governors. The Russian Federation is not a failed state. This chapter shows that it has successfully gained popular support for an undemocratic regime.

Support with and without democratization

The common characteristic of most regimes created since the fall of the Berlin Wall is that, by one means or another, they have consolidated support. However, post-Communist political elites have differed in the type of regime that they have supplied: Some are democratic and some are not. Ten Central and East European countries have had the consolidation of their democratic credentials confirmed by admission to membership in the European Union. By contrast, leaders of Soviet successor states have rejected European models of democracy in theory and fact. The people's democracy of the Communist era, in which the Communist Party was the highest political authority, has been succeeded by a sovereign "democracy" consistent with undemocratic national traditions and with the interests of the current ruling elite. The rhetorical invocation of democracy in undemocratic regimes shows that political elites believe it is a useful symbol for rallying support, but leaves open how their citizens and subjects interpret this symbol.

Empirical responses to democracy as symbol

Given the history of the tsarist, Prussian, Habsburg, Ottoman and Soviet empires, democracy can be characterized as a system of government that was absent from the many regimes that have ruled in Central and Eastern Europe and Soviet territory up to the fall of the Berlin Wall. Interwar experiments with democracy were limited in duration. In the Soviet Union, the imposition of a totalitarian party-state made democracy an attractive symbol to subjects who rejected the Communist system. But this also meant that there was no way in which people could gain experience of what life in a democracy was actually like. Television offered a vicarious window on democracy to subjects of the German Democratic Republic living within range of transmitters of West German stations, and Estonians had opportunities to watch Finnish television. Communist regimes did their best to prevent their subjects from following news from democratic political systems, albeit for some this made it worth the risk to be clandestine listeners to Radio Free Europe and the World Service of the British Broadcasting Corporation.

Democracy became immediately salient with the fall of the Berlin Wall, since political elites, whatever their background and personal preferences, had to agree on new institutions that could hope to obtain the support of their citizens. In Central and Eastern Europe, the introduction of democratic institutions was seen as the best way to get both elite agreement and popular support (cf. Rustow, 1970; di Palma, 1990). It was also consistent with the goal of "returning" to Europe, which by this time had become both democratic and prosperous (Rose, 1996b).

The freedom to undertake research on political issues and the importance of understanding how newly enfranchised citizens saw democracy stimulated empirical enquiry. A team of social scientists within the region, led by a group at the Hungarian Academy of Science, produced the earliest and most comprehensive empirical study. Altogether, eleven national surveys were undertaken within a year or two of the fall of the Berlin Wall. Their starting point was to ask an open-ended question: What does democracy mean for you? Big majorities, ranging from 66 percent in Romania to 87 percent in Czechoslovakia, were able to give a short answer to this question. For more than half of respondents, the word best summarizing their thinking about democracy was that it meant freedom. This pattern is consistent with theories of freedom from the state as being the first step in the development of Western democracy (Berlin, 1958; Marshall, 1950). References to elections and to social welfare were a distant second and third (Simon, 1998: 105ff.).

Because a full description of democracy covers a multiplicity of characteristics, a complementary question asked post-Communist citizens to say how strongly they associated a range of conditions with democracy. The replies confirmed the high importance of liberty and the rule of law (Figure 4.1). Having multiple parties competing for popular support ranks third. A growing economy, very evident to East Europeans comparing the command economy of their one-party state with the prosperity of West European democracies, also ranked higher than jobs and social equality.

When the New Russia Barometer asks about important characteristics of democracy, big majorities see it as recognizing freedom from the state, a choice between parties at an election, and government

Q. *People associate democracy with diverse meanings. Can you please tell me whether each of these phrases shown has a lot, something, nothing much or nothing at all to do with democracy?* (Replies scored from 4, a lot, to 1, nothing at all.)

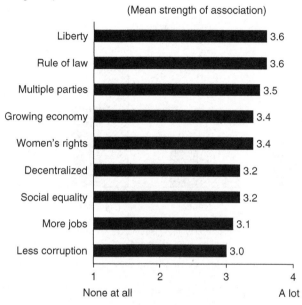

(Mean strength of association)

Liberty	3.6
Rule of law	3.6
Multiple parties	3.5
Growing economy	3.4
Women's rights	3.4
Decentralized	3.2
Social equality	3.2
More jobs	3.1
Less corruption	3.0

None at all   A lot

Sources: Simon, 1998: 100; pooled results of national surveys in Bulgaria, Czech Republic, East Germany, Estonia, Hungary, Lithuania, Poland, Romania, Slovakia, Slovenia, Ukraine and Krasnoyarsk, Russia, November 1990–November 1992; total number of interviews, 12,365.

Figure 4.1 What post-Communist citizens associate with democracy

provision of social welfare. The chief difference is whether a given characteristic is regarded as important or essential (see e.g. Rose, Misher and Munro 2006: Table 7.1; White, 2011: Table 8.5). The importance given to liberty and multiple parties competing for office is common to citizens in many countries. The provision of social welfare is not just a legacy from Communist times; it is also cited by social democrats around the world (see e.g. Dalton *et al.*, 2007; Diamond and Plattner, 2008).

Russians not only have a clear idea of what democracy is about; they also have a clear desire to be governed democratically. When people are asked how they would like Russia to be governed, the majority preferring democracy to dictatorship has been consistently high. After two decades of experiencing the tumultuous administration of Boris Yeltsin and order under Vladimir Putin, 82 percent were positive about

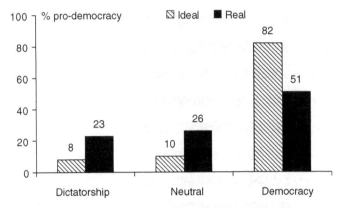

Q. Here is a scale ranging from 1 to 10, where 1 means complete dictatorship and 10 complete democracy. Where would you like our political system to be? And where would you place it at the present time (2009)?

Source: Centre for the Study of Public Policy, New Russia Barometer XVIII (June 2009). Pro-democracy replies: 6 to 10 on scale

Figure 4.2 Gap between democratic demand and elite supply

democracy and only 8 percent thought that dictatorship was the better form of government (Figure 4.2).

When people are asked whether the starting point for transformation, the Soviet regime, was democratic, the answer is negative. In reply to a question asking people to place the regime before *perestroika* on a scale with one end representing a complete dictatorship and the other a complete democracy, 72 percent unambiguously characterized it as a dictatorship and an additional 16 percent assigned it to the psychological middle of the ten-point scale. Only 12 percent described the Soviet regime as democratic.

Although elections have been held on schedule, Russians have not seen their government as engaged in democratization. At the midpoint of President Yeltsin's second term, the New Russia Barometer asked people to say whether the new regime was closer to a full democracy or a complete dictatorship. The largest bloc was close to the midpoint and the overall mean rating was 5.3, just below the arithmetic mean. The mean rating for democracy as an ideal was 7.4. After two terms of the Putin presidency, more than four-fifths of Russians were in favor of democracy as the kind of government that they wanted, while only half thought the regime was more democratic than dictatorial (Figure 4.2).

The democratic model of support predicts that high support for the democratic ideal ought to make government produce a regime that its citizens view as democratic. However, this has not happened in Russia. There is a big gap between how Russians would like to be governed and how they are governed. Such a gap is consistent with Robert Dahl's (1989) polyarchic model of democratic support. In a polyarchy, there is a gap between democracy as an ideal and the regime as it actually is. As long as the regime is democratic, then citizens have the resources to put pressure on governors to reform institutions to bring them closer to the democratic ideal (Rose, Shin and Munro, 1999). However, in an undemocratic regime, governors do not have to respond to the preferences of subjects. When the gap is substantial, Ted R. Gurr (1970) hypothesizes that subjects can become frustrated and even rebellious. However, if the political elite holds firmly to an undemocratic course and offers appropriate sticks and carrots to induce support, then subjects will learn to support what the new regime supplies.

Measuring support

Endorsement of the democratic ideal is not the same as the evaluation of a system of government as it actually is. In an established democratic system, asking people whether they are satisfied with the way that democracy is working identifies a group of dissatisfied democrats who support the regime but would like to see it reformed. However, in an undemocratic regime such a question rests on a false premise, namely, that the regime is democratic when this is not the case (for further discussion, see Rose, Mishler and Haerpfer, 1998: ch. 5; Canache *et al.*, 2001).

The realist approach is used in the CSPP Barometer surveys: It asks people about the regime that political elites have actually supplied. It does not label it as democratic or undemocratic. While support is a word that is easy to understand in everyday conversation, the difference between the regime as a set of durable institutions and the government of the day is not so easy to distinguish. In a consolidated democracy, the great majority of people cannot conceive of being governed by a regime any different from what they have known all their lives as "the American way" or "the Swedish way." However, political transformation gives concrete significance to differences between types of government, since it involves a very public change between regimes.

Our questionnaire is defined ostensively, that is, by pointing at what is there; it thus avoids using a label that subjects may consider unsuitable, such as calling it a democracy. Ostensive definition also avoids linking a system of government that is meant to be durable to transient personalities, as is done in American references to the Obama administration or British references to the Cameron coalition government. It also avoids confusing institutions of the regime with its outputs, as is the case if a question asks about satisfaction with the performance of government. Such a phrase can be interpreted as referring to how well the government of the day is managing the economy. The Barometer surveys ask people to evaluate performance in a parallel set of questions about the economy and about whether the regime respects freedom.

In a new regime people must accept or reject the whole package of institutions supplied by the elite; they cannot pick and choose between parts. Therefore, our Barometer questionnaires treat the regime holistically because transformation is about a pervasive change in central institutions of the state. Like most political packages, the institutions of a new regime are a mixture of attractive and unattractive parts. However, evaluating a new regime is like voting in a referendum: A person must either support or reject what is on offer without alteration. In a consolidated democracy, by contrast, surveys may ask about support for specific institutions, such as the courts, the legislature or the president. Indications of dissatisfaction with particular institutions are sometimes "overinterpreted" as indicating a threat to the regime. In fact, such statements are no more and no less than a demand to reform institutions or change leaders (cf. Dalton, 2004: vii, 6ff.).

When the Centre for the Study of Public Policy began its New Europe Barometer (NEB) surveys about regime support in Bulgaria and what was then Czechoslovakia in spring 1991, the collapse of Communist regimes meant that the future could not be a simple projection of what had gone before. Many countries had yet to adopt a constitution and in some the boundaries of the state were contested. Questions about political support had to take into account the novelty of the present system of government, uncertainties about the future, and the past being known but no more. To provide a durable baseline for trend analysis, support questions had to avoid mentioning current events, parties or personalities that could (and often did) soon leave the political scene. To be useful for comparative analysis, the questions had to focus on generic political concepts applicable in many countries yet immediately meaningful to people confronted with a new political system. The preparation of key questions was carried forward in Austria, Poland, Hungary and Romania in autumn and concluded in Moscow in November 1991. By 2009 more than one hundred surveys had included support questions in democratic and undemocratic post-Communist regimes.

The NEB questionnaire asks about regimes in the sequence in which people have experienced them (Rose, 2009c: chs. 12, 17). It starts by requesting people to evaluate the former Communist regime. It then asks people to evaluate the current political system with free elections and parties. The avoidance of adjectives such as "democratic" or "national" makes the question meaningful in countries where the regime is not, or no longer is, democratic, and in multi-ethnic societies such as the Baltic states. References to parties and elections were included in order to give concrete meaning to the abstract term "system." Since every NEB respondent has experienced two contrasting regimes, the sequence makes clear that the focus is on two different regimes. A third question asks people to rate their system of government in five years. This time frame is far enough into the future to offer the potential for substantial change and, especially in new regimes, uncertain enough to tap the subjective hopes and fears of individuals about their support for the direction of a regime in transition.

Offering a scale ranging from minus 100, the worst, to plus 100, the best, gives people who are anti-Communist or strongly against the current regime an opportunity to show just how "anti" they are. In the first NEB round in 1991, more than one-quarter of Romanians and Czechs gave their previous regime a rating of minus 100. The scale also offers a neutral midpoint, 0, for people who have mixed views about their system.

By 2004 what was once the very distant and uncertain future in the aftermath of the fall of the Berlin Wall was now the everyday experience of hundreds of millions of people. In ten Central and East European countries people were no longer subjects of a Communist regime or post-Communist citizens; instead, they had become citizens of the European Union. NEB surveys found that, while a majority in all ten countries supported their regime, there were crossnational differences (Figure 4.3). In four countries, Estonia, Lithuania, Slovenia and the Czech Republic, 70 percent or more were positive about their current regime. However, in Bulgaria and Romania only 51 percent showed support, and the European Commission, while not

*Q. Here is a scale evaluating how well the political system works.
The top, plus 100, is the best and the bottom, minus 100, is the worst.
Where on this scale would you put our present system of governing
with free elections and many parties?*

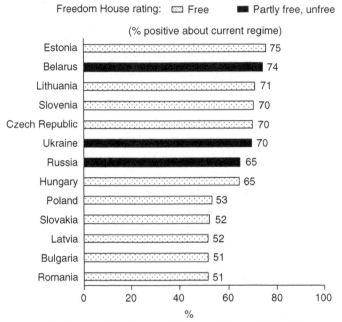

Freedom House rating: ▨ Free   ■ Partly free, unfree

(% positive about current regime)

Country	%
Estonia	75
Belarus	74
Lithuania	71
Slovenia	70
Czech Republic	70
Ukraine	70
Russia	65
Hungary	65
Poland	53
Slovakia	52
Latvia	52
Bulgaria	51
Romania	51

%

Source: Regime classifications from Freedom House, 2004; all New
Europe Barometer surveys from 2004 except Ukraine, February 2005.

Figure 4.3 Popular support for post-Communist regimes

questioning their democratic credentials, postponed their admission to
the union until 2007 (see Rose, 2008).

Regimes in post-Soviet states had also had time to demonstrate
what they were like. Freedom House rated Belarus as unambiguously
undemocratic, and Russia had been downrated to the category of
unfree political system. The trajectory of Ukraine has been less clear-
cut, fluctuating between being free and unfree. At the time of the NEB
survey, the Orange Revolution had turned an incumbent president out
of office in favor of a democratic hopeful. Since then, Ukrainians have
turned the Orange Revolution out of office and restored a president
associated with a less-than-free regime. In all three regimes there was a
high degree of support shown by their subjects: 74 percent in Belarus,
70 percent in Ukraine and 65 percent in Russia.

Although post-Communist regimes have diverged in major respects, differences in popular support have not been along the lines differentiating democratic from undemocratic regimes. In the ten new EU member states, an average of 61 percent are positive about their democratic regime. Since another 8 percent are neutral, there is a two-to-one balance in favor of the new regime. In post-Soviet states closest to Europe geographically, support is even higher. An average of 70 percent endorse their new regime and, after taking into account the 7 percent who are neutral, the balance in favor is more than three to one. NEB evidence reinforces the conclusion in Chapter 1 (Figure 1.3): Undemocratic as well as democratic regimes can mobilize popular support. Thus, an in-depth examination of the experience of Russians is important not only in itself but also because it deals with the experience of many countries around the world today.

Dynamics of regime support

In a regime in the process of transformation, the dynamics and direction of support for the regime are more important than the absolute level of support. Theories of democratization assume that a new regime will be responsive to its citizens and that this will produce a positive dynamic consolidating the regime. The object of an undemocratic regime is the same – increasing the support it receives from its subjects; only the methods used are different.

Contrasting elite evaluations of change

Replacing the hammer-and-sickle Soviet flag with the red, white and blue banner of the Russian Federation and removing statues of Marx and Lenin from prominent plinths made palpable to Russians that a new regime had come into being. However much such symbols may stir emotions, they cannot tell us the direction of the replacement regime. This has been revealed with the passage of time. However, there is no consensus between the international community and Russia's governing elite about what the new regime has become.

When Mikhail Gorbachev took office as general secretary of the Communist Party of the Soviet Union, Freedom House placed the country at the bottom of its seven-point scale rating countries from completely free to completely unfree. Categorizing it as a complete dictatorship was consistent with Soviet history. Gorbachev's initiatives resulted in Freedom House upgrading its rating, but within the category of unfree regimes. After competitive elections began to have serious consequences, the expiring Soviet regime was raised to the ranks of the partly free. The launch of the Russian Federation resulted in further improvements in its ratings, albeit the regime was still categorized as partly free. While changes did not match those of Central and East European countries, nonetheless this advance could be interpreted as the start of a process of democratization. At the start of his first term of office President Bill Clinton of the United States enthusiastically identified Russia as a democracy and pledged support to Boris Yeltsin in promoting democratization. However, during his second term of office, Clinton had come to support Yeltsin as the "least bad" Russian president there was (Marsden, 2005: ch. 2).

Freedom House ratings began to reverse by 1999 and in Vladimir Putin's first year as president the regime's rating had fallen to the borderline separating partly free from unfree regimes. By the start of his second term of office, the regime was once again placed in the unfree category and has remained there since, along with countries such as Algeria, Cameroon, and the United Arab Emirates. The country's Freedom House rating is now the same as when Gorbachev launched his reform initiative. However, Gorbachev achieved this rating through liberalizing a very undemocratic regime whereas the Putin administration achieved it by reversing tendencies to democratization.

Western social scientists initially treated the new regime as engaged in democratization or even as having achieved "a highly imperfect democratic order" (McFaul, 2001: 17). However, this has been followed by dropping the use of democracy from the compound labels that are used to describe what is variously called an "unconsolidated autocracy" (Way, 2005) or a "plebiscitarian autocracy" (Rose, Mishler and Munro, 2006: ch. 2). Whatever hybrid categories are used, there is a consensus that it is misleading to characterize the Russian regime as engaged in democratization (for reviews, see Fish, 2005: ch. 2; White, 2011: ch. 8).

The abruptness of Russia's regime change meant that there was no preparation for the challenge of creating a new regime, whether democratic or undemocratic. The political education of Boris Yeltsin and his team of advisors was gained within the Communist Party of the Soviet Union. In the words of Anatoly Sobchak, mayor of St. Petersburg and a mentor of Vladimir Putin, "To fear Communists

Q. *What kind of democracy does Russia need?*

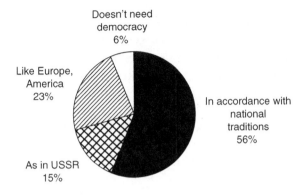

Doesn't need
democracy
6%

Like Europe,
America
23%

In accordance with
national
traditions
56%

As in USSR
15%

Source: White, 2011: Table 8.7, 2010 survey.

Figure 4.4 The kind of democracy that Russia needs

does not make sense, because we were all Communists. We had 20 million members." There was no agreed policy among ex-party members about what the new regime should or could be like (White *et al.*, 1997: 242ff.). President Yeltsin was forced to proceed in a trial-and-error experiment in political innovation. His main goal was to maintain his hold on power. The new regime accepted one essential element of democracy, elections, as the means to decide who should govern. However, insufficient regard for the rule of law undermined a claim to being a democratic regime. In a book published near the end of Yeltsin's first term, *Democracy from Scratch*, Fish (1995; 2005: 5) foresaw two alternatives, "democracy by default," that is, a "fairly open political regime with weak institutions for translating popular preferences into policy," or "moderate authoritarianism," that is, a regime that tended to be closed to the expression of popular preferences.

The Putin administration responded to the Yeltsin legacy by seeking to consolidate a regime that could act effectively and secure the compliance of its subjects (Figure 4.4). It did so by strengthening institutions of the state and closing down channels for expressing criticisms of the new regime:

Democracy should not be accompanied by the collapse of the state and the impoverishment of its people. I'm sure that democracy is not anarchy and laissez faire. (quoted in R. Watson, 2005)

The formulation "sovereign democracy" emphasizes Putin's rejection of the right of foreign governments or critics "to use the democratic lexicon to influence our internal and external politics" (quoted in Hutcheson, 2010: 18). It is also consistent with the thinking of a majority of Russians. While only one in six would regard the Soviet system as the form of democracy (*sic*) suited to Russia, less than one in four think a Western-style democracy is suitable. A majority regard the country as needing a special kind of democracy according with national traditions. While this language is vague enough to include freedom or respect for the rule of law, such characteristics of government have been absent from Russian history.

The changing views of Russians

Because planning and analyzing a survey can take several years, by the time it is published the opinions studied are part of the past. In a book about a stable political system, this is unlikely to make a substantial difference to conclusions. However, in a regime that undergoes the shock of transformation, it can make a big difference whether the time examined is the first months of high uncertainty, an economic boom, or a time when the economy is in recession. The inexperience of the Russian people with anything other than Soviet rule at the time Boris Yeltsin took power and the subsequent efforts of Vladimir Putin to institutionalize an effective regime imply substantial changes in support during the unsteady evolution of the Russian regime, and this is the case.

When the first New Russia Barometer went in the field, the Russian Federation was four weeks old. While the old regime was gone, the new regime was a blank. The new regime started off with a big majority of Russians disliking it: 74 percent gave it a rating between minus 1 and minus 100, while only 14 percent showed positive support and 12 percent expressed no opinion (Figure 4.5). Statistically, this implied that the new regime's support could only rise from a low base. However, politically it implied that the new regime was vulnerable to collapse.

After a year Russians had had at least a little experience of what their new regime was like: 36 percent gave positive support to it and the median Russian was neutral. For the rest of the decade support fluctuated: A plurality of respondents were negative while the median respondent was neutral about the new regime. A politically significant line was crossed in 2003. For the first time the percentage of Russians

Q. Here is a scale evaluating how well the political system works. The top,
plus 100, is the best and the bottom, minus 100, is the worst. Where on this
scale would you put our present system of governing?'

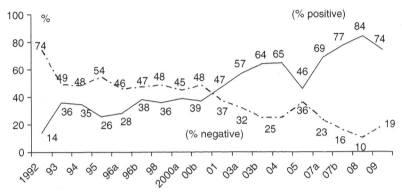

Source: Centre for the Study of Public Policy, New Russia Barometer data base.
Neutral replies (0) not shown.

Figure 4.5 Trends in support for Russia's regime

positive about the new regime outnumbered those who were negative.
While support for the regime has risen substantially since its early
years, there is nothing inevitable about this trend. From one survey to
the next support has risen significantly in nine years, while it has fallen
or not altered significantly in almost half the NRB surveys. However,
the changes have not canceled each other out. After almost two
decades of experiencing how the Russian Federation is governed,
three-quarters to five-sixths now positively support their regime. This
has produced the consolidation of an undemocratic regime.

The upward trend in popular support for a regime that has become
more undemocratic is a striking challenge to theories of the inevitability
of democratization. It is also a caution against assuming that the
absence of democratization means the "failure" of political authorities.
In the case of Russia, it demonstrates the clear success of the regime's
leaders in securing positive support for an undemocratic regime.

Variability of support

While generalizations are frequently made about Russian attitudes as
if everyone thought the same, NRB surveys consistently show that
Russians divide into three groups: those who support the regime, those

who do not and those who are neutral. However, neutral subjects are consistently the smallest of the three blocs of opinion. Thus, even though the mean rating of the regime tends to hover around the midpoint, most Russians are not neutral; the population divides into supporters and critics of the regime.

Because the New Russia Barometer measures support on a 201-point scale it is easy for people to register their degree of enthusiasm or disapproval of the regime. There is no polarization of extreme attitudes. In the first NRB survey, when the greatest proportion of Russians were negative about the new regime, only 5 percent gave it the worst possible score, minus 100, and when the majority supporting the regime was highest in 2008 only 1 percent gave it the highest possible rating of plus 100. Instead of generalizing about what all Russians are supposed to think, we need to understand differences between individuals who are more or less enthusiastic or lukewarm supporters or critics of the regime.

Statistically, the standard deviation is the appropriate measure of the extent to which Russians cluster or are polarized in evaluating the regime. The two-thirds within one standard deviation of the mean form a middle mass of supporters near the mean while one-sixth are even more positive about the regime and one-sixth less. In the first decade of the new regime, the standard deviation tended to be high, reaching a maximum of 55 points in 2000. This meant that there was usually a substantial proportion giving support and a substantial proportion withholding it (cf. Figure 4.6). Concurrently, there was also a significant minority neutral about the new regime, rising to as much as 26 percent in early 1996. Thus, from 1993 to 2001 there was usually no majority opinion for *or* against the regime; the median Russian was neutral.

A consensus in support for the regime began to develop by 2003 and peaked in 2008. The standard deviation fell to less than the overall mean for support, plus 33 on the 201-point scale. Five-sixths of Russians gave positive support to the regime while only one in ten did not. Even though the mean level of support fell by 10 points in 2009, this did not destroy the consensus, for 74 percent of Russians continued to be positive about the regime and the two-fifths who were very positive at the top half of the support scale outnumbered those who were very negative by a margin of three and one-half to one.

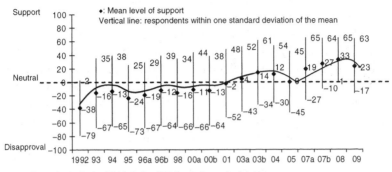

Q. Here is a scale for ranking how our system of government works. The top, plus 100, is the best; the bottom, minus 100, the worst. Where on the scale would you put our current system of governing?

Source: Centre for the Study of Public Policy, New Russia Barometer data base.

Figure 4.6 Wide dispersion in support for the regime

From its launch, the regime has had lots of "floating" supporters and critics. Exposure to the performance of a new regime is a stimulus to rethink attitudes among those initially predisposed to support or reject it and this has very clearly happened in Russia. The ups and downs in support for the regime over the span of a few years reflect the fact that a majority of Russians have changed their evaluation at least once. That is the only way in which support could rise from 14 to 84 percent in the course of almost two decades while those critical fell by a similarly great amount. This implies that many subjects do not have permanent commitment to support the new regime.

A lifetime of learning and relearning

Whether and why an individual supports a regime can be modeled as the outcome of a lifetime-learning process. This model summarizes the effect on regime support of the accumulation of old and new experiences (Mishler and Rose, 2002; Rose, Mishler and Haerpfer, 1998: 117ff., 194ff.). Logically, the political values and norms that an individual learns first are more important because they establish criteria by which the subsequent performance of the regime is evaluated. In a steady-state regime that does not change during an individual's lifetime, the values learned early in life can be used to justify support in old age too. However, the political system governing Russia has not been in a steady state throughout the lifetime of New Russia Barometer respondents. Since 1991 all Russian adults have been subject to intensive resocialization through the quadruple transformation of state, regime, economy and society. By 2008 the median adult will have been subject to resocialization in the Federation for as long a period as being socialized in the Soviet Union.

We have developed a model of lifetime political learning *and* relearning to take into account the effects of regime change on support, as well as the changing political, economic and social experiences of individuals. Following Weber's analysis of the manifold influences that affect support (Chapter 1), we do not postulate that there is a single cause of support. Instead, the lifetime learning model leaves open to testing under what circumstances and to what extent a variety of theories – cultural, sociological, political and economic – can help explain regime support (see also Kornberg and Clarke, 1992; Dalton, 2004). Since many individuals are subject to conflicting influences on support, the likelihood of an individual giving support to the regime depends on the priority given to cross-cutting pressures.

Contemporary political scientists differ about which social influences are most important, e.g. family (Butler and Stokes, 1974); education (Dalton, 2008); class (G. Evans, 1999); or generation (cf. Mishler and Rose, 2007). Socialization theories emphasize the persistence of values from one generation to another. Insofar as these values are widely shared within a society they constitute a national political culture. This is assumed to exist by historians who find common values and behavior from one Russian regime to another (Keenan, 1986; Eckstein, 1988; Fleron and Hoffmann, 1993: Part II; Duncan, 2000). The approach is reinforced by studies of continuity between regimes in bureaucratic institutions and behavior (Ryavec, 2003).

Socialization begins in early life to differentiate individuals into different roles in society (Table 4.1). There are substantial differences in how people experience socialization, depending on whether their parents are educated or not, religious believers or indifferent, and so forth. Gender and generation are fixed at birth and education is completed before entering adulthood; in turn, they influence an adult's social class. In this process, youths develop distinctive interests and expectations about how the country ought to be governed. Life cycle theories predict that political attitudes, like much else, change with age. When young, a person will reflect youthful hopes and expectations formed in the home and school; once into middle age

Table 4.1 *What matters for regime support: four hypotheses*

Differences in regime support depend on

1. *Socialization*: What individuals have learned from their roles in society.
2. *Politics*: How individuals evaluate the performance of political institutions.
3. *Economics*: How individuals evaluate household and national economic conditions.
4. *Time*: When individuals make evaluations and how long the new regime has been in place.

experience will alter youthful attitudes; and the change in life style associated with old age will once again alter how people view their political system.

In contrast to socialization theories, institutionalist theories emphasize the importance of changes in political institutions leading to changes in political performance (cf. North, 2005; Hall and Taylor, 1996). Moreover, political leaders can be judged not only in terms of their personality but also by their performance in office (Mishler and Willerton, 2003). People will decide whether to give support to a regime depending on how they evaluate its political performance, for example, whether it is corrupt or trustworthy (cf. Newton, 1999) or by whether it respects or ignores the rights of its citizens. Weber's (1947) discussion of justifications of support and legitimacy calls attention to the importance of the absolute and instrumental values that are used to evaluate the performance of its institutions.

Political economy theories stress a regime's performance in delivering material economy. Individual support is hypothesized to depend on a regime's performance in managing the economy and maintaining social welfare (e.g. Przeworski, 1991; cf. Stokes, 2001). The rational choice theory of Ronald Rogowski (1974) postulates that governments "buy" support. The shift from a command to a market economy has produced both winners and losers in material terms. Moreover, since 1992 the radical contraction and then expansion of the Russian economy have made many people at different points in time losers and then winners. Individuals can assess economic performance in terms of their own circumstances or according to the state of the national economy. While there tends to be a correlation between the two, it is not great, since some people can prosper even when times are hard, while others can fare badly when the national economy is booming. The question thus arises: Which economy – the macro- or the household economy – is most influential (Kinder and Kiewiet, 1981; Duch and Stevenson, 2008)?

Achieving durable support is a process that takes time. Studies of the oldest democracies declare that centuries may be required to create the institutions and values that sustain a consolidated democracy (Dahl, 1971). However, the Federal Republic of Germany, founded in 1949 as the successor to Adolf Hitler's Nazi regime, achieved popular support within two decades (Weil, 1987), and the European Union has admitted new democratic regimes such as Spain and Portugal less than a decade and one-half after their launch. The Russian Federation is now two decades old.

If a new regime can survive for a decade, subjects learn to adapt to its ways. Relearning encourages support for a regime because that has become the way we are governed now. A no-longer-new regime creates the expectation that it will remain in place tomorrow. The passage of time thus encourages support through path dependence, that is, the acceptance of the status quo as preferable to the potential benefits of a hypothetical change (Pierson, 2004). Those who hoped that another type of regime could supplant the new regime will increasingly realize that this is unlikely. The longer the old regime fades into the past, the more its onetime supporters realize that it is unlikely to return. Support for an alternative regime is thus not practical politics. At this point a regime may be described as consolidated.

The equilibrium of a consolidated regime is not static; it is open to challenge from any one of a number of sources. Rational choice theories emphasize that individuals frequently recalculate the net present value of a regime in response to changes in their personal circumstances or in the national economy. Theories stressing the role of leadership in mobilizing support imply that a change of leaders could undermine support.

The lifetime learning model provides a theoretical framework for understanding not only why Russians differ in their support for a regime at one point in time but also why support changes over time. Chapter 5 looks at the extent to which the first three hypotheses set out in Table 4.1 affect regime support throughout the whole period.

Chapter 6 looks at the extent to which the passage of time has been important too. Since an equilibrium is not static but dynamic, Chapters 7 and 8 examine the extent to which support was altered by two substantial challenges: the constitutional requirement for Vladimir Putin to leave the presidential office and the 2008 world financial crisis.

5 | Individual influences on regime support

The unity of Russian society is a theme of tsarist and Soviet writers and is invoked by Vladimir Putin as well. However, every society is differentiated in many ways. The liberal idea that individuals choose the positions that divide them politically was explicitly rejected by Karl Marx. He argued in his *Critique of Political Economy* that "It is not the consciousness of men that determines their being but, on the contrary, their social being that determines their consciousness." Although Soviet society claimed to be classless, many social differences could be found and the same is true of Russia today.

Given social differences, the critical question is: *Which* social distinctions influence regime support? Differences significant in one dimension of society – for example, tastes in sports or food – are unlikely to have a direct influence on political support. Combining multiple distinctions to create ideal-type categories – for example, young, well-educated, secular urbanites and old, uneducated rural churchgoers – reduces the size of each to a very small proportion of the total population. The majority of people tend to combine attributes with different political implications: for example, being uneducated but prosperous, or young rural residents. Such crosspressures require careful consideration when relating social differences to regime support.

Through the limitations of language, political theories that discuss concepts in the abstract imply either/or differences: for example, between young and old or men and women. However, statistical analysis invariably shows that political differences are differences of degree. The hypotheses set out in Table 4.1 are not mutually exclusive and may even be mutually supportive. For example, an individual may make a positive evaluation of the new regime on the grounds of both political performance (it provides freedom) and economic performance (it provides a higher standard of living than its Soviet predecessor). We therefore need to understand how much influence each can have when other influences are taken into account.

The extent to which specified social differences actually influence Russians is an empirical question. Multivariate statistical analysis can take into account a number of indicators that may influence regime support and determine, net of all other variables, which actually are important, which have a little influence and which are without significance. Insofar as Russians are crosspressured by different influences, such as an appreciation of freedom, and stressed by the economic costs of transformation, analysis can show the extent to which these influences cancel each other out when individuals are assessing the regime.

In this chapter ordinary least squares (OLS) regression analysis is used to test the extent to which socialization, politics and economic performance matter for Russian support for the current regime. To identify influences consistently important since the founding of the Russian Federation, we pool all 34,071 respondents from eighteen New Russia Barometer surveys since 1992 and weight each survey equally. Since the NRB questionnaire includes a dozen or more potential influences for each hypothesis, a preliminary regression analysis was undertaken to screen out those measures that do not achieve a minimum of statistical significance for regime support: for example, many forms of social capital (Rose, 2000c). Because of their substantive interest, a few indicators such as gender and church attendance have been retained even though their influence is weak. The first three tables in this chapter separately test hypotheses about social, political and economic effects on support. The regression analysis in the concluding section combines all three sets of influences.

Social differences inevitable; their influence is not

In democracies the regime leaves many areas of social life to individual choice and civil society institutions. By contrast, the Soviet party-state aspired to politicize every area of social life. Socialization into Communist values started at a very young age. In a stable political regime, there is little reason for *generations* to differ in support. However, there is no such consistency in Russian history. After a political regime is transformed, beliefs that adults have acquired in youth no longer fit the new regime. The influence of the Soviet past is now outside the personal experience of the youngest generations of subjects of the Russian Federation.

Generational theories emphasize that the political context of a person's youthful socialization has a lifelong influence on individual attitudes: Its impact is expected to inhibit relearning. Instead of changing evaluations in the light of experience, individuals will reinterpret new experiences in the light of the formative experience of their generation. Insofar as this is the case, then each generation's outlook would remain stable from one year to the next and from one decade to the next. We would expect older Russian generations to be less likely to support the new regime and younger people to be more supportive. However, insofar as political relearning occurs, generational differences will be limited or even spurious due to the correlation between generation and other influences, such as education or income.

Theories of generational change imply that the death of the Stalin-era generations and the coming of age of the post-*perestroika* generation will alter the aggregate level of support for the regime (for a lengthy exposition, see Mishler and Rose, 2007). Since the New Russia Barometer spans almost two decades, demographic turnover is particularly relevant as an influence. About one-sixth of the respondents interviewed in the first NRB survey have died since, and almost one-third interviewed in the 2009 survey were school pupils or infants when the first NRB round was conducted.

There are intergenerational differences in political support for the current regime: It tends to be higher in each new generation (Figure 5.1). The youngest generation, born after 1975, has usually consistently been highest in support for the new regime; over two decades 67 percent have supported it. This is 15 percentage points more than the support among those born in the preceding decade. Among Russians born before 1932, the level of regime support has averaged 28 percentage points lower than among the youngest generation.

Although generations do differ in political support, Russians are alike in their ability to relearn in response to the changing performance of the regime. Regardless of when they were born, generations tend to go up and down together in their support for the regime (Figure 5.1). In the mid-1990s the support of young, middle-aged and older Russians went down, while by the year 2000 all generations were becoming more positive about the new regime. Support for the regime among the generation of Russians born before 1932 rose from 16 percent in 1996 to a high of 85 percent in 2008. The youngest

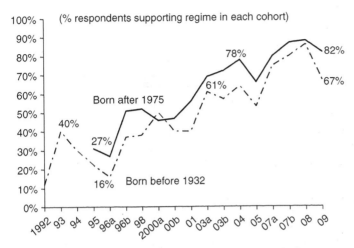

Source: Centre for the Study of Public Policy, New Russia Barometer data base.

Figure 5.1 Generations' support goes up and down together

cohort of Russians has been most responsive to events in the new Federation. Among this cohort, support rose by 61 percentage points between 1996 and 2008 – and the proportion of this cohort in the population doubled.

Within each generation there is nonetheless a division between those who do and those who do not support the current regime. Generational differences are thus a tendency rather than an absolute contrast. This is confirmed by the multiple regression analysis: The oldest generation tends to be significantly less supportive of the regime, while the youngest generation is significantly more supportive (Table 5.1).

Class is a central ideological concept of Marxism, but its application was problematic in Communist societies that were full of status distinctions based on an individual's position in the *nomenklatura* of the party (McAllister and White, 1995). The transformation of the economic system forced a large proportion of the labor force to change their employer, their occupation or both with the prospect of their social status altering too, for worse or for better.

Ambiguities in occupational structures have led many social scientists to regard the subjective assessment that individuals make of their

Table 5.1 *Limited influence of socialization on regime support*

	Adjusted R^2 6.9%		
	b	s.e.	Beta
Born before 1946	−8.19***	.65	−.07
Born 1976–1987	16.82***	.81	.11
Social status	4.43***	.14	.18
Education	.46	.29	.01
Town size	−1.73***	.27	−.03
Female	−2.27***	.60	−.02
Church attendance	3.98***	.31	.08

***Significant at .001. Number of cases: 34,071.
Source: Centre for the Study of Public Policy, New Russia Barometer data base, 1992–2007.

position in society as a better measure of social status than a position assigned on the basis of a sociological theory. The New Russia Barometer employs a subjective measure of class, asking people to place themselves on a social status ladder. The use of numbers avoids giving politically charged verbal labels such as upper-class or working-class. Russians have no difficulty in recognizing differences in social status: only 2 percent are unable to place themselves on the ladder of social hierarchy. The median group does not choose the arithmetic midpoint on the social ladder but places themselves below it. Only 1 percent place themselves at the highest rung of the ladder, and 12 percent on the lowest rung. Subjective social status does significantly influence regime support, after controlling for other social influences (Table 5.1). Support for the regime tends to be higher among Russians who see their social status above average by comparison with those below average.

Education is an alternative measure of status, since more educated people tend to have better jobs, higher incomes and more power in society. This was true in Soviet times and it remains true today. A majority of Russians have gained a vocational certificate as a skilled worker or an academic secondary school diploma entitling them to proceed to higher education. Only one-quarter have failed to obtain any qualification. Those with more education should be better able to adapt and benefit from the opportunities that transformation creates, and thus to favor the new regime. In West European and Anglo-American societies, more-educated people tend to be more in favor of democratic institutions (Dalton, 2008). In the Russian context this implies that more-educated citizens will be more critical of the regime. However, after controlling for the effects of age and occupational status, educational differences fail to achieve any significant effect on regime support.

Marxism dismissed *religion* as a form of superstition inconsistent with its materialist philosophy, and the Soviet regime actively promoted atheism. It allowed the Russian Orthodox Church to continue but only on condition that it supported the regime. When the New Russia Barometer asks people their religion, the population divides into three groups: About half say they are Orthodox; a quarter say they are not believers; and a fifth find it difficult to decide about religion. However, a nominal religious identification is not evidence of religious commitment, since many people identify the Orthodox religion with being a Russian. Church attendance is a more meaningful measure of religious commitment. Almost half of NRB respondents never go to church, including many who are nominally Orthodox. The median person goes to a religious service no more than once a year; only 6 percent report going to church as often as once a month. After controlling for age and education, church attendance is associated with support for the regime (Table 5.1).

Urbanization was a major goal of the Soviet regime. To abolish what Marx had denounced as "the idiocy of rural life," the Soviet regime introduced collective farms that turned peasants into the rural equivalent of factory workers. However, the failings of the command economy resulted in chronic food shortages and encouraged urban residents to grow food. By the end of the Soviet Union, a big majority of Russians growing food lived in cities rather than the countryside (Rose and Tikhomirov, 1993). Larger cities have offered greater opportunities for people to find like-minded friends and insulate themselves from an intrusive party-state, as in the German dictum *Stadtluft macht frei* (city air gives freedom). In the Russian context, living in a larger city has tended to make people less supportive of the current regime, but the effect is limited in size (Table 5.1).

The political significance of *gender* is socially constructed and Soviet society left a distinctive legacy (cf. P. Watson, 1995; Kay, 2006).

In Soviet times the regime's desire to industrialize resulted in the mobilization of a large proportion of women into the labor force. Factories in high-priority sectors of the economy provided many social services, including child care for working women, albeit such services were allocated according to the priorities of the economic plan rather than the needs of employees (Rose, 1996a). However, the Central Committee of the Communist Party of the Soviet Union did not give women political prominence. While women have begun to appear in public life in the Russian Federation, there is no positive policy to promote women in politics and the decline in state-owned industries has reduced the proportion of employers offering special facilities for women with children. The multiple regression analysis found that gender had only a slight influence, depressing support for the regime among women.

The Soviet regime was ambivalent about nationalities. On the one hand, Marxist ideology stressed that ethnic identification was unimportant compared to class differences. Political careers were open to all minorities; for example, Stalin was a Georgian and Trotsky was of Jewish origin. Nonetheless, nationality was inscribed in identity documents; Soviet republics were established for nationalities such as Armenians and Ukrainians; and jurisdictions with ethnic labels were created within the Russian Republic. The 2002 Russian census allowed Russians to give a nationality according to their subjective preference. A total of 79.8 percent were recorded as Russian; 3.8 percent Tatar; 2.0 percent Ukrainian; 1.1 percent Bashkir; 1.1 percent Chuvash; and 1.0 percent gave no answer. The remaining 11.2 percent were dispersed among 178 different nationalities. When NRB surveys ask about nationality, five-sixths say they are Russian and the remainder are scattered. Because Russians are numerically dominant in the population, their support for the regime is virtually the same as that of the population as a whole. Because minority nationalities are diverse, in a representative nationwide sample there are too few respondents of any one minority nationality to provide data for reliable statistical analysis. Hence, it would be inappropriate to include minority groups in the regression analyses.

There is some support for the socialization hypothesis; altogether these influences can account for 6.9 percent of the variance in regime support. However, any attempt to explain regime support solely in terms of social structure would be an exercise in sociological reductionism. While the social characteristics of individual Russians tend to be fixed at birth or early adulthood, support for the current regime has fluctuated greatly.

Political performance matters

The evaluation of political performance involves matching the values of individuals with the performance of the regime. While it is self-evidently reasonable to hypothesize that regime support depends on political values and government performance, this does not specify *which* particular values and what areas of performance matter most. Because every subject holds a multiplicity of political values, there are not only value conflicts between individuals but also within an individual. For example, a Russian can value freedom and yet distrust the political institutions of the regime. When values lead to conflicting assessments of the regime, the critical analytic issue is to identify which have priority in the minds of Russians.

The regime that Russians want

Whereas theories of democratization assume that popular values ought to be democratic, many scholars of Russian history have inferred that centuries of undemocratic rule reflect authoritarian values in the political culture (see e.g. McDaniel, 1996; Duncan, 2000). Survey evidence shows that a big majority of Russians see democracy as a positive ideal, but the pooled survey data find no significant relation between the value placed on democracy as an ideal and how the current regime is evaluated (Table 5.2).

At the launch of the new Russian regime its leaders proclaimed that it was democratic, but Russians have tended to be skeptical about this claim. The median Russian sees the regime as about halfway between a democracy and a dictatorship. This creates an incongruence between the regime that Russians would like to have and how they see it actually operating (cf. Figure 4.2). Statistical analysis confirms that the bigger the incongruence the less individuals are inclined to support the regime (Table 5.2).

Support for the current regime depends not only on how it is evaluated but also on the extent to which there are acceptable alternatives. Since every Russian has lived under at least two different

Table 5.2 *Political influences on regime support*

	Adjusted R^2 26.1%		
	b	s.e.	Beta
Pro old regime	−.04***	.01	−.04
Democracy as ideal	.16	.13	.01
Regime incongruence	−.94***	.14	−.04
Fairness of officials	5.16***	.25	.12
Freedom greater	5.91***	.33	.09
Trusts institutions	1.21***	.23	.03
Corruption	−5.21***	.37	−.08
Rating of president	6.23***	.13	.30
Approves dictatorship	−3.02***	.20	−.08
Approves suspension Duma	−2.32***	.20	−.06

*** Significant at .001.
Source: Centre for the Study of Public Policy, New Russia Barometer data base.

regimes, advocates of changing the regime can argue that "it can happen here." The simplest place for people to look for an alternative regime is to the past. As part of his inclusive political strategy, Vladimir Putin has selectively praised past achievements. Even though Russians endorse democratic ideals and do not see their old regime as democratic, nonetheless they have consistently tended to be positive about the Communist system, and the size of the majority approving it has tended to rise. A month after the Soviet regime disappeared, 50 percent of NRB respondents were positive; by the end of the Yeltsin presidency almost three in four were positive. Endorsement has remained high since: After the 2009 post-economic crisis survey, 71 percent of Russians were favorable about the old regime. As expected, there is a significant but limited effect; those favoring the Communist regime are less likely to support the current regime (Table 5.2).

A positive view of the old regime reflects nostalgia, a statement about how good the old days appear in retrospect; it is not a demand for the return of a regime that is no more (Munro, 2006). When asked directly whether they would like to return to the Communist regime, this change is consistently rejected by a majority. On average, only 32 percent have favored a return to the Communist system. Moreover, those strongly against restoring the old regime outnumber those strongly in favor by a margin of more than three to one.

Whereas demands for leadership pose no threat to a democratic regime, in societies without a democratic tradition strong leadership can be a synonym for dictatorship (cf. Rose and Mishler, 1996). In the uncertain circumstances of the Russian Federation, the NRB asks if people think "a tough dictatorship is the only way out of the current situation." In each survey an absolute majority rejects a tough dictatorship. Notwithstanding the centralization of power in the Kremlin, the minority in favor of a tough dictatorship are less likely to support the current regime than those who reject a dictatorship (Table 5.2). There is even less support for a military dictator; nine-tenths reject this idea. Equally important, the ideology of the Russian army, as in Soviet times, is to defend the regime rather than supplant it.

The strongest form of political rejection is to endorse the abolition of existing institutions without regard for what replaces them. Since parties and the parliament are distrusted by most Russians, it would be logical if a big majority wanted these institutions swept away. However, this is not the case. More than three-fifths would disapprove of suspending parliament and getting rid of parties. Among those in favor of closing down parliament and getting rid of parties, there is a significant tendency to be less supportive of the current regime (Table 5.2).

While many Russians are prepared to think outside the box, that is, contemplate one or another alternative to the current regime, no one alternative is endorsed by a majority. Russians who would readily dismiss the parliament and parties do not agree about what should fill the gap. The Communist Party of the Russian Federation, unlike its predecessor, is not organizing for revolution; instead, many former Communists have adapted to the new economy and are doing what Marx predicted, engaging in opportunities for exploitation that a capitalist economy offers.

The regime Russians get

Given the character of the Soviet regime, Russians do not take freedom for granted. Instead of asking whether people feel free in the abstract, the New Russia Barometer asks whether people feel freer now than in the former regime. Questions cover four different everyday activities: being free to say what you think, join any organization you like, make your own choice about religion and decide for yourself whether to take an interest in politics (cf. Berlin, 1958; Rose 2009c: ch. 10). Whereas in a democratic regime taking an interest in politics is a civic virtue and in a Communist regime feigning political interest was necessary to avoid suspicion, in the post-Soviet context freedom is represented by not having to have a party card or party connections to get on in life.

An unintended consequence of Soviet socialization is that an overwhelming majority of Russians feel freer in their post-regime system. In every NRB round an absolute majority has expressed a greater sense of freedom on each of the four counts. An average of 82 percent feel freer to decide about religious matters; 78 percent to join any organization of their choice; 75 percent feel freer to say what they think; and 71 percent feel freer to decide whether to take an interest in politics. Among the limited minority who do not feel freer, most say things have remained the same rather than worsened. The more inclined people are to feel freer than before, the more they support the current regime. This reflects the fact that while Western-based organizations such as Freedom House judge freedom by the standards of the democratic ideal, Russians judge it by comparison with a regime that tolerated little freedom from its intrusive demands for compliance.

Even if people do not want to become engaged politically, the services provided by the state are so numerous that in the course of the year a family is likely to have contacts with a teacher, nurse, or other officials delivering services in their locality. One definition of good government is that public officials treat everyone fairly (see Galbreath and Rose, 2008). When asked to compare fair treatment under the new regime with the Soviet regime, half think it is much the same, one-quarter regard the new regime as fairer and one-quarter see it as less fair than the Communist regime. Most Russians see public officials in the new regime tending to behave arbitrarily. In the 2009 NRB survey, 73 percent did not think public officials treated people like themselves fairly. The minority who did see it as fairer are more likely to support the regime (Table 5.2).

In theory, trust in political institutions could provide virtual representation, as trusted institutions could act on behalf of the interests of individuals. In established democracies trust in political institutions is considered an important indicator of support for the current regime (Pharr and Putnam, 2000; Norris, 1999; but cf. Mishler and Rose, 2005). Consistently, New Russia Barometer surveys find low levels of trust in political institutions. The two central institutions of representative democracy – the Duma and political parties – are the least trusted. Over the years only one in six have any trust in either institution. The level of trust is less low for three authoritative institutions of the state: the police, the courts and the army. However, none can claim the trust of as many as half of Russians. If trust were as important for political support as is hypothesized in theories of social capital (Putnam, 2000), then support for the current regime should be two-thirds or half what it is today. However, after controlling for the effect of other measures of political performance, trust has only a small effect (Table 5.2).

Corruption shows that a political regime is unable to apply the rule of law to its own officials, and more than four-fifths of Russians see public officials as inclined to take bribes. The chief difference is between those who believe almost all public officials are corrupt and those seeing most as corrupt. However, this negative image is not based on individual experience, for most Russians who have contact with officials do not have to pay a bribe (Rose and Mishler, 2010). The perception of public officials is largely colored by visible signs of corruption at the top of government. The more Russians see public officials as corrupt, the less likely they are to support the regime (Table 5.2).

Contemporary media tend to personalize political institutions, and in Russia the media are under pressure to focus positive coverage on the president and avoid negative coverage. Although the personality of a president is relatively constant, presidential ratings fluctuate during their term of office. This was true of Yeltsin, whose mean rating fluctuated between a so-so position in the middle of the scale early in his first term and an extremely low rating during his second term of office (see Figure 2.3). Within the positive range, Putin's rating has fluctuated too. At the start of his first term, Putin had a rating just above the midpoint of the scale, while during his second term it was usually very high (see Figure 7.1). When only political performance indicators are considered (Table 5.2), the popular evaluation of the president of the day has the strongest effect on regime support. However, when multivariate analysis is undertaken by taking the state of the economy into account, the association declines greatly, because regime support and presidential approval are both affected by evaluations of the national economy (Mishler and Willerton, 2003; Treisman, 2011).

There is strong support for the hypothesis that political performance matters. Measures of political values and performance account for 26.1 percent of the variance in support for the Federation regime (Table 5.2). Even though Russians tend to characterize their regime as corrupt, untrustworthy and undemocratic, these judgments have less influence on support than do evaluations comparing their freedom today and responsiveness of the new regime with its Soviet predecessor. Moreover, negative views of the current regime do not create a demand for getting rid of the parliament and parties or turning to a dictator. This suggests that Russians have low expectations of government. Even if it performs badly, as long as it is viewed as less bad than the Soviet regime, it will not lose support.

The economy that matters

Both neo-classical economists and Marxists hold views consistent with the epigram made familiar by Bill Clinton's campaign staff – "It's the economy, stupid." However, the epigram is indiscriminate: It fails to identify which particular aspect of the economy is influential. Is it the state of the national economy or that of a person who simultaneously faces job insecurity and new opportunities to make money? Conventional Anglo-American economic theories postulate that individuals maximize their welfare, an assumption consistent with Russian distrust of collective institutions. From this perspective, political judgments should reflect an individual's standard of living. Individuals may accept responsibility for their own living standard, whether it is good or bad, but expect the government to be responsible for preventing inflation and promoting national economic growth (Rose, 1998). Marxist theory is collectivist; the economy that matters is the national economy.

By definition, statistics about the downs and ups of Russia's national economy cannot say anything about the distribution of costs and benefits of transformation among Russians. When the national economy grows or contracts by 5 percentage points, this does not mean that every Russian's income rises or falls by that amount. Some people will see an above-average rise in their income while others see it stagnate or move in the opposite direction from the aggregate pattern. Nor can national statistics about conditions that concern everyone, such as inflation, take into account the extent to which inflation affects people differently: for example, hurting people with fixed incomes such as pensioners, while benefiting those who can push up their earnings or have assets in a foreign currency. A major advantage of survey data is that they can identify Russians who have benefited from economic transformation and those who feel its costs most.

The New Russia Barometer questionnaire is explicitly designed to collect subjective evidence about how people evaluate the economic system (Rose, 2002). Russians do so differently than do official statistics produced by Goskomstat in Moscow or by intergovernmental agencies in Washington. For example, in 2005, when the national economy was booming, only 41 percent of Russians gave it a positive rating and in 2009, when the national economy was negatively affected by the world financial crisis, 61 percent were positive.

In a modern economy, income is the normal way to evaluate economic wellbeing. In Soviet times, the combination of artificially controlled prices and the allocation of goods and services through the party or personal connections made income unsuitable as a measure of the ability to acquire goods and services. Transformation devalued the ruble as a meaningful measure of what people could afford. The introduction of the market legalized working for cash in hand in the shadow economy, but not many people could pay cash. Households relied much more on growing some of their food, do-it-yourself repairs and exchanging help with friends and relatives (Rose, 2009c: ch. 8). When the costs of transformation were at a peak in 1996, only 15 percent were relying solely on earnings from the official economy and this proportion was no higher at the height of the boom a decade later.

While juggling activities in multiple economies is important, a ruble income is necessary to buy many goods that people cannot produce by themselves. Given treble-digit annual inflation followed by unstable double-digit inflation, the most appropriate measure of income across time is a household's position in the distribution of income. Whatever the number of zeroes appended to ruble income, NRB respondents can be grouped into five income quintiles. Hypothesis 3 predicts that the higher an individual is in the income distribution, the more likely he or

Table 5.3 *Economic influences on regime support*

| | Adjusted R^2 41.4% | | |
	b	s.e.	Beta
Pro current economy	.62***	.00	.62
Pro old economy	−.02***	.01	−.01
Household econ. situation	1.56***	.24	.03
Destitution	−2.35***	.28	−.04
Income	−.14	.17	.00

***Significant at .001.
Source: Centre for the Study of Public Policy, New Russia Barometer
data base.

she is to support the regime. However, income fails to register a
statistically significant effect on regime support (Table 5.3).

The destabilization of money by inflation likewise makes it problematic to measure poverty in terms of rubles of uncertain value.
Therefore, the New Russia Barometer has created a destitution index
that focuses on whether people have had to go without basic necessities – food, clothing, and electricity and heat – during the past twelve
months. If people are only infrequently doing without basic necessities, they can make temporary adjustments: for example, having a
dinner consisting only of potatoes, or buying secondhand rather than
new clothes. Destitution arises when people frequently go without
necessities. The longer the time period for assessing deprivation, the
smaller the size of the group often doing without necessities. For a
majority of Russians, doing without has been an occasional or rare
event rather than a persisting problem throughout the year (cf. Rose,
2009c: 80ff.). As expected, the greater the frequency of doing without,
the less likely an individual is to support the regime. While the association is statistically significant, it is also limited (Table 5.3).

Socialization into the command economy stressed the material
aspects of building socialism; inadvertently, the deficiencies of the
command economy created chronic shortages in consumer goods that
made Russians very materialistic (Kornai, 1992). When the New
Russia Barometer survey started, questions were asked about the
ownership of consumer goods that were then in short supply, such as
a telephone, a car or a dacha. The dynamism of a market economy has

changed the products indicating how much discretionary income a household has to buy goods costing several months' or more earnings. Buying a color television set was added, then a video cassette recorder or DVD player, and finally home computers and access to the Internet. The change in what consumers could buy has made it inappropriate to monitor consumption trends with a standard list of consumer goods. In the 2009 NRB survey, 37 percent of Russians had a color TV, DVD player or VCR and a car, and only 2 percent were without all three of these "good" household goods. As expected, support for the regime was higher among those who were best-off compared to those with the fewest goods, but the difference is only 7 percentage points.

When economic difficulties were great, 26 percent of Russians nonetheless rated their household's economic conditions as satisfactory. Since then, most households have seen their material standard of living rise but the proportion reporting themselves satisfied with their household's economic situation has averaged only 23 percent. When asked to compare their household's economic situation at present with what it was before *perestroika*, in every NRB survey the largest group of Russians feel that their living standard has fallen. In January 1992, when comparison was between the legacy of Gorbachev and that of Brezhnev, 56 percent said their household's economic situation was worse. In 2009, after almost a decade of prosperity, 42 percent felt their living standard was lower than before transformation.

Even though many Russians are better off in material terms than two decades ago, many nonetheless feel that they are now worse off. There is a statistically significant association between individuals seeing their standard of living improving and regime support, but it is weak (Table 5.3). Thus, contrary to neo-classical economic theories about individual maximization of private benefits being of primary political importance, two of our three micro-level measures have only a weak relationship to regime support and the third, income distribution, fails to achieve statistical significance.

The Soviet regime socialized Russians to think of the national economy as a political economy, for the system made it very evident that political power rather than market forces controlled the allocation of material goods. Since official statistics about the national economy were Potemkin statistics, Russians were much more accustomed to ignoring official statistics than were Western economists inexperienced in the bookkeeping practices of the command economy (Grossman, 1977; Katsenelinboigen, 1977).

While ordinary people cannot follow the convoluted calculations of macro-economic statistics, Russians do experience how the national economy works. When asked to evaluate the pre-*perestroika* economy, the retrospective view is consistently favorable. The only variation is in the size of the majority endorsing it. At the start of transformation, 62 percent viewed the old economy positively, 12 percent were neutral and 26 percent negative. After market mechanisms were introduced, attitudes toward the command economy actually became more positive. Following the economic crisis of 2008, more than four in five were positive about the old economic system. As expected, the more positive people are about the old economy, the less positive they are about the new regime. However, the relationship is limited in strength (Table 5.3).

When people are asked to evaluate the current economic system, a neutral term that avoids ideologically charged references to the market, a very dynamic picture emerges. At the start of transformation, only 10 percent were positive about the new economy and throughout the 1990s less than one in three was positive. It was not until 2003 that as many as half had a positive view of the current economic system. The proportion rose to 81 percent in 2008, before falling back after the global economic crisis hit (see Figure 6.2 for details).

How Russians evaluate the national economic system has an extremely strong effect on support for the regime (Table 5.3). Not only is it statistically significant but its Beta coefficient of 0.62 is far greater than that of any other economic influence. It is the principal reason why economic influences collectively account for 41.4 percent of the variance in support for the current regime, notably more than political measures and very substantially more than the influence of socialization.

Combining influences

Although nineteen different socialization, political and economic performance measures have significant effects on the extent to which people support the current regime, their effects are not equal. Combining all three sets of indicators in a single multiple regression analysis can identify which measures remain significant after controlling for the effect of all others.

Table 5.4 *Combining influences on regime support*

	Adjusted R^2 46.2%		
	b	s.e.	Beta
Economy			
Pro current economy	.52***	.01	.52
Pro old economy	.06***	.01	.06
Household econ. situation	−.52	.23	−.01
Politics			
Pro old regime	−.05***	.01	−.06
Democracy as ideal	.41***	.11	.02
Regime incongruence	−.39***	.12	−.02
Fairness of officials	2.91***	.22	.07
Freedom greater	4.59***	.29	.07
Trusts institutions	1.78***	.20	.04
Corruption	−.75	.32	−.01
Rating of president	2.56***	.12	.12
Approves dictatorship	−1.27***	.17	−.04
Approves suspension Duma	−1.11***	.17	−.03
Socialization			
Born before 1946	−2.49***	.52	−.02
Born 1976–1987	−.70	.65	−.01
Social status	.99***	.12	.04
Education	−.22	.23	−.01
Town size	−.41	.22	−.01
Church attendance	.29	.22	.01

***Significant at .001; **significant at .01.
Source: Centre for the Study of Public Policy, New Russia Barometer data base.

The importance of the national economy for political support is confirmed (Table 5.4). Its Beta coefficient of 0.52 is by far the largest of any indicator. Its unstandardized b coefficient implies that for every 10 points higher a respondent rates the current economic system, their support for the current regime will rise by 5 points. In addition, Russians who are positive about the old economic system tend to be more favorable toward the current regime. However, the effect is limited. The egocentric view that people vote their pocketbook is conclusively rejected; a family's household economic condition has no statistically significant effect.

The rating of the president – whether favorable or unfavorable – is the most important political performance measure. However, the big difference in the ratings given Presidents Yeltsin and Putin makes the impact of this influence very different in the 1990s and in the following decade. On a scale of 1 to 10 in which a score of 1 signifies maximum disapproval, the downward ratcheting of Boris Yeltsin's popularity produced a mean rating of 3.3. By contrast, Vladimir Putin has enjoyed a fluctuating but consistently positive rating as president, with a mean of 6.4. Because Table 5.4 takes into account economic as well as political performance, the statistical effect of the rating of the president is halved from a regression using only measures of political performance.[1]

Altogether, a variety of political performance indicators have a substantial effect on regime support but they push in opposite directions. Awareness of greater freedom under the new regime has a positive influence on regime support. If Russians are among the minority who view their political institutions as likely to treat people like themselves fairly and trust those institutions, then they are more likely to support the regime. However, if people hold undemocratic values, such as favoring a dictatorship or the suspension of the parliament, they are less likely to be supportive of the regime. The authoritarian model of mobilizing support receives indirect endorsement because of the very slight effect on regime support of democratic ideals and incongruence between ideal and reality. It is how the regime makes demands on subjects that determines support rather than the commitment of citizens to democratic ideals.

After controlling for political and economic performance, the relevance of socialization for political support almost disappears. Of the six indicators, only two, socioeconomic status and belonging to a cohort that had been socialized during the Great Patriotic War, achieve statistical significance. In each case the effect is weak. Whereas political and economic performance reflect the pressures of relearning, socialization measures tend to reflect what was learned before the treble transformation of polity, economy and society.

Together, the three sets of influences can account for 46.2 percent of the variance in support for the current regime. This is high in the

---

[1] Controlling for economic performance reduces the b coefficient for presidential approval from 6.23 to 2.56 and the Beta drops from 0.30 to 0.12 (cf. Tables 5.2 and 5.4).

absolute sense. However, because the OLS regression pools surveys undertaken over eighteen years, it cannot take into account the dynamic process by which regime support has changed. Between the first and the latest NRB survey, the proportion of subjects favoring the regime has risen from one in seven to three-quarters or more supporting an undemocratic regime.

6 | *Time tells: there is no alternative*

Support for a regime is never static, as is implied by theories of democratic consolidation. The appearance of stability is caused by a regime being in equilibrium; the tension created by political forces pushing and pulling in different directions holds support at a particular point (Young, 1998). Thus, a change in a single influence will affect the overall equilibrium. If other forces adapt, the net effect is that aggregate support will appear steady as opposing forces continue to cancel each other out. However, substantial changes in determinants of support create a dynamic challenge to an equilibrium. In a democratic political system, challenges can take the form of a new political party emerging. In an undemocratic system, challenge can involve the demand for regime change.

Since society is constantly in flux, the longer the passage of time, the less realistic it is to expect that the influences that substantially affect regime support will remain unchanged or cancel each other out. For those in charge of a regime, anything that increases support for the current regime will be welcomed, while anything likely to decrease support will sound political alarm bells. Even if small, a change in regime support can capture political attention and encourage political commentators to extrapolate a trend. A shock event, such as an armed Chechen band holding schoolchildren as hostages, may temporarily alter the level of regime support. However, if the stimulus of an event is transitory, it will soon disappear and there will be a reversion to the status quo ante.

Cumulatively, seemingly small changes in the same direction can have a big impact on regime support. In what historians call the *longue durée*, the passage of time can itself affect regime support. To have a long-term impact, changes must occur in the limited number of political, economic and social variables that significantly influence support for the regime. The logic of multiple regression analysis is that changes in the mean values of significant independent variables will result in a change in the dependent variable, support for the regime. However, significant influences differ in their dynamic properties. The economy is continuously in flux, and in post-Communist regimes fluctuations are far greater than in the normal business cycle of an established democracy. Over two decades many households have experienced both pains *and* gains (Rose and Bobak, 2010). The passage of time can also increase or decrease the degree to which a significant variable alters regime support. For example, popular perceptions of freedom may remain unchanged but people may begin to take freedom for granted, thus causing it to make less difference to regime support.

In the unprecedented circumstances of a new regime, subjects do not know what to expect to happen next. Therefore, subjective expectations of the future cannot be based on projecting past experience. Instead, they are expressions of hope or fear. Since the future is uncertain, governors can assert that today's costs will be rewarded by a better tomorrow, while their opponents can argue that the costs of transformation are but a down payment on worse to come. With the passage of time, people can adjust their evaluation of the regime in the light of experience.

Regime change puts pressures on individuals to rethink political values formed early in life. For example, the Gorbachev reforms taught Russians that an election need not be an occasion for a passive show of support. Instead, it can offer a choice between candidates who differ fundamentally about how the country should be governed. Subsequently, voters learned about what elected officials did once in office and that, just because you vote for prosperity, you don't always get what you want. In some cases, however, new experiences can be interpreted as confirmation of previous judgments. For example, people who regarded politicians as corrupt in the Soviet era can draw the same conclusion about politicians in the current regime.

The passage of time slowly pushes people to adapt to new institutions. In the early years of the new regime, Russians who said they would never adapt outnumbered those who had adapted. The regime's persistence has steadily increased the proportion adapting to new institutions and reduced the proportion saying they will never do so (Figure 6.1). By autumn 2000 a majority reported that they had adapted; by 2009 almost two-thirds had done so and more than one-fifth expected to adapt in the coming years. Once a new regime demonstrates that it can persist, support is increased by political

Q. *Have you and your family already adapted to the changes that have
happened in the country during the past ten years?*

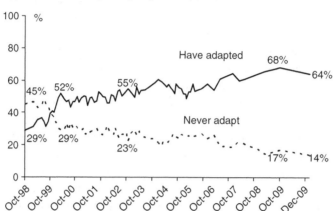

Source: Levada Center nationwide surveys, October 1998–December
2009. Not shown are respondents saying they will adapt in the near future.
Don't knows, 4 percent on average, are excluded.

Figure 6.1 Russians adapting to transformation

inertia, that is, the cumulative force exerted by the passage of time.
Individuals can support a no-longer-new regime as a matter of fact
independent of any normative commitment. The persistence of a
regime also lowers expectations that another regime change is possible, encouraging resigned acceptance of the status quo.

Stable and variable influences

If a society did not have some stable characteristics, then it would be
chronically disorderly. However, if a regime does not alter as the world
around it changes, it will be disrupted due to the failure of leaders to
adapt to external pressures. Demographic change is a textbook
example that, even when the aggregate population is stable, there is
change within it as older people die and children are born. Russia today
has a combination of a low birth rate and a high death rate together
producing a steady contraction of the country's population. However,
the year-to-year turnover of generations is slight. Equally important,
the effect of generational differences on political support is weak and
generations react much the same to changes in the regime's economic
and political performance (see Figure 5.1, Table 5.4).

Since the past is past, the Soviet regime cannot change. However, people can alter their evaluation of the past. The past can look better to people who are disappointed with the performance of the current regime or it can be negatively re-evaluated if Russians become aware of the price that they have paid by comparison with Western market economies and democracies. In fact, Russian attitudes toward the political past tend to be stable. New Russia Barometer evaluations of the pre-*perestroika* Soviet regime have consistently been positive. The chief fluctuation is in the proportion with a favorable view.

Since the ideal of democracy is a "timeless" value, we would expect that people most committed to such ideals will hold to them whatever the change in their personal circumstances. However, if a new regime that is expected to be democratizing falls far short of these ideals, as the Russian regime has done, then people could abandon their commitment rather than suffer frustration from living under an undemocratic regime. In practice, the size of the Russian majority committed to democracy as an ideal has remained constant, while the actual practice of government by the new regime has become more undemocratic.

Corruption in everything from the highest levels of the state bureaucracy to the local police appears to be a persisting feature of Russian life. In Soviet times party members used their position to extract benefits from their political position, whereas in the current regime billionaire "*biznesmen*" collaborate with public officials to their mutual advantage. The fact that Vladimir Putin has repeatedly railed against corruption indicates that the most powerful official in the regime has been unsuccessful in efforts to reduce it. Since the NRB began asking questions about corruption, popular views have tended to be stable.

People who have spent much of their lives as subjects of an authoritarian regime do not take for granted the big gains in freedom that occurred when the Soviet regime collapsed. However, the Putin administration's attacks on critical media and civil society organizations have given Western observers grounds for charging that freedoms have been curtailed. The New Russia Barometer finds that this view is not held by Russians. Consistently, three-quarters or more say they now feel freer than under the Soviet regime.

Economic conditions are subject to fluctuations down as well as up. This is spectacularly the case with the price of oil and other natural resources that are a substantial portion of Russia's GDP and foreign currency earnings. In turn, these earnings are used for everything from importing grain and consumer goods to re-exporting billions of dollars to opaque offshore accounts of Russian billionaires whose firms control extractive industries – as long as they do not fall foul of the Kremlin (cf. Goldman, 2008; Gaddy and Ickes, 2009). For much of the 1980s and 1990s world oil prices did not produce wealth for the Soviet economy. After the 1998 ruble crisis, oil prices began to rise and the 2001 terrorist attacks in the United States maintained this benefit. However, the price of oil has remained volatile (see Figures 3.1, 9.3).

In an established market economy, small, short-term fluctuations are described as a business cycle in which there is a higher rate of growth and inflation, followed by a slowing down of growth and more stable prices. Political business cycle theories assume that in a democracy the popularity of the government of the day will fluctuate as it overspends in pursuit of popularity before a general election and imposes cuts once an election victory is achieved. However, the shift from a nonmarket to a market economy is not a cyclical adjustment but a structural transformation. The scale of economic change in Russia has been much greater and the direction of change has been much more erratic than in a normal market economy.

Over two decades the performance of the official economy has been spectacularly U-shaped. In the last year of the Soviet Union and the first year of the new regime the official economy contracted by 19 percent. By the time of the 1996 presidential election the official economy was beginning to stabilize – albeit at a level two-fifths below that of the official 1990 base. One reason why this did not cost President Yeltsin the election is that the official economy was not the only economy on which Russians relied (Rose, 2009c: ch. 8). After the 1998 collapse of the ruble, officially measured GDP was only 57 percent of what it had been in 1990. Paradoxically, the ruble crash was doubly beneficial. It made foreign imports so expensive that domestic producers benefited, and it increased the value to Russia of the dollars it received for its energy and natural resource exports. Concurrently, these commodities began to rise in price. By 2007 official statistics showed that Russian GDP had almost doubled since 1998. Even after the economic crisis of 2008 had taken its toll, the official economy remained strong by comparison with the preceding decade (Figure 6.2).

Q. *Here is a scale for ranking how the economic system works: the top,*
plus 100, *is the best; the bottom, minus* 100, *the worst. Where on this*
scale would you put our current economic system?

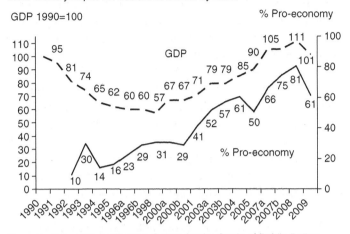

Sources: Economic evaluation: Centre for the Study of Public Policy,
New Russia Barometer data base; GDP: EBRD, 2001: 59; EBRD,
2004: 38; EBRD, 2010.

Figure 6.2 Economic change and evaluations of the economy

Russian evaluations of the new economic system have followed
different trajectories in the 1990s and in the subsequent decade
(Figure 6.2). At the beginning of 1992, when the turbulence of transformation was at its greatest, only 10 percent were positive about the
new economic system. Notwithstanding the continued contraction in
the official economy, in the next half-dozen years endorsement of the
economic system rose. This reflected the gap between the official
economy and the multiple economies on which Russians relied, where
goods were now increasingly available, albeit at high prices. Since a
shortage of money had replaced a shortage of goods, the proportion of
Russians positive about the new system was still less than one in three
in the year 2000. The rise in endorsement of the new economic system
while the national economy was contracting demonstrates that subjective evaluations of the economy cannot be inferred from nominally
objective macro-economic measures such as GDP. With the passage of
time, popular evaluations rose to a peak of 81 percent positive shortly
before the 2008 financial crisis.

Evaluations of political personalities have not only differed between
presidents but also fluctuated up and down during a president's term

of office. This is true of Western political leaders such as Tony Blair and Barack Obama. Boris Yeltsin was increasingly unpopular during his term of office while public opinion has been positive about Vladimir Putin (see Figures 2.3, 7.1). Putin's move from the presidency to the prime ministership has not affected the high evaluation that he receives from the Russian public. It has also consistently been above that of his nominal successor, Dmitry Medvedev.

Compared to the irreversible shock of transformation, political events are much more frequent. To meet the incessant demands for headlines, the media will manufacture events to fill their schedule morning, noon and night. Some major political events can be staged: for example, Vladimir Putin makes public statements to exploit Russian holidays with contradictory political implications, such as Orthodox religious holidays and Stalin-era phenomena. Political events can also be bad news, such as the sinking of a nuclear submarine. Events of interest within the ring roads of Moscow can, however, be ignored by ordinary people who have little interest in politics. Given popular experience of controlled media, the truth of what is reported can be heavily discounted. However, by definition a crisis is a short-term event and is likely to have a long-term influence only if its consequences ramify and persist with the passage of time.

Events are not interpreted in a political vacuum. People respond according to pre-existing political values developed over a long period of time. Thus, an event may simply reinforce rather than override what has gone before. For example, the collapse of the ruble in August 1998 was undoubtedly a major economic event. However, it did not cause a major fall in the evaluation of the new economic system, since it was already very low. In a New Russia Barometer survey undertaken five months prior to the ruble devaluation, only 31 percent were positive about the economic system. Because an economic boom followed the ruble's devaluation, the short-term effect was soon dissipated.

Expectations of change

In a stable political system people are likely to expect tomorrow what they experience today. This will encourage support for the current regime because any alternative is "not practical politics" and opposition is seen as futile. The immediacy of transformation forces people to live from day to day. If there is a widespread expectation that another change in regime could occur, this can encourage support for it to happen. Taking expectations into account introduces the possibility of a gap between how people would like to be governed and what they expect to get. Gurr's (1970) demand-side theory of political support predicts that if people want a democratic regime but do not expect the regime to become democratic, this incongruence will create frustration and lead to aggressive behavior that disrupts the political equilibrium. By contrast, a supply-side approach predicts that if subjects are not governed as they would like, they will avoid frustration by lowering their expectations to match what the regime supplies (see Figure 1.1).

The logic of transformation was that the current costs of getting rid of the Soviet legacy would be followed by future benefits. A few benefits, such as gaining greater freedom, could be delivered immediately, but the economic benefits of creating a market economy amidst the wreckage of a command economy were certain to require years to achieve. As the advance toward communism had been slow during seventy years of Soviet rule, Russians had learned to accept patiently whatever the future would bring. Hence, New Russia Barometer surveys have asked people about expectations of their national and household circumstances in five years rather than just a year ahead.

Because the future is not known, expectations cannot be classified as true or false; they are subjective assessments of what people think is most likely to come about. Expectations may be a projection of hopes, fears or uncertainty. For example, when asked in 1994 how long it would take before they would be satisfied with the new political system, 65 percent said that they did not know and 64 percent were likewise uncertain about whether they would ever be satisfied with the economic system. By 2009 conditions had changed sufficiently so that most Russians did expect society to become normal, albeit the median person thought it would take up to ten years for this to come about (Rose, 2009c: ch. 18).

The percentage of Russians optimistic about the economic future has always been greater than those positive about the current economic system, while the size of the gap has fluctuated. In 1992 a total of 42 percent had positive hopes for the economy in five years, compared to 10 percent positive about the current system. By 1996 a majority had become optimistic about the future economy. At the height of the boom in early 2008, nine in ten Russians were optimistic about the future of the national economy. After the 2008 economic

Q. Some people think this country would be better governed if parliament
were closed down and all parties were abolished. How likely do you think
this is to happen in the next few years?

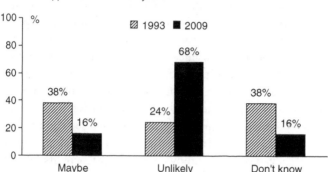

Source: Centre for the Study of Public Policy, New Russia Barometer II
(June–July 1993) and XVIII (June 2009). The maybe group includes a small
percentage saying very likely. Unlikely combines those saying not very and
not at all likely.

Figure 6.3 Expectation of suspension of the parliament

crisis, the level of optimism about the future of the economy fell by
20 percentage points, but a majority was still positive.

Expectations about the future economic situation of the household
are consistently less positive than for the national economy. The
largest group, averaging two in five households, expect their economic
conditions to remain the same in future. Since households tend to be
dissatisfied with their current economic situation, expectations of no
change are a lesser evil compared to a worsening in family fortunes.
Those uncertain about their economic future are substantial too.
In 2009 the 32 percent who did not know what their circumstances
would be in five years were the largest group of NRB respondents.

In addition to asking whether people would like the Duma to be shut
down and parties dissolved, the New Russia Barometer also asks
whether people expect this to happen. While so dramatic a political
event is rare, it has a historical resonance in Russia. When asked about
the prospect of getting rid of parliament a few months before the shoot-
out that ended the life of the Congress of People's Deputies in October
1993, a total of 38 percent thought it might or was very likely to happen
(Figure 6.3). The former group turned out to be right. The upshot was a
new presidential constitution making the Duma subservient to the
threat of dissolution by the president. Since then, there has been a

continuing decline in popular expectations of the Duma's suspension. By the 2009 NRB survey, two-thirds thought it unlikely that the Duma could be suspended and only one in six thought it might happen.

The logic of expectations endorses the hypothesis that people who think the economy will be better in future will be more inclined to support the regime, because they discount current costs in expectation of future benefits. Consistent with this, a regression analysis finds that people more optimistic about the country's economic future are, after controlling for other factors, more likely to support the regime. However, the effect of attitudes toward the national economic system today is five times stronger than expectations of what it will be like five years hence (Table 6.1). The household's future economic condition fails to achieve statistical significance. As predicted, Russians who think the Duma could be dismissed are less likely to support the regime but their number is small. Altogether, adding expectations to the model of support for the current regime makes little difference (cf. Tables 5.4 and 6.1). What Russians experience here and now is far more important for regime support than what they think might happen in future.

Context and time

Our regression analyses so far have highlighted individual influences that should consistently affect support for the regime by pooling together all NRB respondents between 1992 and 2009. However, during this period the political and economic context has altered greatly. The lifetime learning model postulates that, as the performance of the regime changes, people will think again about how they evaluate it, and this will be reflected in changes in regime support (see Table 4.1). In other words, political support is determined not only by individuals altering their assessments of the regime but also by changes in its performance.

The performance of a regime is shown by what it does – that is, administer public policies honestly or corruptly, and successfully or unsuccessfully manage the economy – rather than by what it is, a presidential or a parliamentary system or a federal or unitary state. While institutions tend to remain constant, performance is subject to short-term change. Moreover, institutional arrangements are more likely to affect ordinary citizens indirectly by their influence on the regime's economic achievements and political competence.

Table 6.1 *Adding expectations to a model of regime support*

	Adjusted R^2 47.1%		
	b	s.e.	Beta
Economy			
Pro current economy	.46***	.01	.46
Pro old economy	.06***	.01	.06
Household econ. future	−.24	.41	.01
Politics			
Pro old regime	−.05***	.01	−.05
Democracy as ideal	.10	.13	.00
Regime incongruence	−.49	.12	−.02
Fairness of officials	3.57***	.25	.08
Freedom greater	3.64***	.29	.06
Trusts institutions	1.03***	.22	.03
Corruption	−.39	.31	−.01
Approves president	2.66***	.12	.13
Approves dictatorship	−.55***	.17	−.02
Approves suspension Duma	−1.35	.44	−.02
Socialization			
Born before 1946	−1.54***	.55	−.01
Social status	.84***	.12	.03
Future expectations			
Pro economic future	.09***	.01	.08
Expect suspension Duma	−4.75***	.36	−.08

*** Significant at .001. Number of cases: 34,071.
Source: New Russia Barometer data base, 1992–2009.

Politically, the Russian regime has changed substantially over two decades. Initially, Freedom House characterized it as partly free, and liberals hoped that changes would be part of a process of democratization. In fact, it has become less free, and support has concurrently risen. Transparency International estimates the extent to which regimes are perceived as honest or corrupt. The performance of the Russian regime has not changed. Since Transparency International began evaluating corruption in Russia in 1997, the country's rating on a ten-point scale has been between 2.1 and 2.8, barely 1 point away from the most corrupt position on the scale. The economic context has shown a double reversal. First, the economy contracted dramatically, and then it has grown substantially (Figure 6.2). Calculating the cumulative change in the economy from 1992 to 2009 captures both its big dip and big recovery since.

Economic and political contexts vary across time because of what the government does and because of the cumulative effect of the persistence of a new regime. Over and above changes in political and economic performance, the passage of time by itself can encourage people to become increasingly resigned to a new regime as they see it as ever less likely to go away. The more years that pass, the greater the cumulative impact, for while economic and political performance can alter in different directions, the pages of the calendar are always turned in the same direction. This steady process creates political inertia.

Combining contextual measures of political and economic performance with the passage of time in an aggregate time-series regression makes it possible to identify which contextual influences have the greatest effect on differences in the aggregate level of regime support in Russia over time. Because there are only eighteen aggregate cases, that is, NRB surveys, we use a 0.10 probability level to indicate statistical significance. By this standard, four of the five indicators have significant effects on support (Table 6.2).

Consistent with the inertia hypothesis, the duration of the regime in months is by far the most important contextual influence on aggregate support. However, the fact that months squared is also significant and negative indicates that the effect of time is curvilinear. This cautions

Table 6.2 *Contextual influences on regime support, 1992–2009*

Adjusted R^2 93.6%	b	s.e.	Beta
Month	.541**	.221	.45
Month-Squared	−.001*	.0005	.27
Cumulative GDP	.513*	.298	.17
Freedom House (Highest = Most free)	15.43*	7.96	.27
Transparency	3.06	9.21	.04

** Significant at .05; * significant at .10.
N = 18

that the longer the regime is in place, the less additional support it gains from the passage of time. This is consistent with the ceiling of 100 percent on regime support and its having reached a very high level within a decade and one-half of the regime's founding.

The cumulative change in the economy also has a significant but somewhat smaller effect on aggregate support. When the economic context was negative, the aggregate level of support tended to decline, and when it turned positive support rose. The Freedom House rating of the regime has similar effects. In the 1990s, when the economic performance of the regime was pushing support down, the fact that the regime was partly free, a big improvement on its predecessor, pushed support up. Conversely, in the Putin years the decline in political freedom tended to push support down, but this was significantly counterbalanced by the cumulative growth of the economy. Because corruption has tended to be a steady factor in Russia, it cannot account for the very unsteady movement in regime support.

Combining context and individual evaluations

To appreciate fully why regime support fluctuates we must take into account both the characteristics of individuals subject to it *and* the context in which they are asked to give support. Combining context-ual and individual measures makes ordinary least squares estimation procedures problematic. It artificially reduces the standard errors for aggregate-level variables and seriously inflates estimates of the statis-tical significance of aggregate-level measures (Steenbergen and Jones, 2002). The problem increases in proportion to the ratio of individual-level cases to higher-level cases. Given more than 34,000 individual NRB respondents, this problem is especially severe here. Furthermore, OLS procedures assume that causal relationships in the data are constant or "fixed." However, the "nesting" of individual-level cases (Russians) within aggregate-level units (i.e., years) raises the possibil-ity that individual-level intercepts or slopes or both will vary system-atically across higher-level units (i.e., time). For example, endorsement of democracy as an ideal may have a different effect on political support when the regime appears to be democratizing than when it is going in the opposite direction. The use of hierarchical linear modeling (HLM) procedures facilitates the analysis of random effects while correcting the standard errors associated with the aggregate-level time series variables (Raudenbush and Bryk, 2002; Gelman and Hill, 2007).

Because the New Russia Barometer data base has only eighteen aggregate units, that is, survey years, this limits the aggregate-level degrees of freedom and restricts the number of variables that can be included in the HLM analysis. Therefore, we use the OLS regression analyses in Tables 5.4 and 6.1 to identify those individual characteristics with a substantial effect on support for the current regime. Since a large number of socialization influences lack significance, they can readily be excluded and the same is true of measures of individual economic conditions. A larger number of political measures register statistical significance, but some can be screened out because they have only a very small effect on support. Where influences are borderline, we have undertaken preliminary HLM analyses to determine whether they have any effect when controls are introduced for the passage of time. An incidental advantage of screening out unimportant social, economic and political characteristics is that attention is thereby focused on those indicators that, on both theoretical and empirical grounds, have an impact on regime support. The HLM analysis shows that *both* the passage of time *and* individual differences have important effects on support for the regime (Table 6.3). At the individual level, 40.1 percent of the variance is accounted for and the Level II analysis of two aggregate influences reduces aggregate variance by 29.0 percent.

The effect of the passage of time on political support is cumulatively big. The restricted maximum likelihood (RML) coefficient in Table 6.3 shows the difference that a single month makes for regime support. Net of other influences, it results in an increase of 0.38 points on the 201-point regime support scale. While this appears small, as Aristotle noted, it is a sophist fallacy to believe that, just because each unit is a little, the total is little. In the course of a single year, political inertia increases support for the regime by almost 4.6 points.[1] Moreover, when fluctuations in individual attributes are taken into account, the effect of time is constant and cumulative over the years. Thus, the

---

[1] This impact is calculated by multiplying the RML coefficient, 0.38, by the relevant number of months. Thus, the impact of the passage of time on regime support over a year is 12 months × 0.38 or 4.56 points.

Table 6.3 *Taking time into account: an HLM analysis*

	RML coeff't	s.e.	P-value
Level II Variance reduction:	29.0%		
Passage of months	.38	.06	.001
Freedom House rating	2.11	1.04	.050
Level I Variance reduction:	40.1%		
Fairness of officials	6.23	.87	.001
Democracy as ideal	5.94	1.14	.001
Democracy as ideal X month	−.03	.01	.001
Regime incongruence	−1.08	.24	.001
Corruption	−1.46	.59	.050
Pro current economy	.42	.02	.001
Pro economic future	.05	.01	.001
Pro economic future X month	.00	.00	.010
Social status	.70	.23	.010

Source: Hierarchical linear model of Centre for the Study of Public Policy, New Russia Barometer data base, 1992–2009.

inexorable force of political inertia steadily raises Russian support for the regime. By the end of Boris Yeltsin's two terms of office, the fact that the regime had survived for eight years gave a boost of 37 points to support. By the end of Vladimir Putin's eight years as president, the cumulative effect of the passage of time doubled to 74 points before taking other influences into account.

How people evaluate the national economy has a big effect too. Net of other influences, a 1-point change in the 201-point scale evaluating the economy creates a change of 0.42 points in support for the regime. But unlike the passage of time, the effect of the economy fluctuates depending on popular judgments of economic conditions. In the vacuum created by the transition from a command to a market economy in 1992, the evaluation of the economic system was at its worst; the mean rating was −0.47. This depressed regime support by 20 points[2] net of all other influences. Although the economy continued to deteriorate for half a dozen years, popular ratings of the

_____

[2] That is, the mean rating (−46.6) multiplied by the RML coefficient (0.42) equals −19.57.

economy became less negative. Since 2003 the evaluation of the economy has made a positive contribution to political support, adding almost 10 points to it at the height of the economic boom. The evaluation of the economy in future is significant too, but the size of its impact is limited; its RML coefficient is less than one-eighth that of the evaluation of the current economy.

Because of statistical multicollinearity, changes in aggregate GDP cannot be included in the same HLM analysis as individual evaluations of the economic system. To verify that this does not lead to the omission of an important contextual influence, we have conducted a separate HLM analysis including GDP and excluding individual evaluations of the economy. Although aggregate GDP registers a statistically significant influence, it is much weaker than that of individual evaluations. To see whether growth in GDP has a cumulative influence on support for the regime, it was included in a separate HLM analysis. It failed to register a significant effect.

Comparing the effect of economic evaluations and time on political support shows that the passage of time has cumulatively trumped the impact of the economy (Figure 6.4). Four years after the launch of the Russian Federation, the passage of time was adding more to regime

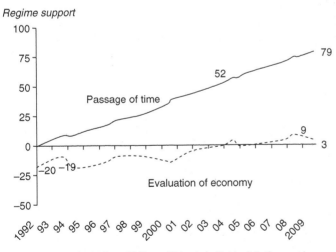

Source: Calculated from RML coefficients in Table 6.2, the number of months since the regime started and, for each NRB survey, the mean score for the evaluation of the current economy.

Figure 6.4 Differential impact of time and economy, 1992–2009

support than was being subtracted by negative evaluations of the economy. The survival of the regime to the end of President Yeltsin's second term doubled the effect of political inertia. Concurrently, the improvement in popular evaluation of the national economy began to augment the impact of the passage of time. At the height of the economic boom in March 2008, the positive evaluation gave a 10-point boost to regime support on the 201-point scale. However, this was far less than the 73-point boost given by the cumulative passage of time.

Whereas most regimes do not change greatly over a short period of time, Freedom House has made a categoric change in its evaluation of Russia, moving it from a rating of partly free to the category of unfree. The actions taken by Russia's leaders that caused Freedom House to downgrade the regime have had a significant effect on regime support. However, the impact of this macro-political change is limited. In the early 1990s when Freedom House rated the regime as partly free this added 9 points to political support. The downgrading of this rating has reduced its contribution to regime support to 5 points since 2005 (Figure 6.5).

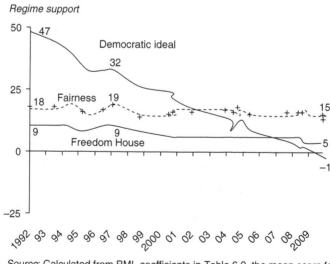

Source: Calculated from RML coefficients in Table 6.2, the mean score for a variable in a given NRB survey and, where there is interaction with time, the number of months from the first survey.

Figure 6.5 Dynamics of political influences, 1992–2009

The extent to which Russians endorse democratic ideals has a substantial and dynamic impact on support for the regime.[3] Russians have consistently been positive about democracy as an ideal. In 1998 the mean endorsement was 7.4 on a ten-point scale; in 2009 the mean was only a tenth of a point less. When the new regime was first launched, democratic idealism gave a 47-point boost in support to a regime that they hoped was going to democratize. This hope more than offset the negative impact on support of dissatisfaction with the national economy. While idealism has remained high, over time Russians committed to democratic ideals have became disillusioned about the regime and less supportive. The coefficient measuring impact declines by 0.03 points each month.[4] Although the high level of democratic idealism has not significantly altered over two decades, its impact on regime support halved by the year 2000 and has continued to contract since. By 2009 commitment to democratic ideals was actually beginning to push support for the regime down (Figure 6.5).

The incongruence between the regime that Russians would like to have and the regime that political elites supply also has a negative effect on political support. However, the RML coefficient is small by comparison with that for democracy as an ideal and it is not altered by the passage of time. Thus, the incongruence between what people want and the regime they get has not caused frustration leading to aggressive protest (cf. Gurr, 1970).

Although most Russians doubt the fairness of public officials, the minority who are favorable are substantially more likely to support the regime. The large RML coefficient boosting support has not altered over time. Since judgments of fairness are fairly stable, the impact of fairness on regime support has been within the narrow range of 14 to 19 points.

As expected, the perception of corruption has a negative effect on regime support, but it is only marginally significant and its impact is slight (Table 6.3). In an analysis of the first fourteen NRB surveys

---

[3] It did not do so in the OLS regression analysis because pooling surveys from all years meant that no allowance could be made for its changing influence over time.

[4] After one year the RML coefficient is reduced by 0.36 (-12 months $\times$ -0.03) from its initial value of 5.94 to 5.58. Between the first and last NRB survey, the RML coefficient turns negative (5.94 $-$ (216 months $\times$ $-.03$).

(Rose, Mishler and Munro, 2006: 178ff.), the passage of time intensified the negative influence of corruption. However, this is no longer the case. It appears that Russians have become inured to the continuance of corruption under the current regime as well as its predecessors.

Although presidential approval exerted a strong and significant effect on support for the regime in the OLS regressions in Chapter 5, it is influenced by many of the same economic and political performance variables that strongly influence popular support for the regime. Because of the resulting multicollinearity, presidential popularity is not reported in the HLM model in Table 6.3. In preliminary analyses that control for the effect of time and other performance variables, presidential popularity lacks a significant independent effect. It is the political and economic performance of the government that has contributed greatly to regime support and to Vladimir Putin's personal popularity.

The multilevel model confirms previous findings that social structure has little effect on support for the regime. In the HLM analysis, socioeconomic status is the only variable that is even marginally significant statistically and its impact is slight, adding only 3 points to the 201-point regime support scale. Moreover, even though individuals go up and down the social status ladder, in aggregate the distribution of the Russian population into higher, middle and below-average status groups tends to remain constant with the passage of time.

The level of political support at a given point in time is the result of multiple influences pushing in opposite directions (Figure 6.5). By 2009 four individual characteristics – fairness, the current and future evaluations of the economy, and socioeconomic status – exerted a positive influence on regime support. Collectively, they boosted it by 23 points. At the same time, the incongruence between individual ideals of what the regime ought to be and what it is and the perception of corruption reduced regime support by 8 points and the fall in the Freedom House rating subtracted another 4 points. Together, positive and negative individual characteristics gave regime support a net boost of only 11 points on a 201-point scale.

When people evaluate their regime is at least as important as *how* it is evaluated. The rise in support for the regime has been primarily due to the passage of time turning a new regime into a familiar fact of life. Between 1992 and 2009 its cumulative impact increased regime support by 79 points. In the early days of the new Russian regime, the positive effect of democratic idealism was a countervailing influence against negative views of the economy. Today, the opposite has become the case: A positive evaluation of the economy tends to offset the effect of the disillusion of idealists.

Although the passage of time today accounts for a high level of support, projecting this into the future depends on all other conditions remaining constant. Such a statement is a reminder that the political equilibrium is threatened with disruption when all other conditions do not remain equal. The replacement of Vladimir Putin by Dmitry Medvedev as president and the abrupt contraction in the national economy due to the 2008 world financial crisis are reminders that the passage of time also brings challenges.

7 | *Finessing the challenge of succession*

In a new regime, the fluidity of institutions makes political succession a challenge. In a consolidated regime, "When things go wrong, you change the rulers, not the regime," but in a new regime the opposite can happen (Huntington, 1991: 266–267). Whether the decision about who governs is taken by the electorate or by an unaccountable elite, if leaders are twice changed within the rules then Huntington considers this evidence of a regime's support being consolidated. Two turnovers show that both the founders and their initial opponents are now committed to an orderly succession in office rather than wanting to reopen past conflicts. It also allows for the passage of time to encourage popular support or, at least, resigned acceptance, if not positive support. Control of government did not initially change hands between parties until twenty years after the founding of the Federal Republic of Germany and twenty-three years after the founding of the French Fifth Republic.

Huntington's two-turnover test is equally applicable to authoritarian regimes. Throughout its history the Soviet Union successfully met the challenge of leadership succession. Normally, the tenure of the leader was for life. The first turnover occurred after Lenin's death and the second did not occur until Josef Stalin died after thirty-one years in which he had institutionalized a strong party-state. In the next three decades there were six changes in the leading position in the regime, the general secretaryship of the Communist Party.

The political success of Vladimir Putin has encouraged scholars as well as the media to identify him with Russia's regime. There are at least five books in English with *Putin's Russia* invoked in the title (Shevtsova, 2005; Jack, 2005; Herspring, 2007; Politkovskaya, 2007; Sakwa, 2008a). They differ only in whether there is a qualifying subtitle such as *Past Imperfect, Future Uncertain*. Such tributes to the personal standing of a leader imply that the departure of Putin from power would put the regime at risk.

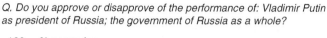

Q. Do you approve or disapprove of the performance of: Vladimir Putin
as president of Russia; the government of Russia as a whole?

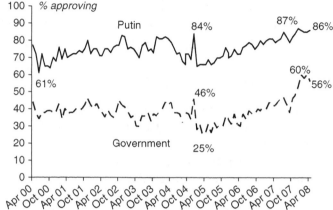

Source: Results from regular nationwide surveys of the Levada Center.
For the full series, see Rose, 2009b: Appendix Table 2.

Figure 7.1 Gap in approval of Putin and of government

Ordinary Russians readily distinguish between Vladimir Putin
and Russia's government. The Levada Center regularly asks separate questions about approval of the two. Consistently, it finds a big gap between
approval of the president and of the government that he heads (Figure 7.1;
Rose, 2009b: Appendix Table 2). Over the years, Putin's approval rating
has averaged 76 percent, while that of the government has averaged
42 percent. The gap between the personification and the institutions of
government was as high as 46 percentage points in November 2003.

Three terms in office would be entirely consistent with democratic
practice; Margaret Thatcher and Tony Blair were each three-term
prime ministers and Franklin D. Roosevelt won four successive American elections. However, in the post-Soviet context circumstances were
different. To prevent a president from becoming a dictator by holding
office for life, as has occurred in some successor states of the Soviet
Union, the 1993 Russian constitution explicitly limits a president to
two terms of office. Article 81.3 declares, "No one person shall hold
the office of President of the Russian Federation for more than two
terms in succession." President Yeltsin's poor health as well as his
unpopularity precluded his attempting a third term. Although the first
succession to the presidency was peaceful and technically consistent

with the constitution, the way it was handled was not. President Yeltsin unexpectedly resigned at the end of 1999 and, in accordance with the law, Prime Minister Vladimir Putin became acting president. This gave him all the advantages of incumbency in the Kremlin and pre-empted conventional procedures for popular choice.

The problem of term limits

The pressures on Vladimir Putin to leave office did not come from the electorate. If the constitution had not had a two-term limit, then opinion polls gave Putin every reason to be confident of winning a third term in office with a big majority in the first-round ballot. However, the language of the Russian constitution appeared to make President Putin ineligible to seek a third term, thus mandating a test of the two-turnover hypothesis by requiring a change in 2008. As the end of Putin's second term loomed, there was recurring speculation about whether he would surrender office or create a means to remain president. If he decided to leave office, this would create a pressing problem of career planning for a physically fit 55-year-old politician.

Speculating about alternatives

Given the existence of a constitutional barrier to running for re-election, Putin had three broad alternatives short of suspending the constitution. Amending the constitution offered a straightforward and formally correct way to stay in office. It could be justified as allowing the electorate to decide how long a person should stay in office. Amendments require endorsement by two-thirds of the members of the Duma; three-quarters of the members of the upper chamber, the Federation Council; and two-thirds of the regions of the Federation. Having created United Russia as a party of power, Putin could be confident that any constitutional amendment he proposed would be endorsed. Supporters of Putin such as Sergei Mironov, speaker of the upper house of the parliament, publicly called for President Putin to initiate such an amendment. Such calls were variously interpreted as a trial balloon from Putin or as an attempt to press him to do what would maintain his staff's privileged positions in the Kremlin, which would be jeopardized by the election of a new president.

Secondly, the duration of the president's term could be extended. A term of up to seven years would follow Charles de Gaulle's design for the French Fifth Republic, albeit the French presidential term has since been shortened to five years. A term as long as ten years would invite the suspicion that Putin was thinking of becoming president for life. However, an extension of the second term for a few years would postpone rather than remove the problem of term limits.

A third alternative would be to "bend" the constitution by unanticipated actions that were not explicitly forbidden. In Latin America such a strategy is called an *autogolpe*, that is, a "self-coup" by which an elected ruler perpetuates himself in office. For example, renaming the office and giving it selectively enhanced powers would have offered Putin another two terms in an office purpose-built to his tastes. If Putin wanted to concentrate on international politics, then becoming head of the Commonwealth of Independent States might have provided a platform to do so. Events threatening the security of Russia, such as terrorist attacks in Moscow, might be used to justify the president in declaring a national emergency and suspending elections. However, the law of 2001 allowed emergency measures to last only for thirty days without renewal. To declare a prolonged state of emergency would be seen as a dictatorial coup. The failure of the August 1991 Communist putsch and the bloodshed of the October 1993 confrontation between the Kremlin and the legislature were precedents cautioning of the risk of losing support by bending the constitution to the point at which it broke.

Although Vladimir Putin's popularity remained consistently high, public opinion was divided between those wanting to have a free choice of leader and those favoring Putin making the decision for them (Figure 7.2). Less than a year before the presidential election, 44 percent favored giving voters a choice. However, an equally large group wanted the constitution changed in some way to allow Putin to stand again or Putin to appoint his successor. While don't knows were few, don't cares were numerous. When the Levada Center asked people in October 2007 how their family would be affected if Putin retained substantial influence for many years, half had no opinion or said it would make no difference. Among those with a view, four-fifths thought Putin remaining in office would have a positive impact on their family while one in five saw its impact as negative. In short, Russians were ready to give resigned acceptance, if not positive

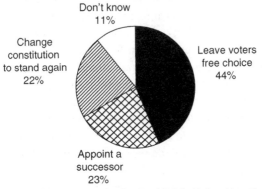

Q. At present, the constitution says that Vladimir Putin is ineligible to be a candidate for a third term as president in 2008. What should he do in this situation?

Don't know 11%

Change constitution to stand again 22%

Leave voters free choice 44%

Appoint a successor 23%

Source: Centre for the Study of Public Policy, New Russia Barometer XV (April 2007).

Figure 7.2 Choices facing Putin: the public's view

support, to whatever Putin decided about who should govern Russia for four years or more.

Ending uncertainty

From early in his first term Vladimir Putin consistently said that he had no plan to repeal term limits. When asked after four years in office what he thought was the optimal period to hold the presidency, Putin carefully balanced arguments for a longer term and the countervailing argument that changing the constitution could create "an element of destabilization. And that's much worse than a four-year term" (Lenta.Ru, 2004).

Denials did not stop speculation that the president was planning by one means or another to retain his hold on office. In his own interest, Putin avoided identifying a successor; members of the government who showed signs of wanting to claim that position were sidelined. The absence of an obvious successor increased speculation that Putin would remain in the presidency after the date of the next election.

Eight days after United Russia's landslide victory at the December 2007 Duma election, Putin announced in a stage-managed television interview that he would leave office. He proposed as his successor a protege from St. Petersburg, Dmitry Medvedev, who was then first deputy prime minister. A week later delegates to the Party Congress of

United Russia endorsed Medvedev as their presidential candidate by a vote of 478 to 1. Thus, for the first time the presidency would not be held by a person who had run as an independent. However, United Russia is not a party with a network of civil society institutions or a caucus of Duma notables who could hold their leader accountable or remove him if they lost confidence. Instead, it is an ingenious institution devised by Putin to maintain his power in government (see Chapter 4).

By ceasing to be president in 2008, Vladimir Putin became constitutionally eligible to succeed President Medvedev at an uncertain future date. This led to speculation that his protege would remain in office only long enough to create a short interruption in Vladimir Putin's presidency. If Medvedev resigned after a year or so, Putin would be eligible to seek election for another two terms as president. A Levada Center survey in October 2007 found public opinion divided: 43 percent disapproved of this happening, 33 percent favored it and the remainder had no opinion.

In announcing his departure from the presidency, Putin volunteered to continue to serve the state as Chairman of the Government, the Russian term for prime minister. The constitution gives the government responsibility for the federal budget, managing the economy, formulating social policy, legislating on matters of the state's defense and security, and issuing decrees subject to veto by the president. The prime minister's role is to be in charge of what ministries do. The president is constitutionally charged with nominating the prime minister; directing foreign policy and national security; and acting as commander-in-chief of the armed forces. The president can also veto Duma legislation. In accepting the presidential nomination, Medvedev pledged to carry on Putin's program and expressed delight that Putin would remain in government.

While the constitution sets out formal powers, politics dictates how they are used. The complaint often made against President Yeltsin was that he took too little interest in what "his" government was doing and, reciprocally, that too much was left to his longest-serving prime minister, Viktor Chernomyrdin. By contrast, President Putin was, within the limits of time and political resources, involved in a range of government policies and made good use of his contacts in the federal security agencies. In addition, Putin actively pursued a role in international relations. However, as president he was hesitant about "interfering" in departments of government with strongly entrenched bureaucratic interests: for example, the military remained unreformed and corruption continued at a high level (see e.g. Sakwa, 2008b).

Russians favor a system of checks and balances. Consistently, NRB surveys find that a majority endorses the president having the power to suspend the Duma and rule by decree if he considers it necessary, but a majority also favors the Duma having the right to stop the president taking decisions that it considers wrong. As Putin's second term neared its end, 45 percent endorsed strong checks, being in favor of the president ruling by decree and of the Duma being able to overrule him. Only one-third endorsed the president being able to rule by decree without the Duma; 9 percent favored the Duma being able to check a president without decree powers; and 11 percent rejected both alternatives.

By moving from the presidency to the prime ministership, Putin remained true to his public statements; he did not change the constitution. However, he finessed the challenge of term limits by taking the most important office for which he was eligible. In doing so, he raised the question whether the office confers power on a politician or whether a politician can make an office powerful. Many studies of Putin's conduct imply that it was his personal skills that made the presidency so commanding. Insofar as this was the case, he can continue to dominate the government as prime minister. However, institutionally minded political scientists emphasize that the office makes the man, implying that Medvedev would gradually take control of "his" government.

Organizing the right result

Free and fair elections are the first condition of a regime being democratic (www.freedomhouse.org). An election is free if many parties compete and there is the possibility that the opposition can emerge as the winner (Przeworski *et al.*, 1996: 50–51). It is fair if electoral procedures provide a level playing field to competing parties (Levitsky and Way, 2010b). These are not the same criteria as those of governors of an undemocratic regime: They are primarily concerned with getting the "right" result, making sure of victory by whatever means are necessary. As Andreas Schedler (2010: 78) notes, "Contemporary electoral autocracies have given up the longstanding battle against the establishment of representative institutions. They have shifted their authoritarian energies from repressing formally democratic institutions to manipulating them."

The electoral process involves many procedures set out in rules and laws concerning everything from the eligibility of parties to appear on the ballot to rules governing the counting of ballots and the declaration of the result. A procedurally fair election requires that rules are impartially administered by bureaucrats according to laws setting out what parties and voters must, may or cannot do. Impartiality is particularly important for opposition parties, because they lack the advantages of incumbency. If officials enforce election laws that involve procedures that the opposition regards as substantively unfair, for example, gerrymandering electoral districts, this makes fairness a political rather than a procedural issue (see e.g. Goodwin-Gill, 2006; OSCE, 2005).

Fairness can also be defined in substantive terms: The party that wins the most votes ought to be the winner, and public opinion and exit polls offer social science evidence of which party has the most popular support. However, the term "ought" can be interpreted in partisan terms, as identifying the party that its backers believe deserves to win. Marxist-Leninist doctrine was very clear about which party ought to win an election: the party that represented the true interest of the working class. From this perspective, to offer a choice between parties would be ideologically wrong, because it would be a choice between truth and error; therefore, only one party was on the ballot (Rosa, 1949; Pravda, 1978).

Unfairness can take many forms, ranging from rigging election laws in favor of the party in power; showing partiality or even contempt in administering election laws; campaign practices that are heavily biased in favor of the government; intimidation of voters; systematic maladministration of polling stations to the disadvantage of the opposition; and fraudulent casting or counting of ballots (Boneo, 2000; Elklit and Reynolds, 2005). Normative standards can be used to describe elections as unfair, for example, if the threshold to qualify for proportional representation seats is so high that it excludes parties that receive a nontrivial share of the vote. In the cynical maxim of a onetime American party strategist, "If you can't steal an election before election day, you don't deserve it."

From the introduction of national elections in 1905, Russia has had a tradition of elections in which the "right" result was assured, because elections were unfree and unfair (see Emmons, 1983). The definition of who ought to win was determined by the powers that be. In tsarist times, officials infiltrated and disrupted political parties as well as manipulating the published results. Soviet elections went beyond unfairness: They were unfree because there was no competition (Furtak, 1990). In the Russian Federation the administration of election procedures is in the hands of a Central Election Commission composed of members nominated in equal numbers by the president, the Duma and the Federation Council (www.cikf.ru/eng).

Russian administrators and voters were initially unaccustomed to conducting free and fair elections. Observers from the Organization for Security and Cooperation in Europe criticized electoral administration but also noted improvements (OSCE, 2000). The 2004 presidential election was procedurally unfair. To demonstrate their resentment of unfairness, the Communist presidential candidate was not the party leader but a former Agrarian Party member and the presidential candidate of the Liberal Democratic Party was the chauffeur of the party leader. These two candidates, who were critics of the Kremlin, together polled 7.9 percent. One candidate, Sergei Mironov, speaker of the upper house of the parliament, actually endorsed Putin. Ivan Rybkin, who had held high positions under President Yeltsin, was nominated by a group bankrolled by the exiled billionaire Boris Berezovsky, but after going missing for five days during the campaign he withdrew his name from the ballot. Independent opinion polls left no doubt that Putin was the candidate favored by a substantial majority of voters. The outcome was substantively fair: The candidate with the most popular support in the opinion polls, President Putin, secured 71.3 percent of the vote (Colton, 2005; Oates, 2006).

Every Russian election has been accompanied by allegations of fraud. Official results can be challenged on the grounds that they are not what they ought to be. Such challenges rest on "two unknown and unobservable variables – popular preferences and authoritarian manipulation" (Schedler, 2006: 7). Some allegations are supported by official statistics showing results in a specific locality that appear "too good to be true." Statistical comparisons between the official results and predictions of what the result ought to have been if voters had behaved according to a priori assumptions are also cited in allegations of electoral manipulation. However, Mikhail Myagkov,

Peter Ordeshook and Dimitri Shakin (2009: 24) caution, "There is no single magical pattern in the numbers that flags an election as fraudulent or fraud free."

Substantively, voters endorse Putin's choices

In the strict sense, the 2007–8 round of Russian elections was not about Vladimir Putin: His name was not on the presidential ballot and the Duma ballot offered a choice between party lists. While the Communist Party and the Liberal Democratic Party had fought every election since 1993, United Russia was different. It was fighting only its second Duma contest and it had not fielded a presidential candidate before. In the official record of the Central Election Commission, United Russia was registered as a political party; in practical political terms, it was a support group for Vladimir Putin.

In the 2007 Duma election United Russia achieved a big victory. Its share of the list vote rose by more than 26 percent and it took more than two-thirds of Duma seats. Complaints that the Duma election was not a free and fair contest implied that the vote for United Russia ought to have been less than the 64.3 percent with which it was credited. However, the substantive outcome was in line with the independent Levada Center's final pre-election poll; it estimated United Russia would receive 67 percent of the vote. Substantively, the outcome of the Duma vote was fair, that is, the party favored by the majority of Russians won the election.

The contrast between institutionalized party support and per-sonalized support is shown by regression analysis of Duma voting behavior (Rose and Mishler, 2010a: Table 3). By comparison with both Communist and Liberal Democratic voters, who tended to have longstanding commitments to these well-established parties, United Russia's support came from electors who were much more likely to have decided recently. United Russia's voters were much less likely than others to identify with an ideology, be it pro-market, Communist or nationalist, and they were far more motivated by approval of Vladimir Putin.

The presidential ballot was different, for it explicitly asked voters to endorse an individual, and Putin's name was not on the ballot. Dmitry Medvedev, the official candidate of United Russia, received 70.3 percent of the vote. Substantively, the election was fair, since opinion polls showed that Medvedev was endorsed by a large majority of those intending to vote. The Levada Center's final pre-election poll found no doubt about who was favored, but confusion among the electorate about who was running for president. A total of 62 percent named United Russia's official candidate, Medvedev, as their preference and an additional 22 percent spoke of voting for Putin. When people were asked to give approval of named politicians, Putin's name led all the rest.

Even though a big majority cast their presidential vote for Medvedev, this was not an indication of the candidate's personal appeal; trust in Putin was by far the strongest influence on voting for Medvedev. By contrast, ideological and programmatic attachment to the Communist Party was by far the most important influence on voting for the Communist candidate (Rose and Mishler, 2010a, Table 4; cf. Colton and Hale, 2009). Voters for Medvedev were also positively motivated by approval of the current economic system and by their household's economic situation. Medvedev could not take credit for either achievement, since both were associated with Putin's presidency. Of those who voted for Medvedev, 73 percent saw him as a surrogate who would be subordinate to or share power with Putin. Thus, even though Vladimir Putin no longer holds the office of president, his finesse of term limits has left him the biggest man in government in the minds of the Russian public.

Contrasting views of electoral fairness

Before the 2007–8 round of elections, the Russian government imposed major restrictions on election monitoring by foreign groups. Therefore, the OSCE Office for Democratic Institutions and Human Rights (ODIHR) refused to send observers to the Duma election. It thus relegated Russia to the category of countries such as Turkmenistan, Tajikistan and Uzbekistan, whose restrictions on the freedom of election monitors have also been great. The Parliamentary Assembly of the Council of Europe (PACE) and its EU counterpart did send monitors. They assessed the Duma election as "not held on a level playing field" because of the merger of United Russia with the state, harassment of opposition parties, barriers to new parties appearing on the ballot, and strong media bias (Council of Europe, 2007). Some academic judgments have been harsher;

Mikhail Myagkov, Peter C. Ordeshook and Dimitri Shakin (2009: ch. 1) described the 2007 Duma contest as fraudulent.

In advance of the 2008 presidential election, the ODIHR again refused to send observers on the grounds that the conditions laid down by the Russian government would not permit independent assessment. PACE again sent observers. After President Putin's handpicked candidate won an overwhelming victory, the Council of Europe group described the result as "a reflection of the will of the electorate whose democratic potential was, unfortunately, untapped" (Harding, 2008). In particular, it criticized the domination of the media by Putin's candidate. However, the PACE delegation did not challenge the substantive result.

Any assessment of electoral fairness that omits the views of the electorate is incomplete. Insofar as fraud is widespread, a substantial portion of the Russian electorate ought to have witnessed or heard about fraud from trusted sources such as friends and relatives. Even if hearsay exaggerates the extent of fraud, popular perceptions are important, insofar as unfair behavior by officials reduces support for the regime.

When asked about the 2007 Duma election, three-fifths of New Russia Barometer respondents described it as more or less fair, one-fifth said it tended to be unfair and almost one-fifth had no opinion (Table 7.1). This assessment is consistent with the experience of respondents. Only 15 percent said that they noticed some sort of pressure being put on people to vote for a particular party; usually the pressure came from bosses or coworkers. Only 9 percent thought the Duma results were falsified. In short, Russians disagreed with international election observers about whether the Duma election was fair (see also Hutcheson, 2010).

The NRB survey after the presidential election similarly found that a clear majority, 58 percent, described the election as definitely or somewhat fair, as against one-quarter calling it somewhat or definitely unfair (Table 7.1). Only 10 percent reported irregularities around polling day such as election administrators advising people whom to vote for or individuals casting ballots for other family members, familiar practices in Soviet times. In all, 68 percent thought the ballot was secret, as against 17 percent believing officials could find out how people voted. Moreover, only 15 percent thought they could be pursued if they did not vote as the authorities would like. The positive

Table 7.1 *Evaluation of fairness of elections*

Q. Would you say that the recent election of the (Duma/president) was conducted fairly or not?

	Duma %	Presidency %
It was fair	16	14
To some extent fair	45	44
(Fair)	(61)	(58)
To some extent unfair	16	20
Definitely unfair	6	6
(Unfair)	(22)	(26)
Don't know	17	16

Source: Centre for the Study of Public Policy, New Russia Barometer XVI (December 2007) and XVII (March 2008).

evaluation that Russians make about the fairness of elections is not because they are afraid to criticize government (Rose, 2007). The continuing characterization of the regime as corrupt and periods of low support for the regime show that this is not the case.

On procedural as well as substantive grounds, most Russians saw the 2007–8 round of elections as fair. However, the judgment was qualified. In each contest the median elector thought that the election was to some extent fair rather than completely fair. Likewise, among the minority seeing the election as unfair, those seeing it as to some extent improper outnumbered those viewing it as definitely unfair by a margin of almost three to one (see Table 7.1).

Politics influences perceptions of fairness

To explain why Russians differ in evaluating electoral fairness we need to add the hypothesis "partisanship matters" to those used for regime support. The partisanship hypothesis assumes that it is the substantive outcome of an election that determines assessments. Those who vote for the winning party are more likely to see an election as fair while those voting for losers or nonvoters are more likely to see it as unfair. In other words, whether your party wins is more important than how it wins (Riker, 1980; Anderson *et al.*, 2005; Rose and Mishler, 2009).

Table 7.2 *Influences on perceived election unfairness*

	2007 Duma election			2008 presidency		
	Adjusted R^2 24.3%			Adjusted R^2 23.6%		
	b	s.e.	Beta	b	s.e.	Beta
Partisan voting						
Voted for opposition	.44***	.07	.17	.65***	.07	.23
Did not vote	.54***	.06	.24	.56***	.06	.23
Rating of president	−.20***	.03	−.18	−.14***	.03	−.13
Politics						
Democracy as ideal	−.01	.01	−.02	−.03	.01	−.07
Regime incongruence	.05***	.01	.10	.02	.01	.03
Freedom greater	−.07	.02	−.06	−.19***	.03	−.15
Corruption	.17***	.03	.13	.14***	.03	.10
Economy						
Pro current economy	.00	.00	−.05	.00	.00	−.02
Pro old economy	.00	.00	.02	.00	.00	−.02
Pro economic future	.00***	.00	−.13	.00***	.00	−10
Household econ. situation	−.03	.02	−.03	−.06	.03	−.04
Socialization						
Born before 1946	−.20	.07	−.07	−.20	.07	−.07
Social status	−.01	.01	−.01	−.01	.01	−.01
Education	.05	.03	.05	.02	.03	.01

*** Significant at .001; ** significant at .01. N = 1,601 (2007); N = 1,603 (2008).
Source: Centre for the Study of Public Policy, New Russia Barometer XVI (December 2007) and XVII (March 2008).

Views about electoral fairness can be tested with data from NRB surveys after the Duma and presidential elections. Separate OLS regression analyses for the Duma and presidential elections produce strikingly similar accounts of what influences the assessments of fairness reported in Table 7.1. In all, 24.3 percent of the variance is accounted for in the Duma election and 23.6 percent in the presidential election (Table 7.2).

Partisanship has the biggest effect on how electors assess the fairness of elections. Virtually everyone knew who won the Duma and presidential elections, but they disagreed about whether this was the "right" result, that is, consistent with the party they voted for. The higher the approval rating given Vladimir Putin, the stronger the tendency for people to see the Duma and presidential elections as fair. In a complementary way, those who voted for losing parties and candidates tend to see elections as less fair, and this is also true of nonvoters.

How people evaluate the performance of government has a major effect too. If people feel freer now than under the Communist regime, this encourages the view that Russian elections are fair. However, if people see government as corrupt, they tend to judge elections as unfair. In the Duma election, seeing an incongruence between the ideal and the actual regime significantly encourages people to assess the election as unfair. In the presidential election, Russians more committed to democracy as an ideal are more likely to see that election as fair.

Even though economic evaluations are important for regime support, they have little influence on assessing the fairness of elections. In both analyses the rating of the current economic system fails to achieve statistical significance and the same is true of evaluations of the old economic system. However, having a positive view of the future of the economy discourages people from seeing elections as fair. This suggests that people who are most optimistic about the prospect for the market in Russia are more aware of political manipulation.

Socialization and social structure have little effect on how Russians see the fairness of elections. Education, which ought to make people more informed about and critical of the conduct of elections, fails to achieve significance for either ballot. Nor do Russians of higher social status, who should be more confident of exerting political influence, have a more positive evaluation of election fairness. The oldest cohort of Russians are marginally more likely to see elections as fair; this may reflect their use of the conduct of Soviet elections as a benchmark for assessing fairness.

Influence of election unfairness on regime support

In the democratic model of regime support, elections are the primary means by which citizens give direction to government and governors respond in ways that encourage support (Figure 1.1). Undemocratic regimes use elections to mobilize a show of support, as was evidenced by the regularity with which elections with predetermined results were held in Communist countries (see e.g. Rose and Mossawir, 1967; Furtak, 1990). However, when elections do not allow citizens to express their views fairly and freely, this may stimulate people to reduce their support for the regime. Likewise, people who vote for opposition parties can be expected to be less likely to support the regime (Anderson *et al.*, 2005).

A narrow focus on electoral processes, however, does not take into account the effect of other influences on support such as the economy. Thus, the relevant question is: How much effect do electoral and partisan influences have on regime support after controlling for all other influences? Since people can best evaluate election fairness in the immediate aftermath of a contest, we answer this question with data from New Russia Barometer surveys fielded just after the 2007 Duma and the 2008 presidential elections. The two OLS regressions give similar accounts of influences on regime support, and they are consistent with patterns identified in previous pooled regression analyses (cf. Tables 7.3 and 5.4, 7.1).

Seeing an election as unfair does significantly reduce support for the regime. However, views about fairness are only one of eleven significant variables affecting regime support in the post-Duma election survey and only one among eight influencing support in the post-presidential election. After controlling for unfairness and partisanship, the performance of the Russian government, especially the credit it was taking for the country's economic boom at the time of the December 2007 and March 2008 elections, is by far the most important influence on support for the regime (Table 7.3). For the Duma election, the Beta coefficient for the effect of the current economy on regime support is almost four times greater than that of unfairness; for the presidential survey, it is more than three times larger. Popular expectations of the economy in the future and of the old economic system also significantly affect regime support.

Partisanship influences regime support too. In the Duma survey, regime support is depressed by 5 points among the minority voting for Communist, Liberal Democratic or other opposition parties, and by 3 points among nonvoters. Approving Vladimir Putin gives support a limited boost. In the post-presidential election survey, partisan demobilization – seeing the election as unfair and not having voted – depressed regime support. The most frequently cited reason for not voting is not political disaffection but the inconvenience of getting to the polls on election day (Hutcheson, 2010: Table 7). The incongruence between the desire for democracy and what the regime supplies

Table 7.3 *Effect of unfairness on regime support*

	2007 Duma election			2008 Presidency		
	Adjusted R^2 50.4%			Adjusted R^2 42.1%		
	b	s.e.	Beta	b	s.e.	Beta
Partisan voting						
Elections unfair	−3.93***	.71	−.12	−4.28***	.63	−.15
Voted for opposition	−5.03	1.91	−.06	−1.02	1.87	−.01
Did not vote	−3.31	1.63	−.04	−4.80	1.56	−.07
Approves Putin	2.75***	.77	.07	.67	.68	.02
Economy						
Pro current economy	.42***	.02	.46	.41***	.02	.46
Pro old economy	.04	.01	.06	.10***	.01	.15
Pro economic future	.13***	.02	.13	.09***	.02	.10
Household econ. situation	.04	.64	.00	.31	.87	.01
Politics						
Democracy as ideal	1.81***	.37	.11	.56	.32	.04
Regime incongruence	−2.49***	.40	−.14	−1.45***	.37	−.09
Freedom greater	1.69	.70	.05	2.96***	.75	.08
Corruption	−.26	.81	−.01	−.56	.80	−.01
Socialization						
Born before 1946	−1.63	1.83	−.02	−3.67	1.67	−.04
Social status	1.31***	.39	.07	.21	.35	.01

*** Significant at .001; N = 1,601 (2007); N = 1,603 (2008).
Source: Centre for the Study of Public Policy, New Russia Barometer XVI (December 2007) and XVII (March 2008).

and an appreciation of freedom register significant effects on support, while socialization has little influence.

The contrast between Russian and Western evaluations of the same elections implies that the idea of fair elections does not have the same meaning everywhere. The contrast is also found in the post-election evaluation by the Commonwealth of Independent States Executive Committee of the 2008 presidential election. Whereas Western observers found the election wanting in procedural terms, the delegation from post-Soviet states reported that it was free, the nomination of candidates "competitive" and media coverage "positive in tone" (CIS Executive Committee, 2008). In short, people who are heirs to the Soviet legacy appear readier to evaluate elections in terms of their substantive outcome rather than by the procedural norms common in Western conceptions of democracy.

The dynamic implications of an unfair election depend on what has preceded it. If subjects are accustomed to Soviet-style one-party elections, then a ballot that offers a choice of multiple parties and allows opposition parties to get a quarter or more of the vote may appear as an improvement on what went before. Moreover, while seeing elections as unfair is a mark against the regime, it is not a major drawback. The regression analysis shows that its negative tendency is overwhelmed by the influence of economic performance. This raises the question: What happens to the capacity of the regime to deliver support if the economy gets into trouble? Unlike the passage of time, which moves in only one direction, the performance of the national economy can reverse.

8 | *The challenge of economic reversal*

The reversal of world economic conditions is trebly significant for Russia. First, it has been severe because the economic boom that preceded it was heavily dependent on the rise in the world market price of exports such as oil, gas and natural resources (Rutland, 2008; Goldman, 2008). Secondly, the consolidation of support for the new regime has been significantly influenced by the decade-long economic boom following the 1998 ruble crisis (see Figure 6.2). Thirdly, dissatisfied Russians cannot alter the government at the ballot box. An economic crisis originating in the epicenter of capitalism, Wall Street, could encourage Russians to view the Kremlin as offering protection against the turbulence of world capitalism.

In medicine, the term crisis connotes a turning point at which a patient is most vulnerable to suffering the worst effects of a threatening clinical condition, for example, a serious heart attack. If the point is passed successfully, then recuperation follows. The unexpected abruptness of the 2008 economic crisis was analogous to a severe heart attack. At this point the correspondence stops, for while a patient can die rather than recover, an economy goes on and on. While its dynamic character implies that there can be a recovery after a reversal, this may come after economic contraction has damaged political support.

The economic crisis that erupted in 2008 shocked political regimes in ways that differ in kind from the marginal fluctuations of the political business cycle. Not only did it produce contractions in market economies unprecedented since the 1930s, but also it called into question fundamentals of a global financial system in which democratic regimes have become deeply embedded. Given social science theories that assume that regime support reflects macroeconomic conditions, the shock raised questions about whether democratic regimes can maintain political support. The challenge also confronts authoritarian regimes.

The 2008 economic crisis was not the first that Russians have experienced. However, crises have been different in kind, and so have the political responses. The nonmarket command economy of the Soviet era produced recurring stress at the workplace and among consumers who had to search from shop to shop in order to buy goods in short supply. However, the Soviet regime was able to mobilize a show of support from its subjects. The Russian Federation was founded amidst the transformation of a command economy into a market economy. The turbulence of transformation culminated in the collapse of the ruble in 1998. Since the world economy was functioning normally in 1998, the ruble crisis of that year was specific to Russia. That was followed by a sustained economic boom that created benefits for the mass of the population as well as for the billionaires who gained most from the unequal distribution of Russia's new wealth. The 2008 crisis occurred when the passage of time had generated a solid base of support for the regime. However, inasmuch as it is perceptions of the national economic system rather than household living conditions that are important for support, then a crisis at the top of the economy may have a big impact on the regime's base of political support.

Crisis at the top

The 2008 economic reversal was first of all a global macro-economic crisis. It started at the top of the international financial system and quickly spread into major national financial institutions such as central banks and ministries of finance. The crisis disrupted the normal patterns of economic change and created uncertainty about the capacity of major economic actors to continue business as usual. Given that the nominal assets of financial institutions are reckoned in the tens of billions of rubles, the losses to Russian banks, major borrowers and the government threatened to run into hundreds of billions. These figures are large in the absolute sense, even though their size is not so large relative to an economy with a gross domestic product valued in many trillions of rubles.

The size of the reversal triggered by the crisis can be seen by comparing macro-economic data about the state of the national economy just before and since its effects were most acute. In 2007 official statistics reported an 8.1 percent annual growth in the national

Table 8.1 *Ups and downs in Russian economy after crises*

	Dec 07	Dec 08	Mar 09	Jun 09	Sep 09	Dec 09	Mar 10	Jun 10	Sep 10
GDP growth, %	8.1	5.6	−9.8	−10.4	−9.9	−7.9	3.15	4.2	na
Inflation, %	11.9	11.6	13.3	7.3	7.9	8.8	3.1	4.3	6.1
Unemployed, %	6.1	7.8	9.2	8.3	7.6	8.2	8.6	6.8	6.6
Ruble/$ exchange rate	25.6	24.8	34.7	31.0	30.8	31.7	29.6	31.2	30.8

Sources: World Bank, 2010b 24. GDP and inflation figures are year-on-year changes. Unemployment (International Labour Organization definition) and ruble/dollar exchange rates for December 2007, 2008, 2009 are annual means; other entries refer to the year-on-year change for the month cited.

economy and growth had been similarly high for more than half a dozen years previously. Thus, GDP had increased by more than four-fifths since the 1998 ruble crisis. In the first part of 2008 a high rate of growth was sustained. However, the sharp contraction in autumn meant that the annual growth rate was down and falling fast. By June 2009, GDP had contracted by 10.4 percent from its level twelve months previously (Table 8.1). While it began to recover from this nadir, by December 2009 the contraction in the economy had wiped out all the growth of the previous year and a portion of the gains in 2007.

By 2007 officially recorded unemployment had fallen by half from the 12 percent level at the time of the ruble crisis. However, in response to the following year's financial crisis, employers reduced their demand for labor. By March 2009 the official unemployment rate had risen to 9.2 percent, half again more than it was in the boom year of 2007. However, by autumn 2010 it had fallen to near its pre-crisis level.

The abrupt transition from a controlled economy to an economy in which supply and demand set prices was followed by treble-digit inflation, and the 1998 ruble crisis fueled further inflation. In reaction, the government managed to reduce inflation to close to 10 percent by the middle of the next decade. In many market economies an incidental consequence of the economic recession was that inflation halted or there was even a short-term fall in the price index. In Russia this has hardly been the case. From the end of 2007 to the end of 2009 prices were up by more than one-fifth. The economic crisis caused a flight from the ruble by Russian billionaires as well as by foreign investors and speculators. It fell from around 25 rubles to the dollar to a low of 36 rubles. After recovering, it had still lost more than one-fifth in value in a year. Concurrently, there was a reduction of more than $100 billion in the foreign currency reserve that the government accumulated from its energy revenues. In January 2010, Finance Minister Alexei Kudrin declared that the abnormally high annual rate of growth since 2000 could not be sustained. However, since the economy had almost doubled in size in the previous decade, a substantial reduction in the annual percentage rate of growth could still yield a larger absolute growth in the economy than before.

The volatility of the Russian economy is a sign not only of its vulnerability to world market conditions but also of its resilience. By the second half of 2009 macro-economic statistics were no longer registering a big contraction in the national economy. Similarly, foreign exchange reserves once again started to rise; between March and December 2009 reserves increased by $55 billion (World Bank, 2010a: 5).

Politically, the Russian government has exploited the short-term effects of the crisis for its long-term advantage. During the economic boom Russian businessmen had speculated by borrowing large sums in dollars. When the financial crisis hit, loans had to be repaid and the Russian businessmen lacked the ready cash to do so. When they turned to the state for financial assistance, the state took advantage of them by demanding assets in return (Goldman, 2008: ch. 7). The substantial recapture of control of energy assets by the regime has important implications for the balance of power between the state and billionaires; however, it does not affect the economic circumstances of ordinary Russians.

Vulnerability at the bottom

Although NRB surveys have consistently found that how people evaluate the national economy is of primary importance for regime support, this generalization is qualified by the statement "all other

conditions remaining equal." By definition the abruptness and inten-
sity of the financial crisis meant that all other conditions have not
remained the same. A macro-economic crisis directly or indirectly
affects everyone in society, but it does not affect everyone in the same
way. The extent to which individuals are vulnerable depends in part
upon their economic difficulties before the crisis. In addition, the crisis
gave a new twist to vulnerability; for example, pensioners have a more
secure income than people in work, for the latter are vulnerable to
becoming unemployed. It also created fresh issues such as whether the
national government or foreign governments are to blame for Russia's
economic difficulties.

Crisis creates new anxieties

The June 2009 New Russia Barometer survey interviewed people
when official statistics showed that the country's GDP had contracted
by almost 10 percent in the previous twelve months. We thus added
new questions to take account of the economic crisis. The low percentage of don't know replies to these questions showed that the great
majority was aware that the national economy faced difficulties.
However, people differed in how they evaluated these difficulties and
related them to their own lives.

Having experienced the shocks of transforming a nonmarket into a
market economy, Russians were aware of greater economic extremes
than Westerners who had been led to expect an era of continuing
prosperity. Seven-eighths of Russians had anxieties about a big rise
in prices and more than two-thirds had concerns about mass
unemployment (Figure 8.1). When asked if a repeat of the 1998 ruble
crisis was likely, almost three-fifths thought it was possible. However,
only 15 percent thought there would definitely be a repeat of the ruble
crash a decade earlier.

Since the economic crisis was international in origins, the Kremlin
followed the practice of many West European leaders: It blamed
foreigners for its problems. This could encourage a "rally round the
Kremlin" effect by asking people to accept discomforts as a necessary
cost of resisting foreign pressures. This strategy was also in harmony
with fears of foreigners cultivated by Vladimir Putin's nationalist
appeals. A "sovereign" economy is, after all, a logical corollary of a
sovereign democracy. When offered a list of groups that could be

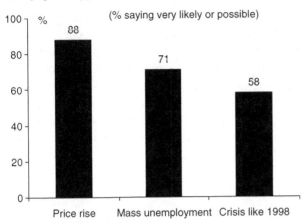

Q. How likely do you think any of the following are this year: (a) mass unemployment? (b) An economic crisis like 1998? (c) a big rise in prices?

(% saying very likely or possible)

Source: Centre for the Study of Public Policy, New Russia Barometer XVIII (June 2009).

Figure 8.1 Popular economic anxieties, 2009

blamed for Russia's economic difficulties, 53 percent of those with an opinion blamed foreign governments. However, even more, 69 percent, blamed the government of Russia. No other group was blamed by a majority. Two in five blamed businessmen and 30 percent blamed Prime Minister Putin. The group least likely to be blamed were the traditional scapegoats, Jews; they were said to be at fault by 15 percent of Russians.

In ordinary times many features of the economy are taken for granted, for example, having a job. However, when there is a major reversal in the economy, then what is normal may become a source of vulnerability (Rose, 2009c: ch. 6). For example, in a crisis economy more people are at risk of being unemployed, but in order for this to be the case a person must be in the labor force. In Russia participation in the labor force has historically been high because Soviet policy was to mobilize both men and women to do the heavy work of building socialism. The 2009 NRB survey found that two-thirds of Russians age 18 or above were in the labor force and one-third were not. Of those in the labor force, 51 percent were fulltime or occasionally part-time workers, 10 percent were working students or pensioners, and 6 percent unemployed. Nine percent of those employed at the time of interview said they had been unemployed at some point in the previous twelve months.

Jobs in the private sector typically offer higher salaries than jobs in the public sector, while also carrying a greater risk of becoming unemployed. Transformation meant that many workers in industry became private sector employees, holding better-paying but less secure jobs. By the time the financial crisis hit Russia, 37 percent were working in public institutions such as schools and hospitals or in state-owned enterprises; 44 percent were in one or another type of private sector firm; and the remainder were employed in organizations with mixed forms of ownership. Workers in the private sector were now more vulnerable to the risks of the economic crisis, because their employers could not rely on the state's tax revenues and central bank to pay their wages.

A major symptom of crisis is that people in work are not paid by their employer when they should be paid. Just before the 1998 ruble crisis, 76 percent of those in work reported that they had not been paid regularly or not at all during the past year. Once the economy began to boom, paying wages became normal; by 2007 only one-sixth were having trouble being paid regularly. However, the financial crisis meant that employers had trouble getting bank credits needed to pay wages: The fraction of Russian workers receiving wages late or not at all rose to one in three.

In boom times pensioners can be at a disadvantage because their income does not rise as fast as the earnings of people in work. Even if pensions are indexed to take inflation into account, the adjustment tends to lag behind the rising cost of living. However, in an economic recession pensioners are less vulnerable than those in work. Pensioners are not only without a job to lose but also they can rely on the taxing power of the state to guarantee them a monthly income. This is a much more reliable source of income than employment. The 2009 NRB survey found 30 percent of Russian adults were drawing a pension; of these, one-quarter were also in work.

Household size not only affects expenses, such as the amount of groceries that must be bought each week, but also income. Households with two or more incomes benefit when purchasing for their common use household goods such as a color television set. They are also better protected against recession. If one member of a household loses a job while another remains in work or draws a pension, then unemployment reduces household income less than if there is only one income in the household. The high rate of employment of women as well as men makes a two-income household the norm in Russia as in many Western countries. The long-term shortage of housing increases the incidence of multiple-income households in which young adults in work live with their working parents or a widow drawing a pension lives with a working offspring.

In a conventional market economy people are accustomed to putting purchases on a credit card, buying a car with monthly payments, or buying a home on a mortgage and borrowing from a bank in order to finance a high level of consumption. A legacy of the Soviet era is that banking and credit facilities are not so widespread, and Russians rely on informal social capital networks to meet unexpected financial difficulties. The 2009 NRB survey found 57 percent of Russians felt that, if they needed to do so, they could probably borrow as much as a month's wage or pension. Such loans are usually made on the understanding that repayment will be made only when the borrower is no longer in difficulty; this reduces financial pressures. Hardly any Russians need worry about making mortgage repayments because, to replace the Soviet practice of state or enterprise ownership of housing, the new regime transferred ownership of accommodations to their residents. The 2009 NRB survey found that, of the 84 percent of Russians who are now homeowners, only 1 percent were buying their home on a mortgage.

Depression more subjective than objective

In the distinctive circumstances of Russia, consumption indicators provide a suitable measure of how much or how little the international macro-economic crisis has reached down to cause problems in individual households. The threat of destitution ought to be expected to rise, while consumer durables should remain steady or households might even lose goods that they had bought on credit.

Frequently doing without food, clothing, and heat and electricity are indications of destitution. The NRB's Destitution Index ranges from a high of 3 for frequently doing without all these necessities to 0 for never doing without any in the past year. Just before the 1998 ruble crisis, the mean score on the Destitution Index was 1.2, showing that the average Russian occasionally did without one of three necessities. The uneven distribution of benefits from the economic boom left the Destitution Index at 1.2 in 2007. However, the great majority of households appear insulated from the macro-economic crisis. In the 2009 NRB survey, the mean Destitution Index actually fell to 0.9 and only 9 percent of respondents were often doing without all three household necessities.

Owning familiar household goods such as a color television set, a car or a DVD or VCR reflects a family's ability to accumulate sufficient savings to make purchases equivalent to several months' or a year's wages. Together, these goods form a three-point Consumer Goods Index. In 1998 Russian households had an average of 1.5 of these goods; by 2007 the average was 2.0 consumer durables. Notwithstanding the macro-economic reversal, the possession of consumer durables has continued to rise. By 2009 the average was 2.1. Only 2 percent of households lack all consumer durables while three in eight have a car as well as a color TV and a DVD or VCR. In short, when the global crisis hit, most Russians had already accumulated enough consumer durables so that their homes were not bare if they had to pause before spending on buying another consumer durable.

Subjective evaluations of a household's living standards do not match objective indicators. In the midst of economic turmoil in 1998, when the benefits of transformation had yet to become widespread, 27 percent of Russians said that they were satisfied with their household's economic situation. By 2007, when the nation's GDP had almost doubled, there was an increase of only 3 percentage points in those satisfied with their household's economic situation. Media reports of bad news about the world economy did not alter attitudes. In the 2009 NRB survey, the percentage satisfied with their household's current economic situation was the same as in the pre-crisis survey two years earlier.

From the trough of the economic crisis to the peak of the economic boom, there has been a big rise in popular endorsement of the current economic system (Figure 6.2). In the spring of 2008 endorsement of the current economic system peaked; 81 percent were positive. The abrupt reversal of the world economy that followed was accompanied by a fall in popular evaluations of economic performance. But just as the downturn did not destroy most of the country's GDP, so the effect on public opinion was to modify rather than reverse popular attitudes toward the economic system. Even though popular approval of the current economic system dropped, in June 2009 three-fifths of Russians still viewed it positively. Future expectations have been affected less. Instead of seeing the crisis as the start of a prolonged deterioration in the Russian economy, four in five remain positive about what they expect the economic system to be like in five years.

Altogether, the NRB evidence shows that the shocks of the macro-economy have not greatly affected the material conditions of Russian households: Those who lived in households that were better off before the crisis remain better off and the minority at risk of destitution has not increased. However, media attention to the economic crisis has made Russians feel that the national economy is not doing so well and, given the evidence of previous chapters, this implies a substantial reduction in support for the regime.

The economy reverses, support remains high

An unexpected event such as the 2008 financial shock adds a crisis hypothesis to the list of determinants of political support. A crisis can affect support in at least three different ways. Novel conditions specific to the crisis can be important; a crisis can increase or decrease the mean value of a significant influence; or an influence that was previously unimportant can become significant or vice versa. While changes have had a disturbing effect on the Russian macro-economy, they have not caused a major alteration in the condition of Russian households.

Political support predictably affected by crisis

Given that political support has declined from its pre-crisis high, the analytic challenge is to identify how much the decline is predictably due to the effects of indicators identified in previous chapters and how much is due to new anxieties stimulated by the crisis itself.[1]

The way in which people evaluate the current and future economy continues to have big effects on regime support (Table 8.2). For each 1 point change in the evaluation of the economy, political support is likely to go up or down by just under half a point. The impact of the

---

[1] A preliminary regression analysis tested the potential effect on support of all the indicators described previously. We have therefore excluded those influences that had no significant effect on support except for a few of theoretical relevance.

Table 8.2 *Economic crisis and regime support*

	Adjusted R^2 42.2%		
	b	s.e.	Beta
Economy			
Pro current economy	.45***	.02	.50
Pro economic future	.09***	.03	.09
Crisis			
Crisis factor	−2.44	.86	−.06
Blame foreign governments	−.21	.67	−.01
Politics			
Freedom greater	4.84***	1.08	.09
Fairness of officials	3.52	1.16	.07
Regime incongruence	−1.05	.49	−.07
Democracy as ideal	.66	.62	.03
Corruption	−1.94	1.10	−.04
Socialization			
Social status	2.09***	.46	.10

*** Significant at .001; N = 1,601.
Source: Centre for the Study of Public Policy, New Russia Barometer XVIII
(June 2009).

future economy on support is one-sixth that.[2] The one feature of a household that has a significant influence on regime support is not economic but social: The higher a person's social status, the more likely they are to favor the regime.

Anxieties about the return of a crisis like that of 1998, inflation and mass unemployment tend to be correlated; hence, they are combined in a single measure of crisis anxieties. The more inclined Russians are to see the country facing a major macro-economic crisis, the less likely they are to support the current regime. However, the effect is much less than that forecast by doom-mongers who draw inferences based on the assumption that a short-term change in some macro-economic indicators will leverage a massive

[2] An OLS regression with spring 2007 NRB data finds much the same. The Beta for the effect of current economic evaluations is 0.44, compared to 0.48 in 2009, while for the future economy it is 0.17 compared to 0.05 in 2009.

fall in support for the regime or create a demand for a new regime. Efforts of political leaders to mobilize support by blaming foreign governments for the country's economic problems are completely lacking in significance.

The economic crisis has not annulled the influence of political performance; three measures continue to influence political support (Table 8.2). Almost two decades after the disappearance of the Soviet regime, Russians who see themselves as enjoying greater political freedom today than under the old system remain more likely to be positive toward the new regime. On the other hand, the greater the incongruence between the political system that people would like to have and where they place the current regime on the democracy/dictatorship scale, the less its support. People who see public officials acting fairly in dealings with people like themselves are also more likely to be positive about the new regime.

Crisis evaluations of the economy

Even though the economic situation of an individual has no direct effect on regime support, it is possible that micro-economic influences can exert an indirect effect on political support. This will be the case if individual conditions have a big impact on how people evaluate the national economy, which in turn has a big impact on support for the regime.

Two features of an individual's micro-economic situation significantly influence evaluations of the economic system (Table 8.3). The judgment that people make about their household's current economic situation is strongly associated with their evaluation of the national economy. Among the minority threatened to a substantial extent with destitution, there is a more negative attitude toward the national economy system. However, the complement is not true: People with more consumer goods are not significantly more likely to be positive about the national economy.[3]

The financial crisis, as expected, has had a significant influence on how people evaluate the current economic system. Among the

---

[3] A preliminary regression tested whether an individual's income quintile, being a pensioner, working in the public sector or being unemployed influenced how people evaluated the current economy. Consistent with earlier findings, none of these influences was significant so they are not detailed in Table 8.3.

Table 8.3 *Influences on economic evaluations*

	Adjusted R^2 11.6%		
	b	s.e.	Beta
Economy			
Household economic situation	6.95***	1.11	.16
Extent of destitution	−3.27	1.29	−.07
More consumer goods	−3.70	4.20	−.02
Pro old economy	−.10***	.03	−.09
Crisis			
Crisis factor	−6.37***	1.02	−.14
Problem getting paid	−8.12	2.61	−.07
Blame foreign governments	−.61	.92	−.02
Socialization			
Born after 1975	7.39	2.42	.07
Born before 1946	−4.79	3.09	−.04
Social status	.97	.61	.04

***Significant at .001; **significant at .01; N = 1,601.
Source: Centre for the Study of Public Policy, New Russia Barometer XVIII (June 2009).

ten independent variables in the regression equation, the anxieties combined in the crisis factor are second in their effect (Beta −0.14). The increase in the late payment of wages has made the crisis more salient to popular attitudes. Whereas in the 2007 NRB it had no significant influence on endorsement of the current economic system, the crisis has resulted in people who have problems getting paid being significantly more negative about the current economic system. Although Russians are generous in blaming governments for the economic crisis, again this has no significant effect on their evaluation of the national economic system.

Even though young people are especially vulnerable to an economic crisis because they are least likely to have a steady job, they are more positive about the current economic system. This may reflect being more adaptable in times of crisis, including lowering their expectations about what work they can find. Insofar as there are generational differences, they are indirect, being registered by those most positive about the old command economic system being more negative about the new economic system. Socioeconomic status has no significant influence on evaluations.

The economic crisis lowered but did not disrupt support for the political regime because its negative effects were offset by long-term countervailing influences. The HLM analysis in Table 6.3 identifies political inertia as cumulatively the most important and steadiest influence on regime support. An arithmetic calculation of its impact on regime support between the March 2008 and June 2009 NRB surveys suggests that while the lower evaluation of the economy reduced political support by about 9 points, the countervailing effect of the passage of time gave it a boost of about 7 points in the opposite direction.

By the time the financial crisis occurred, what was once a new regime had become a familiar set of political institutions. The radical changes induced by transformation had such a pervasive effect on everyday life that the great majority of Russians have been forced to adapt; this has included giving positive or passive support to the regime. Although the rise in prices and unemployment resulting from the world financial crisis created anxieties, it lowered but did not reverse popular evaluations of the political regime.

9 | Maintaining a regime – democratic or otherwise

The intent of an authoritarian regime is not to prepare the way for democratic rule but to maintain its power. While the actions of Communist reformers had the unintended consequence of destroying their regime, there are many examples of long-lived authoritarian regimes. Thus, it is important to understand to what extent undemocratic regimes are durable.

A multiplicity of causes can put an end to a regime. A war gives victors the opportunity to replace the defeated regime with one more consistent with the winner's interest. Thus, after World War II the three Western allies promoted the establishment of the democratic Federal Republic of Germany, while the Soviet Union promoted the establishment of a Soviet-style and grossly misnamed German Democratic Republic. National independence movements have succeeded in voiding undemocratic colonial regimes. However, many regimes in newly independent states have been undemocratic. Civil wars pit domestic supporters of competing regimes against each other; the victor may introduce a dictatorship, as in Franco's Spain, or disputes may be transferred to the ballot box, as in Northern Ireland. In an undemocratic regime a falling out within the political elite can lead to the repudiation of the regime. However, the successor regime need not be democratic. Middle Eastern countries have frequently had changes in regime, as one undemocratic regime replaces another (Posusney, 2004). Turkey and some Latin American states have shown that it is possible to oscillate between short-lived military rule and rule by elected politicians.

Undemocratic regimes that hold elections can secure substantial popular endorsement (Chapter 7). But sometimes the results of unfree and unfair elections turn out differently than rulers expect. For this to happen the regime's diverse opponents must agree and pursue a common strategy in seeking popular support. However, there are many obstacles to achieving opposition unity in the face of a regime following a "divide and rule" strategy (Bunce and Wolchik, 2010). Developments in Ukraine after the Orange Revolution's 2005 electoral victory illustrate how short-lived a successful democratic protest can be.

The Russian regime established at the end of 1991 has already lasted longer than many democratic and undemocratic regimes and it has achieved a high level of popular support from its subjects. The critical question to ask about such a regime is not whether Russia is a democracy, for this is hardly the case. Instead, we need to consider how Russia's rulers can maintain support for their regime and what predictable or unpredictable circumstances might undermine it. Since, as Chapter 1 showed, Russia is not the only undemocratic regime that has achieved a substantial amount of popular support, the concluding section asks: How much difference does popular support make for the political and economic performance of an undemocratic as against a democratic regime?

Maintaining an undemocratic regime

Vigilance is not only the price of liberty; it is also the price that authoritarian rulers must pay to maintain their regime. To maintain an undemocratic regime does not require repression; it can be done with political skills that are relevant in many types of political regimes. Niccolò Machiavelli's advice to troubled rulers of Renaissance Florence about how to maintain power remains relevant today (cf. Neustadt, 1960), for example, preventing insurrection by offering patronage to would-be opponents as well as friends and paying attention to feedback from subjects.

Containing would-be opponents

In an undemocratic regime, the chief challenge comes from within the political elite. Instead of the visible loss of popular support through electoral defeat or mass demonstrations, undemocratic governments are more vulnerable to a palace coup, a military takeover, or a power struggle following the death of a dictator. In an undemocratic regime, those who hold power must be consistently vigilant to prevent ambitious associates from combining to mount a putsch that ousts them from power (Bueno de Mesquita *et al.*, 2003).

In all kinds of regimes, governors find that "converts and opportunists flock to those in power" (Geddes, 2006: 156). By giving potential opponents office, the party in power offers recipients of patronage the choice of supporting the regime as it is or forfeiting the power, prestige and profit that go with doing so. In post-Communist regimes there was an additional reason to retain in office many who served the old regime. They were experienced in administering the everyday activities of government whereas those who were excluded by the old regime were not. Insofar as political support depends on the effectiveness of the regime in maintaining services, competent officials must be kept in place. Many officials of the old regime were only incidentally party members; they were more committed to tasks such as running hospitals or building roads while political dissidents were usually inexperienced in doing so.

The visible centralization of power in the Soviet regime made it easy to remove from office the few who symbolized it while leaving in place the many responsible for the everyday activities of government. Since a party card was necessary to hold almost every position of authority, being a party member was associated with a government job. By the time the Soviet regime fell, few party members were committed to the ideological doctrines of Marxism and Leninism (Rose, 2009c: ch. 13). Insofar as people were motivated to join the Communist Party because it offered a good job, prestige and power, these same motives could justify their serving a post-Communist regime. An additional reason for recruiting people who had served the previous regime was that they were numerous while dissidents were relatively few. In the Russian Federation every prime minister from the first, Yegor Gaidar, to the current incumbent, Vladimir Putin, had been a member of the Communist Party of the Soviet Union.

An undemocratic regime can license criticisms that it finds useful. The idea of inviting subjects to write "letters to the editor" was endorsed by Lenin as a way of using the media to improve the effectiveness of the regime. Although Stalin clamped down on published criticism (Inkeles and Geiger, 1952), Brezhnev allowed dissatisfied subjects to voice their complaints in letters to party newspapers (White, 1983). As long as the complainant blamed individual local officials rather than national leaders or the principles of the regime, such criticisms could be utilized to remove officials whose actions weakened support for the Soviet system. The Chinese Communist Party continues to license such forms of criticism (Marsh, 2005).

In order to hold elections that appear competitive, opposition parties must be tolerated or even created in order to show how limited their support is. In Russia today, no opposition party presents a challenge to the regime (Dimitrov, 2009; www.RussiaVotes.org). The Communist Party of the Russian Federation appeals to older and less well-off Russians who look back nostalgically to the past; even among those who vote Communist only one-fifth think the Communist system could return (Munro, 2006). Vladimir Zhirinovsky's party voices a populist appeal to a limited audience. The fourth Duma party, Fair Russia, was formed by a merger of four small parties and endorsed Dmitry Medvedev's presidential candidacy in 2008. Divided opponents prevent the emergence of an undemocratic but potentially popular "red–brown" opposition party. It is an old Russian tradition for the regime to engage in *chernyi piar* (dirty tricks) in order to keep the opposition divided. By splitting the vote that does not go to United Russia, the opposition parties collectively perform the role of what Lenin described as "useful idiots."

When major political issues arise, differences of opinion can be found within government. Some reflect institutionalized competition between different ministries for money and influence. Others reflect differences within the ranks of United Russia about the priority to be given to economic and political reform. President Medvedev has spoken about the need to end "stagnation" (*zastoi*), a term with echoes of the Brezhnev era (Lloyd, 2010). He has called for a reform of the country's "backward" economy so that it does not have a "primitive reliance on oil and gas," and becomes instead an "innovation economy." Medvedev has also endorsed freedom as a better basis for achieving economic reform as against what he has called the Chinese model of authoritarian capitalism (Clover, 2010). By contrast, Putin has continued to stress the importance of stability and caution: "We don't need any kind of leaps, we don't need leaps to the left or the right, because we used this strategy before and it didn't work" (Buckley, 2010).

As the March 2012 presidential election approaches, speculation increases about whether Putin will run for the presidency. He has repeatedly insisted that this will be decided in accordance with the constitution. As he is not the incumbent president, he is now eligible to run for two successive six-year terms as president. Putin has also stressed that the decision about who will be United Russia's candidate for the presidency will be decided in accordance with the "real situation." The reality is that the party can nominate only one presidential candidate and Putin has constructed United Russia so that it is *his* party. At the previous presidential election, the little-known Medvedev did not run for the party's nomination; instead, Putin nominated him as United Russia's candidate. As prime minister, Putin has continued to control United Russia and Medvedev has not sought to wrest control of the party apparatus from him.

Russian law does allow candidates to form a new party or a candidate to run for the presidency as an independent. However, the requirements are onerous and subject to scrutiny by the Central Electoral Commission and the courts. The geographical expanse of Russia and large population require substantial money to create a nationwide organization that can challenge a party of power. An undemocratic regime can deny media publicity to a demonstration at a single factory, university campus or town square, thus inhibiting emulation elsewhere, a necessary condition of a nationwide demonstration. While there are enough Russian billionaires with the money and opinions to criticize the regime, the Putin administration has shown billionaires that if they bankroll opposition groups, their wealth rather than the regime is at risk.

Gaining support from skeptics and the compliant

A new regime is likely to start with a modicum of support, especially if the old regime was unpopular. The need is greater if the old regime was popular. As time passes, citizens who supported the old regime do not have to change their positive evaluation of what the old regime was like. The key issue is whether they will support the new regime too. Insofar as this happens, instead of society being polarized between supporters of different regimes, the dominant mode of public opinion will be compliance with whatever regime demonstrates the stamina to persist (Rose and Mishler, 1994).

Insofar as the intrusive activities of the Communist regime raised political consciousness, this produced two strong but contrasting reactions to its successor. Those whose values and interests made them positive supporters of the old regime are initially likely to be *reactionaries* opposing the new regime. In a complementary manner, individuals negative about the old regime may be *pro-change*. Subjects whose experience has bred distrust of political authority will be ready to reject the old regime but hesitate to support its replacement without any experience of what it is like. Individuals who are doubtful about supporting their new regime and negative about the old are *skeptics*. Their complement are those who went along with the old regime and are ready to support the new powers that be, whether democratic or undemocratic. This group is *compliant*.

The challenge to the leaders of the new regime is to consolidate rather than dissipate its support. If reactionaries are the largest group, the primary goal is to increase the proportion of compliant subjects positive about the new as well as the old regime. Since skeptics lack commitment to the old regime and do not hold a negative attitude toward the new, they are open to becoming supporters of the new regime or at least prefer it as the lesser evil.

When asked to evaluate old and new regimes in the first month of the new regime, Russians divided into two almost equal groups. A total of 44 percent were reactionaries, positive about the former regime and negative about the new, and two-fifths were skeptics, withholding support from both. Only 7 percent were so against the old regime that they supported the new regime sight unseen. A similarly small group was so compliant toward the powers that be that they showed support for both the old and new regimes (Figure 9.1).

The trajectories of support for old and new Russian regimes are very different. Support for the old regime has consistently been high. In every NRB survey an absolute majority has been positive about the regime as it was before *perestroika*. Amidst the turbulence of transformation in the 1990s, endorsement of the old regime rose from 50 percent in 1992 to as high as 73 percent in 2000. Since then it has fluctuated around two-thirds positive. Over two decades Russians have learned from experience what the new regime is like and they have become increasingly positive about it too (Figure 4.5).

With the passage of time, compliant subjects have become an absolute majority. Russians supporting both the old and new regimes have increased as half those who initially favored only the Communist regime are now prepared to support the new regime too. Similarly, upwards of half of skeptics have come around to supporting the new regime's performance. The proportion of Russians who exclusively support the new regime is less than one in four. The new regime has not made people change their views of the past; instead, it has encouraged those nostalgic about the past to accept the present regime. This is consistent with Vladimir Putin's inclusive rhetoric, which not only

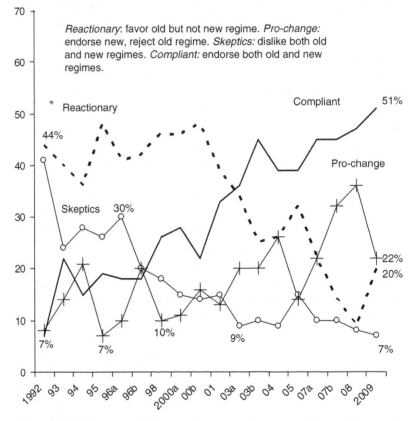

Source: Centre for the Study of Public Policy, New Russia Barometer data base, 1992–2009.

Figure 9.1 Compliance now prime response to regime change

takes credit for present achievements but also pays tribute to Russia's past, for example, describing the collapse of the Soviet Union "as the greatest geopolitical catastrophe of the century" (Putin, 2005; see also Linan, 2009).

Insulation from external influences

Political evaluations reflect what is happening elsewhere in the world as well as what happens within society. The Soviet regime was suspicious of capitalist countries, which it saw as ideological enemies.

Building socialism in one country was a doctrine that justified creating the military-industrial resources needed to defend Russia against attack from whatever direction. Repulsing the 1941 German invasion and winning the Great Patriotic War reinforced both national pride and concern about foreign threats. Marxist-Leninist ideology warned against Western ideas threatening the regime by stimulating "false consciousness" among Soviet subjects. Although Mikhail Gorbachev's endorsement of *glasnost* lowered Soviet barriers to contact with the world outside the Soviet orbit, it did not remove them.

The absence of obstacles to foreign contacts is not sufficient to create commitment to values common in Western societies. Among the Russian elite, many attributed the cost of introducing the market in the 1990s to demands imposed by the International Monetary Fund and Western advice rather than to the legacy of the command economy (but see Winiecki, 1988; Kornai, 1992). In the words of one Duma deputy, "We have twice tried to take Western theories and apply them in Russia: Marxism and liberalism. We must now rely on our own thinking and values" (quoted in Thornhill, 2009). The Putin administration has explicitly rejected Western advice and models. Vladislav Surkov, a member of Putin's staff, accused "centres of global influence" of promoting "managed democracy" by force and deception. In Surkov's words, the Kremlin's alternative of "sovereign democracy" is premised on the fact that "We don't want to be ruled from outside" (quoted in Buckley, 2006).

The collapse of the Communist bloc and the break-up of the Soviet Union have effectively pushed Russia's Western borders a thousand miles east. Now they are with Belarus and Ukraine rather than West Germany. The dissolution of the Warsaw Pact army and the abandonment of Communism have resulted in Russia's regime having less of the "hard power" that Moscow once commanded. It also destroyed the "soft" ideological power (Nye, 2004) it had used to attract followings in other countries. Yet Russia remains a big country in terms of population as well as territory. The domestic resources of a population of 140 million encourage cultural and scientific self-sufficiency and Russian is the leading language for communication with an additional 100 million people in successor states of the Soviet Union. Like the United States, it is big enough to be insular on a continental scale.

Consistently, New Russia Barometer surveys find that the life space that Russians construct tends to be inward-looking (Figure 9.2). When

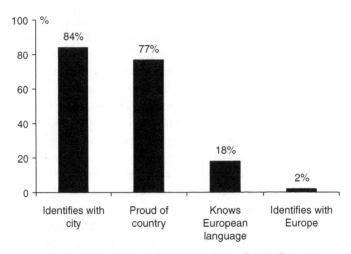

Source: Centre for the Study of Public Policy, New Russia Barometer
XVIII (June 2009).

Figure 9.2 The life space of Russians

asked what place they most closely identify with, 84 percent name
their city as their first or second choice, as against 69 percent mentioning Russia. Nor has the Soviet experience undermined Russians'
national pride, as happened in Germany and Italy after regimes fell
(Almond and Verba, 1963). When asked about pride in being a citizen
of this country, a phrase avoiding ethnic connotations, there is no
significant difference in the expression of pride between Russian and
non-Russian nationalities. Most subjects are satisfied with the extent
to which Russia is open to other countries. In 2009 only 12 percent
favored more openness, 44 percent are content with things as they are,
and 35 percent would prefer Russia to be less open to other countries.

First-hand knowledge of Western societies is very limited. Whereas
84 percent know the name of the governor of their region, only 39
percent know that Brussels is the headquarters of the European
Union and 2 percent select Europe as even a secondary identity (see
Figure 9.2). There are more Russians living in Central Asian states
than in the Baltic states that were once part of the USSR and are now
European Union members. The majority of Russians have family links
with what were once Soviet republics and are now post-Soviet states.
Barely one in eight Russians says that they have any friends or relatives
in the West. This is consistent with seven-eighths of the population

living outside Moscow or St. Petersburg, the two cities where meetings with foreigners are most likely. Even if a Russian happened to meet a Westerner, the chance of having a conversation is limited, since only 18 percent say they know a European language well enough to read a newspaper, including 13 percent claiming a knowledge of English.

Fear as well as pride can bind people to their nation. Geography exposes Russia to more than a dozen neighbors by land and sea, extending from Japan and China through Afghanistan and Iran to the Baltic states and Turkey. In 2009 three-fifths of NRB respondents saw the United States as the biggest threat to Russia's peace and security, compared to 29 percent naming neighboring countries and 14 percent anxious about a threat from Germany. This view is often endorsed by Russia's governors. However, dealing with threats from abroad is not the first concern of Russians: 62 percent think having a high standard of living should be the country's first priority as against 38 percent giving priority to being a great power respected by other countries.

History and geography offer Russia a choice between engagement with the post-Soviet countries of the Commonwealth of Independent States (CIS) and the West (see Lynch, 2005). Because many Russians distinguish between "good" Western Europe and the "not so good" United States (Kolossov, 2003), NRB surveys ask whether people see the country's future being linked more with Western Europe or with the CIS. A total of 71 percent put ties with CIS countries first as against 29 percent giving priority to Western Europe.[1] Moreover, CIS ties are much firmer. Among those with strong opinions, those regarding the country's future as definitely with the CIS outnumber by more than six to one those seeing it definitely with Western Europe (Rose and Munro, 2008).

The development of the Internet is simultaneously strengthening communication within the vast territory of the Russian Federation and encouraging an electronic ghetto. As of June 2009, 33 percent accessed the Internet at least occasionally. While the percentage of Internet users is higher in Western Europe, the absolute number of Russian Internet users is as great as in Germany and much larger than the combined total population of Nordic countries. The Russian-language Internet provides a great variety of Cyrillic websites ranging

---

[1] When Russians are asked about ties with Soviet successor states, friendly attitudes are expressed toward each of the eleven CIS countries and negative attitudes about Estonia, Latvia and Lithuania (White, 2006: 143).

from rock music and sports results to national and world news. In small countries with a distinctive language, such as Finland, the content and variety of websites is limited, encouraging people to look abroad, and language skills are acquired in order to do so. In Russia, by contrast, access to the Internet is not an invitation to cruise the world but to remain within the familiar confines of a vast cyberspace mall in which all the signs are in Cyrillic (Rose, 2005).

Challenges

Sooner or later every regime, whether democratic or undemocratic, faces challenges. Predictable challenges may arise from the political calendar, for example, a constitutional limitation to the term of a president or the need for United Russia to nominate its candidate for the presidential election due in March 2012. Some long-term challenges are already immanent in society, such as the fall in the birth rate. Other developments are unpredictable, for example, the timing, direction and magnitude of changes in world oil prices.

The durability of post-Soviet regimes

The first priority of governors is to maintain the integrity of their state against the challenges of internal disruption and incursions from neighboring lands. The break-up of the Soviet Union at the end of 1991 produced fifteen states with boundaries that were a legacy of the Soviet division of territories. They were not ethnic states, for each had a significant minority differing from the nationality in the title of the new state. In Kazakhstan no nationality was as much as half the population and in another five successor states the titular nationality was less than three-quarters of the resident population. Juan Linz and Alfred Stepan (1996: 424ff.) predicted that the alternative for Estonia and Latvia was to become multinational democracies or be vulnerable to having their regime destabilized by ethnic Russians.

Within the Russian Federation, the chief challenge to its territorial integrity has been from guerrilla forces fighting to establish an independent Republic of Chechnya. There have been two prolonged wars there, which sometimes spill over to neighboring territories or involve terrorist acts by Chechens in Moscow. While the conflict within Chechnya has been brutal, its duration has been less than the four decades of violence in

Northern Ireland and many decades of violence in the Basque territory of Spain. Transborder armed conflicts have created a Russian-controlled Trans-Dniestria region of Moldova; the separation of two regions of Georgia on its border with Russia; and an Armenian-dominated region of Nagorno-Karabakh within Azerbaijan. None of these de facto modifications in national boundaries has been as bloody as the break-up of Yugoslavia or as dramatic as the reunification of Germany. Nor have they been recognized in international law.

In Belarus and Ukraine trends in political support are similar to those in Russia. Initially, CSPP Barometer surveys found that each regime was supported by only a minority but with the passage of time support has become positive. In Belarus, where the regime evolved from being partly free to unfree by the mid-1990s, support rose from 35 percent in 1992 to 75 percent in 2004. In Ukraine, where free elections are regularly held, support has risen from 25 percent in 2002 to 70 percent in 2005 (Rose, 2006: 23).

Leaders of undemocratic CIS regimes have a common interest in countering dissent and Moscow is a near-at-hand example of a successful authoritarian regime. Vladimir Putin has actively sought to exert influence in what is called the "near abroad." This is often welcomed, since Russia is by the criteria of both hard and soft power the leading country in the CIS. It thus offers an alternative to claims that democracy is the only way to achieve order and economic development (Ambrosio, 2009).

The persistence for two decades of post-Soviet regimes that Freedom House labels unfree shows their capacity to maintain at least passive support. Azerbaijan and Turkmenistan have successfully passed the test of political succession following the death of a long-serving dictator. In unfree and unfair elections in Azerbaijan in 2003 the son of the retiring leader, who was then in poor health, was elected president with 76 percent of the vote. In Turkmenistan succession to the deceased president for life was endorsed by 89 percent of the officially reported vote. In Kazakhstan, Tajikistan and Uzbekistan, dictatorships have maintained themselves with little popular show of dissent. In the more open regimes of Armenia, Georgia, Kyrgyzstan and Moldova, which Freedom House labels as partly free, control of the presidency has changed hands. However, the methods used have involved massive street demonstrations, inept attempts to mobilize support by the party in power, and elections of contested validity (see Lane and White, 2009). After reviewing a variety of so-called

color revolutions in the region, Stephen White (2009: 397) concludes
that the irregular replacement of political leaders is not evidence of a
change in kind of their undemocratic regimes.

Challenges, predictable and otherwise

Fluctuations in the price of oil are abrupt, reversible and usually
unanticipated. Because of oil's importance to the Russian economy, this
makes forecasting the future of the national economy abnormally uncertain. Just before the 2008 world financial crisis hit, the price of oil rose as
high as $147 a barrel. However, the crisis then pushed the price as low as
$39 a barrel (Figure 9.3). By spring 2010 oil prices were more than
double the level a year earlier, but down by two-fifths from their

Source: Financial Times Online, http://markets.ft.com/tearsheets/performance.asp
?s=1054972&ss=WSODIssue (accessed 3 December 2010). Price shown is for
ICE Brent Crude on the day of each month showing maximum change from the
previous month.

Figure 9.3 Oil price volatility, 2007–2010

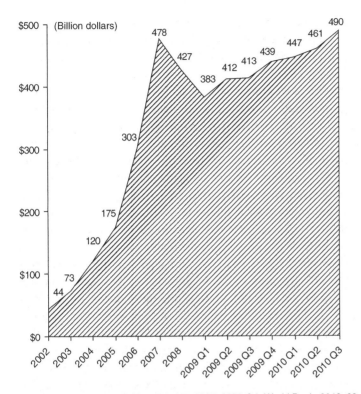

Source: 2002–2006: EBRD, 2008,175; 2007–2009 Q4: World Bank, 2010, 23.
Reserves as of the end of the period covered.

Figure 9.4 Resilience of Russia's currency reserve, 2002–2010

peak two years earlier. The Kremlin has succeeded in controlling much of the revenue generated by the export of energy resources, but it cannot control the price of oil that is set in the world market.

In reaction against the dependence on foreign borrowing of the Gorbachev and Yeltsin administrations, Putin has sought to achieve financial independence. The boom in oil prices during his presidency gave him an opportunity. Between the end of 2002 and 2007, Russia's international reserves increased more than tenfold, as $434 billion was added (Figure 9.4). Thus, when the crisis of the following year produced a heavy drain on this reserve, it still had $383 billion at its "low" point at the end of the first quarter of 2009. The net outflow of reserves then halted and started to recover, until by autumn 2010 reserves were above the pre-crisis peak. Because the volatility of international currency and oil markets remains uncertain, to protect Russia against again becoming dependent on foreign lenders the state holds sufficient foreign exchange to fund five times the claims on its reserves as big as those of the 2008 crisis. However, a big drop in oil prices would cause a big increase in the government's domestic budget deficit, because it is using foreign oil revenues to fund heavy spending on social programs rather than relying on a notoriously opaque tax system.

For more than half a century bad health and a short life expectancy for men have been features of Russian society (Boutenko and Razlogov, 1997). Problems evident under Leonid Brezhnev have continued under all his successors. Repeated campaigns against binge drinking are, like campaigns against corruption, an indication that both are persisting problems (White, 1996). Among young men who ought to be especially healthy, death rates from avoidable causes such as binge drinking or industrial accidents are much higher than in Western societies. The low priority given public health has resulted in the unmonitored spread of HIV-AIDS and a rise in the incidence of tuberculosis (Cromley, 2010). The change of regimes has given some people opportunities to improve their health but these gains are not yet large enough to show up in aggregate health statistics (Rose and Bobak, 2010).

Since the last years of the Soviet Union the number of children borne by Russian women has been below that required to replace generations dying out. In the years following the 1998 ruble crisis the fertility rate fell as low as 1.17; it has risen since but only as far as an average of 1.41 children in 2007 (UNICEF, 2009). It thus remains well below the level required to keep the population stable. The combination of poor health and low birth rates will cause the number of Russians to contract by an estimated 10 million people in the next two decades. To some extent, Russia's relatively favorable economic conditions have been attracting immigrants from other CIS countries. Nonetheless, the median forecast is for a net decrease in the population until 2030 or beyond (World Bank, 2010a: tab. 3.3).

A less healthy and smaller population presents challenges to public policy. The debilitation of people of working age reduces the productivity of a labor force that was already low in Soviet times. This puts a brake on economic growth. Since military conscription is an obligation for young Russian males, a reduction in the number of young people in good health means a smaller and less fit army of conscripts and reserves. Persisting population differences ensure that Russia's military force will remain numerically far larger than that of its neighbors in the CIS, as the 2008 war with Georgia demonstrated. However, it is no longer as substantial as it once was vis-à-vis the behemoths of the United States and China.

While no foreseeable change can alter the predominance of Russians in the Federation, the demographic increase in the Muslim minority has potential political salience. The number of nominal Muslims today varies with definitions, for example, whether religion is inferred from official statistics or from survey data, which estimate about 6 percent of the population is nominally Muslim. Nominal Muslims are divided by ethnicity, language and geography (Dannreuther and March, 2010; Hunter *et al.*, 2004; Rose, 2002). Ethnicity has been the basis of political claims of many nominal Muslims. The largest group of nominal Muslims are Tatars, who, as a legacy from Soviet times, have an autonomous region. A novel feature of suicide bomb attacks in the Moscow underground in March 2010 was that credit was claimed by a small group who described themselves as Islamists waging *jihad* rather than calling themselves Chechen nationalists.

Political support helps undemocratic and democratic regimes

Support promotes durability

While maintaining their regime is the first priority of governors, durability is difficult to achieve. To do so requires more than brute force; it also requires popular support (see Figure 1.1). In short:

- H 1 The higher the level of political support in the population, the greater the durability of the regime.

Theories of democracy postulate that how support is mobilized is important for durability, because the total amount of support that a regime claims may be inflated by a show of support from some who are resigned to accept the powers that be as the lesser evil.

- H 2 The more democratic a regime, the greater its durability.

Political economy theories take a different view, postulating that the most important influence on durability is the level of material benefits that the regime can confer in "buying" support.

- H 3 The higher a country's standard of living, the greater the durability of the regime.

Measuring the durability of regimes is challenging. The longevity of many regimes has been limited by the fact that they govern relatively new states. When the United Nations was founded in 1945 it had only fifty-one members. Membership reached the hundred mark in the 1960s as many former European colonies achieved independence. The UN now has 192 member states. Many states have experienced changes in their regime in the past quarter-century. This is the case not only in Central and Eastern Europe and in what was once the Soviet Union but also in Africa and Asia. Moreover, some older states have undergone regime changes too. In the past century, France has had four different regimes and what is now the Federal Republic of Germany has had five.

While it is a matter of historical fact how long a regime has been in existence, its future duration is open. Since the passage of time has a big cumulative effect on support, there are good theoretical grounds for assuming that a regime that has been in existence for decades is more likely to be durable. Hence, we use the number of years the current regime has been in existence as our indicator of durability. If a system of government has survived for more than a century, this is evidence not only of the capacity of governors to maintain what they have but also of their ability to adapt as the political environment alters. In the extreme case of England, Parliament owes its persistence since the thirteenth century to repeated changes in the regime of which it is a part.

To test the above hypotheses across continents and with as varied a set of regimes as possible, we combine data from multinational Afro Barometer, East Asia Barometer, New Europe Barometer and World Values surveys (for details, see www.afrobarometer.org; www.abdn. ac.uk/cspp; www.asianbarometer.org). Each survey asks a question about support for the current system of government and does so in a neutral way, that is, without labeling the system as democratic or undemocratic. Since surveys differ in how they score replies, results have been standardized to a ten-point scale like that of the World Values Survey, in which 10 shows complete support for the regime and 1 complete disapproval (cf. Figure 1.3). Altogether, ninety-eight countries are covered. The countries surveyed had regimes ranging from a few years old to more than a century old. Freedom House characterized sixty as free, twenty-five as partly free and thirteen regimes as unfree. This range avoids the bias inherent in generalizing about the effects of support from data drawn exclusively from democracies. The countries covered vary in their economic conditions too.

The three hypotheses set out above are not mutually exclusive; for example, there are theoretical grounds to expect that political support will be higher in countries that are prosperous as well as democratic. Combining measures of all three influences in a multiple regression equation can take this into account.

The basic premise of this book is endorsed by the regression: Political support increases the durability of undemocratic as well as democratic regimes (Table 9.1). After controlling for the effect of both Freedom House ratings and economic conditions, regimes in countries where popular support is higher are significantly more likely to be durable. Consistent with many theories, regimes in countries where gross domestic product per capita is higher are also more likely to be durable. However, after controlling for the effects of support and economic conditions, whether a regime is free or unfree has *no* significant effect on its durability. Since support varies among undemocratic regimes (see Figure 1.3), we ran an additional regression with only those countries rated as unfree or partly free. The results confirm that authoritarian regimes that have succeeded in mobilizing more support are significantly more durable than those that lack support.

The longevity of a regime implies that it is not subject to the threat of a coup overthrowing it. Hence, we also test the extent to which political support reduces the vulnerability of a regime to a coup. After

Table 9.1 *Testing the effect of regime support*

	Adjusted R^2 36.0%		
	b	s.e.	Beta
Political support	4.80*	2.20	.18
Gross domestic product	17.72***	2.89	.61
Freedom House	.00	1.89	.00

***significant at .001; *significant at < .05.
Sources: Political support data for a total of ninety-eight countries from AfroBarometer, East Asia Barometer, New Europe Barometer, World Values Survey. Gross national income per capita purchasing power parity adjusted logged: World Bank Development Indicators; Freedom House: rating for year of survey inverted so highest score, 7, is most democratic.

Table 9.2 *Political support and preventing coups*

	Adjusted R^2 17.1%		
	b	s.e.	Beta
Political support	−.08*	.35	−.21
Gross domestic product	−.17***	.05	−.41
Freedom House	.00	.03	.00

*** Significant at .001; * significant at < .05.
Sources: Data on successful and unsuccessful political coups in the five years following the date of the survey.

controlling for other influences, political support significantly reduces the likelihood of a regime being subject to a coup, whether successful or not (Table 9.2). A country's gross domestic product is also significant. Equally important, its Freedom House rating is *not* significantly linked to the incidence of coups. In other words, an undemocratic regime with a high level of popular support tends to be as secure from the threat of a coup as a democratic regime with a high level of popular support. The above conclusions are confirmed by an analysis confined to the incidence of coups in undemocratic regimes.[2]

The leaders of regimes want not only to maintain their power but also to increase their wealth by promoting economic growth. A high rate of economic growth is important in developing countries, where the absolute standard of living is lower than in highly developed economies. In established democracies where average income is high, so too are demands to increase public expenditure and private earnings. Political economy research has found that a favorable political climate has a positive effect on investment that promotes growth. However, this leaves open whether democratic institutions or popular support contribute more to this climate.

The importance of political support for economic growth is endorsed by regression analysis: The higher the level of political support, the higher the annual rate of economic growth (Table 9.3). Moreover, the effect of political support is not due to its being found in

[2] An OLS regression of the forty-seven unfree and partly free regimes accounts for 19.7 percent of the variance in coups. The extent of political support is significant at the 0.05 level (b, −0.15, standard error 0.06, Beta −0.40).

Table 9.3 *Political support and economic growth*

	Adjusted R^2 11.7%		
	b	s.e.	Beta
Political support	.97*	.69	.19
Gross domestic product	−2.82**	1.30	−.25
Freedom House	−1.19	.85	−.16

** Significant at .01; * Significant at < .05.
Sources: As in Table 9.1. Economic growth is measured as the average annual growth rate of the economy in the five years after a political support survey is conducted.

high-income democracies, because the association between a country's gross national product and its rate of economic growth is negative. The fastest rate of growth is likely to occur where a high level of political support is combined with a relatively low level of gross domestic product. Furthermore, this holds whether the regime is democratic or undemocratic. After controlling for political support, a country's Freedom House score again shows no significant influence on the rate of acceleration of economic growth.

Evidence that undemocratic regimes can be long-lived appears to be good news for authoritarian rulers. Thus, the People's Republic of China is not unique in achieving rapid economic growth and being an older regime than more than two-thirds of the states in the United Nations and a majority of member-states of the European Union. But the above statistical analysis also contains a caution. Even though the probability of an undemocratic regime becoming durable is as high as that of democratic regimes in the world today, this does not constitute a certainty. Both democratic and undemocratic regimes are equally vulnerable to the possibility of losing support and disappearing.

The likelihood of a regime becoming durable depends on how political support is achieved as well as how much support it has. In the popular model of democratization, support is taken for granted because governors do what the people want (Figure 1.1). However, this is only half the story, since many new regimes are not trying to democratize. Their first priority is to secure compliance with their demands. However the capacity of a regime to do so is not a full explanation of how a new regime obtains a show of support. It cannot be created by fiat. If a new regime follows a strategy of "soft" authoritarianism, that is, giving subjects greater freedom and being fairer than its predecessor, its performance offers political benefits that were formerly denied. If it limits abuses of the rule of law to marginalizing rather than jailing its opponents, such abuses will not alienate subjects who distrust politicians and parties as a class. If a regime succeeds in promoting economic growth, its economic performance will encourage support too. Altogether, if a new regime can survive the challenges of the first few years, with the passage of time an undemocratic regime can accumulate sufficient popular support to become the only game in town.

Appendix A: New Russia Barometer samples

NRB surveys are conducted by the most senior and established not-for-profit survey research institution in Russia, the Levada Center, initially known as VCIOM, the Russian Center for Public Opinion Research. Its leading personnel are social scientists well versed in both the theory and practice of survey research (see www.levada.ru for details). Continuity in organization and personnel is especially beneficial for the long-term trend analysis reported in this book.

All New Russia Barometer surveys are conducted with multistage stratified samples. The starting point is the division of the population geographically across the whole of the Russian Federation except for war zones and difficult-to-reach extremities, areas with a small percentage of the national population. The data used for stratifying the population come from the censuses and official statistics collected by Goskomstat (www.gks.ru). Initially, the country is stratified into seven to ten large economic and geographical regions, and each is assigned a number of interviews proportionate to its share of the national population. All cities with more than 1 million population are selected, and within each region their center, towns and villages are selected with a probability proportionate to their population. Then, cities are stratified by ward and rural areas by villages in order to select Primary Sampling Units. An average of ten interviews is conducted in a sampling unit, thus ensuring a wide dispersion of interviews within big cities such as Moscow.

Within each Primary Sampling Unit an interviewer is assigned a random address for seeking a respondent and households are approached on a random route basis. Within each selected house, the interviewer normally interviews the person whose birthday comes next; selection may be controlled as well for an age-by-sex-by-education grid. Face-to-face contact in the home is especially important in Russia, since a substantial fraction of the population did not have a home telephone when NRB surveys started and mobile phones create further difficulties for sampling and interviewing.

Levada Center field supervisors verify up to one-fifth of the inter-views by return visits to households, by post or by telephone. Quality checks of the questionnaire are undertaken in the Center's office. The profile of respondents according to age, education and gender is compared with census estimates for the population and, as appropri-ate, weights are calculated to match the census figures.

Fuller details of each sample can be found at www.abdn.ac.uk/cspp/NRBsamples.shtml, and questions and answers are contained in the Studies in Public Policy (SPP) series of the Centre for the Study of Public Policy. The relevant SPP number is given below along with distinctive details of each sample.

New Russia Barometer I: 26 January–25 February 1992 (SPP 205)

The survey was conducted by VCIOM in consultation with Dr. Irina Boeva and Dr. Viacheslav Shironin, economists in the former USSR Academy of Sciences, and supported by a grant from the Centre for Research into Communist Economies, London. The universe con-sisted of Russians in the urban population, 73.3 percent of the total population of Russia in the 1987 census. The effective sample con-sisted of 2,547 persons; a total of 2,106 interviews were completed. The survey was confined to urban areas because of difficulties in the winter of transformation in carrying out fieldwork in rural areas. Comparison of urban and rural respondents in NRB II showed that in the great majority of political questions there was no significant difference between the two groups of respondents, with a few obvious exceptions, such as growing food.

New Russia Barometer II: 26 June–22 July 1993 (SPP 216)

The survey was financed by a grant from the British Foreign Office Know How Fund to study popular response to privatization. The universe of the sample was the population of the whole of the Russian Federation age 16 and above, rural as well as urban. Respondents under the age of 18 were excluded from the analysis. There were a total of 1,975 interviews and a response rate of 83 percent. VCIOM used a multiple regression analysis to derive appropriate weights for gender, age, education and town size.

New Russia Barometer III: 15 March–9 April 1994 (SPP 228)

This survey was a collaboration between the CSPP and the Paul Lazarsfeld Society, Vienna. Fieldwork was undertaken by MNENIE Opinion Service, Moscow, under the direction of Dr. Grigory A. Pashkov. Financial support came from a group of Austrian banks and a grant to the CSPP from the British Foreign Office Know How Fund. The questionnaire was piloted with 100 interviews in Rostov on Don and Petrozavodsk, 26–28 February 1994. The universe for the sample was the population of the Russian Federation age 18 and above. The target number of responses was 3,500; in the event, 3,535 interviews were completed.

New Russia Barometer IV: 31 March–19 April 1995 (SPP 250)

This survey was financed by a grant from the British Foreign Office Know How Fund and, like all subsequent surveys, was conducted by VCIOM and its successor, the Levada Center. A total of 2,770 contacts were made, and 1,998 were interviewed face to face, a response rate of 72.1 percent.

New Russia Barometer V: 12–31 January 1996 (SPP 260)

This post-Duma election survey, organized by VCIOM, was financed by the Centre for the Study of Public Policy. A total of 4,508 contacts were made and 2,426 persons were interviewed, a response rate of 53.8 percent. The data were weighted to match the regional census population in gender, age, education, town size and, because of proximity to the general election, party preference. VCIOM also collected data on the voting preference of its interviewers; they were widely dispersed across the political spectrum. Yabloko was the only party favored by more than a tenth of interviewers; the Communist Party was second and Our Home Is Russia third in interviewer preferences.

New Russia Barometer VI: 25 July–2 August 1996 (SPP 272)

This post-presidential election survey was organized by VCIOM and again financed by the Centre for the Study of Public Policy. The timing of the presidential election shortly before the start of the summer holidays posed a dilemma. To maximize the number of people at home when an interviewer called would have meant postponing fieldwork until September. But given the uncertainties of the president's health and the political situation in Chechnya, as well as completely unforeseeable events, delay would have risked spoiling the study by introducing post-election events into an election survey, as well as decreasing the accuracy of reported voting. That risk was minimized by starting interviewing in late July, even though this invited a lower response rate during the holiday season. Therefore, all interviews were concluded before the presidential inauguration made very visible the state of the president's health and before quarrels about Chechnya had become another running story. In all, 3,379 households were contacted with someone at home; in 965 cases no one at that point met the requirements of the interviewer's age-by-sex-by-education sampling grid. Of the 2,414 households where an interview was sought, there were 1,599 completed responses, 66.2 percent of the total. VCIOM weighted the data to match the regional census population in terms of gender, age, education, town size and, because of the election, voting.

New Russia Barometer VII: 6 March–13 April 1998 (SPP 303)

In addition to standard NRB trend questions, the seventh NRB survey included a lengthy special-purpose section of questions about social capital. It was financed by a grant from the Social Capital Initiative of the World Bank, supported by the Development Fund of the Government of Denmark. Altogether, 5,903 contacts were made with households; 1,868 did not have a respondent matching grid requirements; and in 1,035 cases no one answered. In 3,000 households there was a respondent meeting the sampling specifications, and 2,002 interviews were satisfactorily completed, 66.7 percent of the total.

New Russia Barometer VIII: 13–29 January 2000 (SPP 328)

This survey took place just after the 1999 Duma election and Christmas holidays. It was funded by the British Economic and Social Research Council and fieldwork was conducted by VCIOM. Altogether, 3,055 households were within the sample specifications and 1,940 interviews were completed with adults age 18 or above, 65.6 percent of the sample.

New Russia Barometer IX: 14–18 April 2000 (SPP 330)

The ninth New Russia Barometer survey was funded by the British Economic and Social Research Council. VCIOM undertook fieldwork between 14 and 18 April 2000, promptly after the presidential election, while events were fresh in the minds of Russians and post-election events could not yet influence attitudes. In 2,019 households there was a person meeting the specifications of the sample grid and 1,600 interviews were completed, 79.2 percent of the total.

New Russia Barometer X: 17 June–3 July 2001 (SPP 350)

The tenth NRB survey was funded by the British Economic and Social Research Council with fieldwork by VCIOM. In 3,254 households a resident met sample specifications, and 2,000 interviews were completed, 61.5 percent of effective contacts.

New Russia Barometer XI: 12–26 June 2003 (SPP 378)

The eleventh NRB survey was funded by the Centre for the Study of Public Policy with fieldwork by VCIOM. The survey provides public opinion data from near the end of President Putin's first term of office. In 2,095 households a resident met the sample specifications, and there were 1,601 valid respondents, 76.4 percent of that total.

New Russia Barometer XII: 12–22 December 2003 (SPP 384)

The twelfth NRB survey was conducted as part of the VCIOM–Analytica survey immediately after the Duma election. It was funded by the British Economic and Social Research Council. There were 2,022 contacts within the sampling frame and 1,601 interviews, 79.2 percent of the total.

New Russia Barometer XIII: 18–23 March 2004 (SPP 388)

This survey started a week after the re-election of President Vladimir Putin. It was conducted by the Levada Center, Moscow, staffed by former members of VCIOM, and funded by a grant from the British Economic and Social Research Council. Contacts were made with

2,130 individuals with characteristics fitting the sample design; there were 1,602 completed interviews, 75.2 percent of the effective contacts.

New Russia Barometer XIV: 3–23 January 2005 (SPP 402)

The fourteenth NRB survey was timed to occur after the aura of President Putin's election victory had evaporated. It was funded by a grant from the British Economic and Social Research Council and the Epidemiology Department of University College London Medical School. Of the 3,278 persons eligible for interviewing, there were 2,107 respondents, 64.3 percent of the total.

New Russia Barometer XV: 13–23 April 2007 (SPP 426)

The fifteenth NRB survey was conducted at the climax of President Putin's terms in office. It was funded by a grant from the British Economic and Social Research Council. Of the 2,517 persons eligible for interviewing, there were 1,606 respondents, 63.8 percent of the total.

New Russia Barometer XVI: 7–17 December 2007 (SPP 442)

The sixteenth NRB survey was conducted immediately after the 2007 Duma election. It was funded by a grant from the British Economic and Social Research Council. Of the 2,030 persons eligible for interviewing, there were 1,601 respondents, 78.9 percent of the total.

New Russia Barometer XVII: 14–23 March 2008 (SPP 443)

The seventeenth NRB survey was conducted immediately after the 2008 presidential election. It was funded by a grant from the British Economic and Social Research Council. Of the 1,951 persons eligible for interviewing, there were 1,603 respondents, 82.2 percent of the total.

New Russia Barometer XVIII: 18–24 June 2009 (SPP 462)

The eighteenth NRB survey was conducted after the 2008 global financial crisis had hit the Russian economy. It was funded by a grant from the British Economic and Social Research Council. Of the 2,029 persons eligible for interviewing, there were 1,601 respondents, 78.9 percent of the total.

Appendix B: Coding of variables

	Range of codes	Mean	Standard deviation
Social structure			
Female	1 Women; 0 Men	.55	.50
Age	Age in years	44.1	16.7
Born before 1946	1 Yes; 0 No	.29	.46
Born 1976–1987	1 Yes; 0 No	.13	.34
Education	5 Some university; 4 Technical college; 3 Secondary; 2 Vocational; 1 Incomplete secondary or less	2.35	1.02
Social status	7 Highest; 1 Lowest	4.41	1.99
Church attendance	4 Once a month or more; 3 A few times a year; 2 Once or twice a year; 1 Never	1.86	.96
Town size	4 Cities>1,000,000; 3 Cities 100,000–1,000,000; 2 Towns<100,000; 1 Village	2.36	1.00
Political values & performance			
Pro current regime	+100 Highest; −100 Lowest	−2.9	50.2
Democracy as ideal	10 Complete democracy; 1 Complete dictatorship	7.16	2.26
Regime incongruence (difference between *Democracy as ideal* and *Current level of democracy*)	10 Maximum difference; 0 No difference	2.72	1.92
Pro old regime	100 Highest; −100 Lowest	23.1	51.5
Freedom compared to before *perestroika*. Mean for speech, joining organizations, religion, involved in politics	5 Much better now; 4 Better; 3 Same; 2 Worse; 1 Much worse now	3.86	.77

	Range of codes	Mean	Standard deviation
Fairness of officials compared to before *perestroika*	5 Much fairer now; 4 Better; 3 Same; 2 Worse; 1 Much worse now	2.63	1.15
Trusts institutions. Mean for army, Duma, police, parties, courts	7 Highest trust; 1 Highest distrust	3.10	1.24
Rating of president	10 Maximum approval; 1 Maximum disapproval	5.56	2.41
Corruption	4 Almost all officials are corrupt; 3 Most are corrupt; 2 Corruption limited; 1 Almost no corruption	3.21	.80
Approves suspension of Duma	5 Strongly approve; 4 Somewhat approve; 3 Don't know; 2 Somewhat disapprove; 1 Strongly disapprove	2.70	1.31
Approves dictatorship as only way out of our current situation	5 Strongly agree; 4 Somewhat agree; 3 No opinion; 2 Somewhat disagree; 1 Strongly disagree	2.40	1.38
Economic performance & crisis			
Pro current economy	+100 Highest; −100 Lowest	−13.7	50.2
Pro old economy	+100 Highest; −100 Lowest	34.1	47.9
Household economic situation	5 Very good; 4 Rather good; 3 Don't know; 2 Rather bad; 1 Very bad	2.34	1.04
Income	Household income quintile	2.92	1.37
Destitution. Mean doing without food, electricity or necessary clothing	4 Often; 3 Sometimes; 2 Rarely; 1 Never	2.25	.90
Crisis index	Standardized factor analysis: 2008 crisis seen as bad as 1998; big rise in prices likely; fear of mass unemployment.	0	1

	Range of codes	Mean	Standard deviation
Blame crisis on foreign governments	5 Mainly; 4 Somewhat; 3 Don't know; 2 Little; 1 Not at all	2.75	1.32
Expectations and time			
Pro economic future in five years	+100 Highest; −100 Lowest	14.71	48.52
Household economy in 5 years compared to today	5 Much better future; 4 Somewhat better; 3 Same; 2 Somewhat worse; 1 Much worse in future	3.11	2.08
Expect Duma suspension	5 Very likely; 4 Maybe; 3 Don't know; 2 Not very likely; 1 Not at all likely	2.08	.80
Election fairness			
Election unfair	5 Not at all fair; 4 Not very fair; 3 Don't know; 2 To some extent fair; 1 Definitely fair	2.52	1.10
Voted for opposition in 2007 Duma election	1 Voted for opposition party/ other candidate; 0 Voted for United Russia/Putin, didn't vote, spoiled ballot	.22	.42
Voted for opposition 2008 presidential election	1 Voted for opposition/losing candidate; 0 Voted for Medvedev, didn't vote or spoiled ballot	.20	.40
Did not vote in 2007 Duma election	1 Didn't vote; 0 Voted	.35	.48
Did not vote in 2008 presidential election	1 Didn't vote; 0 Voted	.30	.46
Aggregate context			
Passage of months	Number of months since collapse of Soviet Union	111.5	67.84
Cumulative GDP growth	Annual change in real GDP, 1991=100	83.17	18.42
Freedom House rating	7 Most free; 1 Least	3.42	.86

References

Acemoglu, Daron and Robinson, James A., 2006. *Economic Origins of Dictatorship and Democracy.* New York: Cambridge University Press.

Almond, Gabriel A. and Coleman, James S., 1960. *The Politics of Developing Areas.* Princeton: Princeton University Press.

Almond, Gabriel A. and Verba, Sidney, 1963. *The Civic Culture.* Princeton: Princeton University Press.

Ambrosio, Thomas, 2009. *Authoritarian Backlash: Russian Resistance to Democratization in the Former Soviet Union.* Farnham, UK: Ashgate.

Anderson, Christopher J., Blais, A., Bowler, S., Donovan, T. and Listhaug, O., 2005. *Losers' Consent: Elections and Democratic Legitimacy.* Oxford: Oxford University Press.

Arendt, Hannah, 1951. *The Origins of Totalitarianism.* New York: Schocken Books.

Aron, Leon, 2000. *Boris Yeltsin: A Revolutionary Life.* London: HarperCollins.

Bacon, Edwin, 2004. "Russia's Law on Political Parties: Democracy by Decree?" In Cameron Ross, ed., *Russian Politics Under Putin.* Manchester: Manchester University Press, 39–52.

Bahry, Donna, 1987. "Politics, Generations and Change in the USSR." In Millar, 1987, 61–99.

Berlin, Isaiah, 1958. *Two Concepts of Liberty: An Inaugural Lecture.* Oxford: Clarendon Press.

Blasi, Joseph R., Kroumova, Maya and Kruse, Douglas, 1997. *Kremlin Capitalism: Privatizing the Russian Economy.* Ithaca: Cornell University Press.

Boneo, Horacio, 2000. "Observation of Elections." In R. Rose, ed., *International Encyclopedia of Elections.* Washington, DC: CQ Press, 179–189.

Bonnell, Victoria E. and Breslauer, George W., eds., 2001. *Russia in the New Century: Stability or Disorder?* Boulder: Lynne Rienner.

Boutenko, Irene A. and Razlogov, Kirill E., 1997. *Recent Social Trends in Russia 1960–1995.* Montreal: McGill-Queen's University Press.

Breslauer, George W., 1978. "On the Adaptability of Soviet Welfare-State Authoritarianism." In Karl W. Ryavec, ed., *Soviet Society and the Communist Party.* Amherst: University of Massachusetts Press, 3–25.

2002. *Gorbachev and Yeltsin as Leaders*. New York: Cambridge University Press.

Brown, Archie, 1996. *The Gorbachev Factor*. Oxford: Oxford University Press.

2001. "From Democratization to Guided Democracy," *Journal of Democracy*, 12, 4, 35–41.

2009. *The Rise and Fall of Communism*. London: Bodley Head.

Brownlee, Jason, 2007. *Authoritarianism in an Age of Democratization*. Cambridge: Cambridge University Press.

Buckley, Neil, 2006. "Putin Aide Defends System of Democracy in Russia," *Financial Times*, 29 June.

2010. "Russia's Leaders Split on Reform Pace," *Financial Times*, 10 September.

Bueno de Mesquita, Bruce, Smith, A., Siverson, R. M. and Morrow, J. D., 2003. *The Logic of Political Survival*. Cambridge, MA: MIT Press.

Bunce, Valerie J. and Wolchik, Sharon L., 2010. "Defeating Dictators: Electoral Change and Stability in Competitive Authoritarian Regimes," *World Politics*, 62, 1, 43–86.

Burger, Ethan A., 2009. "Following Only Some of the Money in Russia," *Demokratizatsiya*, 17, 1, 41–72.

Butler, D. E. and Stokes, Donald E., 1974. *Political Change in Britain*. London: Macmillan, 2nd edn.

Canache, D., Mondak, J. and Seligson, Mitchell, 2001. "Meaning and Measurement in Cross-National Research on Satisfaction with Democracy," *Public Opinion Quarterly*, 65, 506–528.

Capoccia, Giovanni and Keleman, R. Daniel, 2007. "The Study of Critical Junctures," *World Politics*, 59, 3, 341–369.

Carey, J. M. and Shugart, M., 1995. "Incentives to Cultivate a Personal Vote," *Electoral Studies*, 14, 4, 417–439.

Carey, Sabine C., 2010. "The Use of Repression as a Response to Domestic Dissent," *Political Studies*, 59, 1, 167–186.

Carnaghan, Ellen, 2007. *Out of Order: Russian Political Values in an Imperfect World*. State College: Pennsylvania State University Press.

Carothers, Thomas, 2004. *Critical Mission: Essays on Democracy Promotion*. Washington, DC: Carnegie Endowment for International Peace.

Churchill, Winston, 1947. "Debate," *House of Commons Hansard* London: HMSO, 11 November col. 206.

CIS (Commonwealth of Independent States) Executive Committee, 2008. *Zayavlenie Missii nabliudatelei ot SNG po rezultatam nabliudeniya za podgotovkoi i provedeniem vyborov Presidenta Rossiiskoi federatsii ot 2 marta 2008*. Minsk: Commonwealth of Independent States.

Clover, Charles, 2010. "Medvedev Makes Case for Reforms," *Financial Times*, 11 September.

Collier, David and Levitsky, Steven, 1997. "Democracy with Adjectives: Conceptual Innovation in Comparative Research," *World Politics*, 49, 3, 430–451.

Colton, Timothy J., 2000. *Transitional Citizens: Voters and What Influences Them in the New Russia*. Cambridge, MA: Harvard University Press.

2005. "Putin and the Attenuation of Russian Democracy." In A. Pravda, ed., *Leading Russia*. Oxford: Oxford University Press, 103–118.

Colton, Timothy J. and Hale, Henry E., 2009. "The Putin Vote: Presidential Electorates in a Hybrid Regime," *Slavic Review*, 68, 3, 473–504.

Colton, Timothy J. and McFaul, Michael, 2000. "Reinventing Russia's Party of Power: Unity and the 1999 Duma Election," *Post-Soviet Affairs*, 16, 3, 201–224.

Conquest, Robert, 1990. *The Great Terror: A Re-assessment*. London: Pimlico.

Cook, Linda J., 1993. *The Soviet Social Contract and Why It Failed*. Cambridge, MA: Harvard University Press.

2006. *Postcommunist Welfare States: Reform Politics in Russia and Eastern Europe*. Ithaca: Cornell University Press.

Council of Europe, 2007. "Russian Duma elections 'not held on a level playing field', say parliamentary observers." Press release, wcd.coe.int/ViewDoc.jsp?id=1221469&Site= (accessed 20 December 2010).

Cromley, Ellen K., 2010. "Pandemic Disease in Russia: From Black Death to AIDS," *Eurasian Geography and Economics*, 51, 2, 184–202.

Dahl, Robert A., 1971. *Polyarchy: Participation and Opposition*. New Haven: Yale University Press.

1989. *Democracy and Its Critics*. New Haven: Yale University Press.

Dalton, Russell, 2004. *Democratic Challenges, Democratic Choices: The Erosion of Political Support in Advanced Industrial Democracies*. Oxford: Oxford University Press.

2008. *Citizen Politics: Public Opinion and Parties in Advanced Industrial Democracies*. Washington, DC: CQ Press.

Dalton, Russell J., Shin, Doh C. and Jou, Willy, 2007. "How People Understand Democracy," *Journal of Democracy*, 18, 4, 142–156.

Dannreuther, Roland and March, Luke, eds., 2010. *Russia and Islam*. London: Routledge.

di Palma, Giuseppe, 1990. *To Craft Democracies: An Essay on Democratic Transitions*. Berkeley: University of California Press.

Diamond, Larry, 2008. "The Democratic Rollback," *Foreign Affairs*, 87, 2, 36–48.

Diamond, Larry and Plattner, Marc F., eds., 2008. *How People View Democracy*. Baltimore: Johns Hopkins University Press.

Dimitrov, Philip, 2009. "Does 'Populism' in Europe's New Democracies Really Matter?," *Demokratizatsiya*, 17, 4, 310–323.

Duch, Raymond and Stevenson, Randolph T., 2008. *The Economic Vote: How Political and Economic Institutions Condition Election Results*. New York: Cambridge University Press.

Duncan, Peter J. S., 2000. *Russian Messianism: Third Rome, Holy Revolution, Communism and After*. London: Routledge.

Durkheim, Emile, 1952. *Suicide: A Study in Sociology*. London: Routledge.

Easton, David, 1965. *A Systems Analysis of Political Life*. New York: John Wiley.

Easton, David and Dennis, Jack, 1969. *Children in the Political System: Origins of Political Legitimacy*. New York: McGraw-Hill.

EBRD, 2001. *Transition Report 2001: Energy in Transition*. London: European Bank for Reconstruction and Development.

2004. *Transition Report 2004: Infrastructure*. London: European Bank for Reconstruction and Development.

2010. *Revised Growth Forecast for Russia*. www.ebrd.com/country/ sector/econo/stats/growth.pdf (accessed 6 April 2010).

Eckstein, Harry, 1966. *Division and Cohesion in Democracy: A Study of Norway*. Princeton: Princeton University Press.

1988. "A Culturalist Theory of Political Change," *American Political Science Review*, 82, 3, 789–804.

Eckstein, Harry, Fleron, F. J. Jr., Hoffmann, E. P. and Reisinger, W. M., 1998. *Can Democracy Take Root in Post-Soviet Russia? Explorations in State–Society Relations*. Lanham, MD: Rowman and Littlefield.

Elklit, Jorgen and Reynolds, Andrew, 2005. "A Framework for the Systematic Study of Election Quality," *Democratization*, 12, 2, 147–162.

Emmons, Terence, 1983. *The Formation of Political Parties and the First National Elections in Russia*. Cambridge, MA: Harvard University Press.

Engerman, David C., 2009. *Know Your Enemy: The Rise and Fall of America's Soviet Experts*. New York: Oxford University Press.

Evans, Alfred B. Jr., 2008. "Russia's Public Chamber," *Demokratizatsiya*, 16, 4, 345–362.

Evans, Alfred B. Jr., Henry, L. A. and Sundstrom, L. M., eds., 2006. *Russian Civil Society: A Critical Assessment*. Armonk, NY: M. E. Sharpe.

Evans, Geoffrey, ed., 1999. *The End of Class Politics?* Oxford: Oxford University Press.

Figes, Orlando, 2007. *The Whisperers: Private Life in Stalin's Russia*. London: Allen Lane.

Finer, S. E., 1997. *The History of Government*. Oxford: Oxford University Press, 3 vols.

Fish, M. Steven, 1995. *Democracy from Scratch: Opposition and Regime in the New Russian Revolution*. Princeton: Princeton University Press.

2005. *Democracy Derailed in Russia: The Failure of Open Politics*. New York: Cambridge University Press.

Fleron, Frederic J. Jr. and Hoffmann, Erik P., eds., 1993. *Post-Communist Studies and Political Science: Methodology and Empirical Theory in Sovietology*. Boulder: Westview Press.

Flora, Peter and Alber, Jens, 1981. "Modernization, Democratization and the Development of Welfare States in Western Europe." In P. Flora and A. J. Heidenheimer, eds., *The Development of Welfare States in Europe and America*. New Brunswick, NJ: Transaction Publishers, 37–80.

Freeland, Chrystia, 2000. *Sale of the Century: The Inside Story of the Second Russian Revolution*. London: Little, Brown.

Friedrich, Carl J. and Brzezinski, Zbigniew K., 1965. *Totalitarian Dictatorship and Autocracy*. 2nd edn. Cambridge, MA: Harvard University Press.

Frisby, Tanya, 1998. "The Rise of Organized Crime in Russia," *Europe–Asia Studies*, 50, 1, 27–49.

Fukuyama, Francis, 1992. *The End of History and the Last Man*. New York: Free Press.

Furtak, Robert K., ed., 1990. *Elections in Socialist States*. New York: Harvester Wheatsheaf.

Gaddy, Clifford G. and Ickes, Barry W., 2001. "Stability and Disorder: An Evolutionary Analysis of Russia's Virtual Economy." In Bonnell and Breslauer, 2001, 103–123.

2009. "Russia's Declining Oil Production: Managing Price Risk and Rent Addiction," *Eurasian Geography and Economics*, 50, 1, 1–13.

Gaidar, Yegor, 1999. *Days of Defeat and Victory*. Seattle: University of Washington Press.

Galbreath, David J. and Rose, Richard, 2008. "Fair Treatment in a Divided Society: A Bottom Up Assessment of Bureaucratic Encounters in Latvia," *Governance*, 21, 1, 53–73.

Gamson, William A., 1968. *Power and Discontent*. Homewood, IL: Dorsey Press.

Geddes, Barbara, 1999. "What Do We Know About Democratization After Twenty Years?," *Annual Review of Political Science*, 2, 115–144.

2006. "Stages of Development in Authoritarian Regimes." In V. Tismaneau, M. Howard and R. Sil, eds., *World Order After Leninism*. Berkeley: University of California Press, 149–170.

Gel'man, Vladimir, 2008. "Party Politics in Russia: From Competition to Hierarchy," *Europe–Asia Studies*, 60, 1, 913–930.

Gel'man, Vladimir, Ryzhenkov, Sergei and Brie, Michael, 2003. *Making and Breaking Democratic Transitions: The Comparative Politics of Russia's Regions*. Lanham, MD: Rowman and Littlefield.

Gelman, Andrew and Hill, Jennifer, 2007. *Data Analysis Using Regression and Multilevel/Hierarchical Models*. New York: Cambridge University Press.

Gibson, James L., Duch, Raymond M. and Tedin, Kent L., 1992. "Democratic Values and the Transformation of the Soviet Union," *Journal of Politics*, 54, 2, 329–371.

Gilley, Bruce, 2010. "Democratic Triumph, Scholarly Pessimism," *Journal of Democracy*, 21, 1, 160–167.

Goldman, Marshall, 2008. *Oilopoly: Putin, Power and the Rise of the New Russia*. Oxford: Oneworld.

Goodwin-Gill, Guy S., 2006. *Free and Fair Elections: International Law and Practice*. Geneva: Inter-Parliamentary Union, 2nd edn.

Grossman, Gregory, 1977. "The 'Second Economy' of the USSR," *Problems of Communism*, 26, 5, 25–40.

Gurr, Ted R., 1970. *Why Men Rebel*. Princeton: Princeton University Press.

Hadenius, Axel and Teorell, Jan, 2007. "Pathways from Authoritarianism," *Journal of Democracy*, 18, 1, 143–157.

Haerpfer, C. W., Bernhagen, P., Inglehart, R. and Welzel, C., eds., 2009. *Democratization*. Oxford: Oxford University Press.

Hale, Henry E., 2007. *Why Not Parties in Russia?* New York: Cambridge University Press.

2008. *The Foundations of Ethnic Politics*. New York: Cambridge University Press.

Hall, Peter A. and Taylor, Rosemary, 1996. "Political Science and the Three New Institutionalisms," *Political Studies*, 44, 5, 936–957.

Harding, Luke, 2008. "Russia Election Not Free or Fair, Say Observers," *Guardian*, 3 March.

Hart, H. L. A., 1961. *The Concept of Law*. Oxford: Clarendon Press.

Havel, Václav, *et al.*, 1985. *The Power of the Powerless: Citizens Against the State in Central Eastern Europe*. London: Hutchinson.

Heller, Mikhail, 1988. *Cogs in the Soviet Wheel: The Formation of Soviet Man*. London: Collins Harvill.

Hellman, Joel S., 1998. "Winners Take All: The Politics of Partial Reform in Postcommunist Transitions," *World Politics*, 50, 203–234.

Hendley, Kathryn, 2007. "Putin and the Law." In Herspring, 2007, 99–124.

Herspring, D. R. ed., 2007. *Putin's Russia: Past Imperfect, Future Uncertain*. Lanham, MD: Rowman and Littlefield, 3rd edn.

Hollander, Paul, 1981. *Political Pilgrims*. New York: Oxford University Press.

Holmes, Stephen, 2006. "The State of the State in Putin's Russia." In T. J. Colton and S. Holmes, eds., *The State After Communism*. Lanham, MD: Rowman and Littlefield, 299–310.

Hough, Jerry F., 1977. *The Soviet Union and Social Science Theory*. Cambridge, MA: Harvard University Press.

Hunter, Shirleen T., Thomas, Jeffrey and Melikishvili, Alexander, 2004. *Islam in Russia: The Politics of Identity and Security*. Armonk, NY: M. E. Sharpe.

Huntington, Samuel P., 1968. *Political Order in Changing Societies*. New Haven: Yale University Press.

1991. *The Third Wave: Democratization in the Late Twentieth Century*. Norman: University of Oklahoma Press.

Hutcheson, Derek S., 2010. *Twenty Years of Post-Communist Elections: The Voters' Perspective*, Studies in Public Policy Number 471. Aberdeen: Centre for the Study of Public Policy.

Inkeles, Alex and Bauer, Raymond A., 1959. *The Soviet Citizen: Daily Life in a Totalitarian Society*. Cambridge, MA: Harvard University Press.

Inkeles, Alex and Geiger, K., 1952. "Critical Letters to Editors of the Soviet Press," *American Sociological Review*, 17, 694–703.

Jack, Andrew, 2004. "Critics See No Room for Dissent in New Duma," *Financial Times*, 5 February.

2005. *Putin's Russia*. Cambridge: Granta Books.

Jennings, M. Kent, 2007. "Political Socialization." In Russell J. Dalton and Hans-Dieter Klingemann, eds., *The Oxford Handbook of Political Behavior*. New York: Oxford University Press, 29–44.

Jowitt, Kenneth, 1992. *New World Disorder: The Leninist Extinction*. Berkeley: University of California Press.

Karl, Terry Lynn, 1999. "The Perils of the Petro-State," *Journal of International Affairs*, 53, 31–48.

Katsenelinboigen, A., 1977. "Coloured Markets in the Soviet Union," *Soviet Studies*, 29, 1, 62–85.

Katzenstein, Peter, ed., 2009. *Civilizations in World Politics: Plural and Pluralistic Perspectives*. London: Routledge.

Kay, Rebecca, 2006. *Men in Contemporary Russia*. Aldershot: Ashgate.

Keenan, Edward, 1986. "Muscovite Political Folkways," *Russian Review*, 45, 115–181.

Kinder, Donald and Kiewiet, D., 1981. "Sociotropic Politics," *British Journal of Political Science*, 11, 129–161.

Klebnikov, Paul, 2000. *Godfather of the Kremlin: Boris Berezovsky and the Looting of Russia*. New York: Harcourt Brace.

Koehler, John O., 1999. *The Stasi: The Untold Story of the East German Secret Police*. Boulder: Westview Press.

Kolossov, Vladimir, 2003. "High and Low Geopolitics: Images of Foreign Countries in the Eyes of Russian Citizens," *Geopolitics*, 8, 1, 121–148.

Kornai, Janos, 1992. *The Socialist System: The Political Economy of Communism*. Princeton: Princeton University Press.

Kornberg, Allan and Clarke, Harold, 1992. *Citizens and Community: Political Support in a Representative Democracy*. Cambridge: Cambridge University Press.

Kryshtonovskaya, Olga, 2008. "The Russian Elite in Transition," *Journal of Communist Studies and Transition Politics*, 24, 4, 585–603.

Kryshtonovskaya, Olga and White, Stephen, 2003. "Putin's Militocracy," *Post-Soviet Affairs*, 19, 4, 289–306.

Kurkchiyan, Marina, 2003. "The Illegitimacy of Law in Post-Soviet Societies." In D. Galligan and M. Kurkchiyan, eds., *Law and Informal Practices: The Post-Communist Experience*. Oxford: Oxford University Press, 25–46.

Lane, David and White, Stephen, 2009. "Rethinking the Coloured Revolutions," *Journal of Communist Studies and Transition Politics*, 25, 2–3, 111–412.

Laverty, Nicklaus, 2008. "Limited Choices: Russian Opposition Parties and the 2007 Duma Election," *Demokratizatsiya*, 16, 4, 343–382.

Ledeneva, Alena V., 2006. *How Russia Really Works: The Informal Practices That Shaped Post-Soviet Politics and Business*. Ithaca: Cornell University Press.

Lenta.Ru, 2004. "Aziatchina kakaya-to! Narod khochet, chtoby Putin ostalsy na tretii srok" [Somehow Asiatic! The people want Putin to stay for a third term], http://lenta.ru/articles/2004/02/05/president7/ (accessed 9 October 2009).

Lentini, Peter, ed., 1995. *Elections and Political Order in Russia*. Budapest: Central European University Press.

Levada, Yuri, 1995. *Democratic Disorder and Russian Public Opinion: Trends in VCIOM Surveys 1991–1995*, Studies in Public Policy Number 255. Glasgow: Centre for the Study of Public Policy.

   2001. "Homo Praevaricatus: Russian Doublethink." In Archie Brown, ed., *Contemporary Russian Politics: A Reader*. Oxford: Oxford University Press, 312–322.

Levitsky, Steven and Way, Lucan, 2002. "The Rise of Competitive Authoritarianism," *Journal of Democracy*, 13, 2, 51–65.

   2010a. *Competitive Authoritarianism: Hybrid Regimes After the Cold War*. New York: Cambridge University Press.

2010b. "Why Democracy Needs a Level Playing Field," *Journal of Democracy*, 21, 1, 57–68.

Lieven, Anatol, 1998. *Chechnya: Tombstone of Russian Power*. New Haven: Yale University Press.

Linan, Miguel Vazquez, 2009. "Putin's Propaganda Legacy," *Post-Soviet Affairs*, 25, 2, 137–159.

Linz, Juan J., 1990a. "The Perils of Presidentialism," *Journal of Democracy*, 1, 1, 51–70.

1990b. "Transitions to Democracy," *Washington Quarterly*, Summer, 143–164.

2000. *Totalitarian and Authoritarian Regimes*. Boulder: Lynne Rienner Publishers.

Linz, Juan J. and Stepan, Alfred, 1996. *Problems of Democratic Transition and Consolidation*. Baltimore: Johns Hopkins University Press.

Lipman, Masha and McFaul, Michael, 2005. "Putin and the Media." In Dale Herspring, ed., *Putin's Russia: Past Imperfect, Future Uncertain*. Lanham, MD: Rowman and Littlefield, 2nd edn., 55–74.

Lipset, S. M., 1959. *Political Man*. New York: Doubleday.

Listhaug, Ole, Aardal, B. and Ellis, I. O., 2009. "Institutional Variation and Political Support." In H.-D. Klingemann, ed., *The Comparative Study of Electoral Systems*. Oxford: Oxford University Press, 311–332.

Lloyd, John, 2010. "Russian Critics Find Their Voice on Net to Blow Holes in System," *Financial Times*, 13 December.

Lopez-Claros, Augusto and Zadornov, Mikhail M., 2002. "Economic Reforms: Steady as She Goes," *Washington Quarterly*, 25, 1, 105–116.

Lukin, Alexander, 2000. *The Political Culture of the Russian "Democrats."* Oxford: Oxford University Press.

Lynch, Allen C., 2005. *How Russia Is Not Ruled*. New York: Cambridge University Press.

McAllister, Ian and White, Stephen, 1995. "The Legacy of the *Nomenklatura*: Economic Privilege in Post-Communist Russia," *Coexistence*, 32, 3, 217–239.

McAuley, Mary, 1984. "Russian Political Culture: One Step Forward, Two Steps Back." In Archie Brown, ed., *Political Culture and Communist Studies*. London: Macmillan, 13–39.

McCauley, Martin, 1998. *Russia Since 1914*. London: Longman.

2001. *Bandits, Gangsters and the Mafia*. Harlow and London: Pearson Education.

McDaniel, Tim, 1996. *The Agony of the Russian Idea*. Princeton: Princeton University Press.

McFaul, Michael, 2001. *Russia's Unfinished Revolution*. Ithaca: Cornell University Press.

Magaloni, Beatriz, 2006. *Voting for Autocracy: Hegemonic Party Survival and Its Demise in Mexico*. New York: Cambridge University Press.

Mainwaring, Scott and Torcal, Mariano, 2006. "Party System Institutionalization and Party System Theory After the Third Wave of Democratization." In R. S. Katz and W. Crotty, eds., *Handbook of Political Parties*. London: Sage, 204–227.

March, Luke, 2009. "Managing Opposition in a Hybrid Regime: Just Russia and Parastatal Opposition," *Slavic Review*, 68, 3, 504–527.

Marer, Paul, Arvay, Janos, O'Connor, John, Schrenk, Martin and Swanson, Daniel, 1992. *Historically Planned Economies: A Guide to the Data*. Washington, DC: World Bank.

Marsden, Lee, 2005. *Lessons from Russia: Clinton and US Democracy Promotion*. Aldershot: Ashgate.

Marsh, Christopher, 2005. *Unparalleled Reforms: China's Rise, Russia's Fall and the Interdependence of Transition*. Lanham, MD: Lexington Books.

Marshall, T. H., 1950. *Citizenship and Social Class*. Cambridge: Cambridge University Press.

Meleshevich, Andrey A., 2007. *Party Systems in Post-Soviet Countries*. New York: Palgrave Macmillan.

Mickiewicz, Ellen, 2006. "The Election News Story on Russian Television: A World Apart from Voters," *Slavic Review*, 65, 1, 1–23.

Millar, James R., ed., 1987. *Politics, Work and Daily Life in the USSR: A Survey of Former Soviet Citizens*. New York: Cambridge University Press.

Mishler, William and Rose, Richard, 2001, "Political Support for Incomplete Democracies: Realist vs. Idealist Theories and Measures," *International Political Science Review*, 22, 4, 303–320.

2002. "Learning and Re-Learning Regime Support: The Dynamics of Post-Communist Regimes," *European Journal of Political Research*, 41, 1, 5–36.

2005. "What Are the Political Consequences of Trust? A Test of Cultural and Institutional Theories in Russia," *Comparative Political Studies*, 38, 1050–1078.

2007. "Generation, Age and Time: The Dynamics of Political Learning During Russia's Transformation," *American Journal of Political Science*, 51, 4, 822–834.

Mishler, William and Willerton, J., 2003. "The Dynamics of Presidential Popularity in Post-Communist Russia," *Journal of Politics*, 65, 1, 111–131.

Moraski, Bryan, 2007. "Electoral System Reform in Democracy's Grey Zone," *Government and Opposition*, 42, 4, 536–563.

Morlino, Leonardo and Montero, José Ramon, 1995. "Legitimacy and Democracy in Southern Europe." In R. Gunther, P. N. Diamandouros and H.-J. Puhle, eds., *The Politics of Democratic Consolidation: Southern Europe in Comparative Perspective.* Baltimore: Johns Hopkins University Press, 231–260.

Moser, Robert G. and Thames, Frank C. Jr., 2001. "Compromise Amidst Political Conflict." In Matthew Shugart and Martin Wattenberg, eds., *Mixed-Member Electoral Systems.* Oxford: Oxford University Press, 254–275.

Munro, Neil, 2006. "Russia's Persistent Communist Legacy: Nostalgia, Reaction, and Reactionary Expectations," *Post-Soviet Affairs*, 22, 4, 289–313.

Myagkov, Mikhail, Ordeshook, Peter C. and Shakin, Dimitri, 2009. *The Forensics of Election Fraud.* New York: Cambridge University Press.

Neustadt, Richard E., 1960. *Presidential Power.* New York: John Wiley.

Newton, Kenneth, 1999. "Social and Political Trust in Established Democracies." In Norris, 1999, 169–187.

Noelle-Neumann, Elisabeth, 1993. *The Spiral of Silence: Public Opinion – Our Social Skin.* Chicago: University of Chicago Press, 2nd edn.

1995. "Juan Linz's Doctoral Dissertation on West Germany: An Empirical Follow-up, Thirty Years Later." In H. E. Chehabi and Alfred Stepan, eds., *Politics, Society and Democracy.* Boulder: Westview Press, vol. II, 13–41.

Norris, Pippa, ed., 1999. *Critical Citizens: Global Support for Democratic Governance.* Oxford: Oxford University Press.

North, Douglass C., 2005. *Understanding the Process of Economic Change.* Princeton: Princeton University Press.

North, Douglass C., Wallis, J. J. and Weingast, B. R., 2009. *Violence and Social Orders.* New York: Cambridge University Press.

Nye, Joseph S., 2004. *Soft Power: The Means to Success in World Politics.* New York: Public Affairs Press.

Oates, Sara, 2006. *Television, Democracy and Elections in Russia.* London: Routledge Curzon.

O'Donnell, Guillermo, 1994. "Delegative Democracy," *Journal of Democracy*, 5, 1, 55–69.

OSCE (Organization for Security and Cooperation in Europe), 2000. *Final Report: Russian Federation Presidential Election 26 March 2000.* Warsaw: ODIHR Election Observation Mission Report.

2005. *The OSCE/ODIHR Election Observation Handbook.* Warsaw: OSCE, 5th edn.

Oversloot, Hans and Verheul, Ruben, 2000. "The Party of Power in Russian Politics," *Acta Politica*, 35, 2, 123–145.

2006. "Managing Democracy: Political Parties and the State in Russia," *Journal of Communist Studies and Transition Politics*, 22, 3, 383–405.

Parsons, Talcott, 1964. "Communism and the West: The Sociology of Conflict". In Amitai Etzioni and Eva Etzioni, eds., *Social Change*. New York: Basic Books, 390–399.

Pempel, T. J., ed., 1990. *Uncommon Democracies: The One-Party Dominant Regimes*. Ithaca: Cornell University Press.

Pharr, Susan J. and Putnam, Robert D., eds., 2000. *Disaffected Democracies: What's Troubling the Trilateral Countries?* Princeton: Princeton University Press.

Pierson, Paul, 2004. *Politics in Time: History, Institutions and Social Analysis*. Princeton: Princeton University Press.

Politkovskaya, Anna, 2007. *Putin's Russia: Life in a Failing Democracy*. New York: Owl Books.

Posusney, Marsha Pripstein, 2004. "Enduring Authoritarianism: Middle East Lessons for Comparative Theory," *Comparative Politics*, 36, 2, 127–138.

Pravda, Alex, 1978. "Elections in Communist Party States." In Guy Hermet, Alain Rouquié and Richard Rose, eds., *Elections Without Choice*. London: Macmillan, 169–195.

Przeworski, Adam, 1991. *Democracy and the Market*. New York: Cambridge University Press.

Przeworski, Adam, Alvarez, Michael, Cheibub, José Antonio and Limongi, Fernando, 1996. "What Makes Democracies Endure?," *Journal of Democracy*, 7, 1, 39–55.

   2000. *Democracy and Development: Political Institutions and Well-Being in the World, 1950–1990*. Cambridge: Cambridge University Press.

Putin, Vladimir, with N. Gevorkyan, N. Timakova and A. Kolesnikov, 2000. *First Person*. London: Hutchinson.

Putin, Vladimir, 2005. "Annual Address to the Federal Assembly: April 25," www.kremlin.ru/eng/text/speeches (accessed 27 April 2005).

Putnam, Robert D. with Robert Leonardi and Raffaella Y. Nanetti, 1993. *Making Democracy Work*. Princeton: Princeton University Press.

   2000. *Bowling Alone: The Collapse and Revival of American Community*. New York: Simon and Schuster.

Raudenbush, Stephen W. and Bryk, Anthony S., 2002. *Hierarchical Linear Models: Applications and Data Analysis Methods*. Thousand Oaks, CA: Sage Publications, 2nd edn.

Reddaway, Peter and Glinski, Dmitri, 2001. *The Tragedy of Russia's Reforms: Market Bolshevism Against Democracy*. Washington, DC: United States Institute of Peace Press.

Reitlinger, Gerald, 1960. *The House Built on Sand*. London: Weidenfeld and Nicolson.

Remington, Thomas F., 2005. "Putin, the Duma and Political Parties." In
    Dale Herspring, ed., *Putin's Russia: Past Imperfect, Future Uncertain.*
    Lanham, MD: Rowman and Littlefield, 2nd edn., 31–54.
Reuter, Ora John, 2010. "The Politics of Dominant Party Formation,"
    Europe–Asia Studies, 62, 2, 293–327.
Riggs, Fred W., 1988. "The Survival of Presidentialism in America: Para-
    Constitutional Practices," *International Political Science Review*, 9, 4,
    247–278.
Riker, William, 1980. "Implications from the Disequilibrium of Majority Rule for
    the Study of Institutions," *American Political Science Review*, 74, 432–446.
Robertson, Graeme B., 2009. "Managing Society: Protest, Civil Society and
    Regime in Putin's Russia," *Slavic Review*, 68, 3, 528–547.
Rogowski, Ronald, 1974. *Rational Legitimacy: A Theory of Political Sup-
    port.* Princeton: Princeton University Press.
Rosa, Ruth Amende, 1949. "The Soviet Theory of 'People's Democracy,'"
    World Politics, 1, 4, 489–510.
Rose, Richard, 1969. "Dynamic Tendencies in the Authority of Regimes,"
    World Politics, 21, 4, 602–628.
    1996a. "Evaluating Benefits: The Views of Russian Employees." In Doug-
    las Lippoldt, ed., *Social Benefits and the Russian Enterprise: A Time of
    Transition.* Paris: OECD, 39–60.
    1996b. *What Is Europe? A Dynamic Perspective.* New York and London:
    Longman.
    1998. "What Is the Demand for Price Stability in Post-Communist Coun-
    tries?," *Problems of Post-Communism*, 45, 2, 43–50.
    2000a. "Uses of Social Capital in Russia: Modern, Pre-Modern and Anti-
    Modern," *Post-Soviet Affairs*, 16, 1, 33–57.
    2000b. "A Supply-Side View of Russia's Elections," *East European Con-
    stitutional Review*, 9, 1–2, 53–59.
    2000c. "How Much Does Social Capital Add to Individual Health?
    A Survey Study of Russia," *Social Science and Medicine*, 51, 1421–1435.
    2002. "Economies in Transformation: A Multidimensional Approach to a
    Cross-Cultural Problem," *East European Constitutional Review*, 11,
    4–12, 1, 62–70.
    2005. "Internet Diffusion Not Divide: A Proximity Model of Internet
    Takeoff in Russia," Oxford Internet Institute Research Report No. 10.
    2006. *Diverging Paths of Post-Communist Countries: New Europe
    Barometer Trends Since 1991*, Studies in Public Policy Number 418.
    Aberdeen: Centre for the Study of Public Policy.
    2007. "Going Public with Private Opinions: Are Post-Communist Citi-
    zens Afraid to Say What They Think?," *Journal of Elections and Public
    Opinion*, 17, 2, 123–142.

2008. "Evaluating Democratic Governance," *Democratization*, 15, 2, 251–271.

2009a. "Democracy and Its Alternatives." In Haerpfer, *et al.*, 2009, 10–23.

2009b. *Russians in Economic Crisis: New Russia Barometer XVIII*, Studies in Public Policy Number 462. Aberdeen: Centre for the Study of Public Policy.

2009c. *Understanding Post-Communist Transformation: A Bottom Up Approach*. London and New York: Routledge.

Rose, Richard, Berglund, Sten and Munro, Neil, 2006. "Baltic Identities and Interests in a European Setting." In John McGarry and Michael Keating, eds., *European Integration and the Minorities Question*. London: Routledge, 308–328.

Rose, Richard and Bobak, Martin, 2010. "Stresses and Opportunities of Post-Communist Transformation: The Impact on Health," *Journal of Communist Studies and Transition Politics*, 26, 1, 80–100.

Rose, Richard and Mishler, William, 1994. "Mass Reaction to Regime Change in Eastern Europe: Polarization or Leaders and Laggards?," *British Journal of Political Science*, 24, 2, 159–182.

1996. "Representation and Leadership in Post-Communist Political Systems," *Journal of Communist Studies and Transition Politics*, 12, 2, 224–247.

2002. "Comparing Regime Support in Non-Democratic and Democratic Countries," *Democratization*, 9, 2, 1–20.

2009. "How Do Electors Respond to an Unfair Election?," *Post-Soviet Affairs*, 25, 2, 118–136.

2010. "Experience Versus Perception of Corruption: Russia as a Test Case," *Global Crime*, 11, 2, 145–163.

2010a. "A Supply–Demand Model of Party-System Institutionalization," *Party Politics*, 16, 6, 801–822.

Rose, Richard, Mishler, William and Haerpfer, Christian, 1998. *Democracy and Its Alternatives*. Baltimore: Johns Hopkins University Press.

Rose, Richard, Mishler, William and Munro, Neil, 2006. *Russia Transformed*. Cambridge: Cambridge University Press.

Rose, Richard and Mossawir, Harvé, 1967. "Voting and Elections: A Functional Analysis," *Political Studies*, 15, 2, 173–201.

Rose, Richard and Munro, Neil, 2002. *Elections Without Order: Russia's Challenge to Vladimir Putin*. Cambridge: Cambridge University Press.

2008. "Do Russians See Their Future in Europe or the CIS?," *Europe–Asia Studies*, 60, 1, 49–66.

2009. *Parties and Elections in New European Democracies*. Colchester, UK: ECPR Press.

Rose, Richard, Shin, Doh Chull and Munro, Neil, 1999. "Tensions Between the Democratic Ideal and Reality: South Korea." In Norris, 1999, 146–165.

Rose, Richard and Tikhomirov, Evgeny, 1993. "Who Grows Food in Russia and Eastern Europe?," *Post-Soviet Geography*, 34, 2, 111–126.

Rustow, Dankwart A., 1970. "Transitions to Democracy," *Comparative Politics*, 2, 337–363.

Rutland, Peter, 2008. "Putin's Economic Record: Is the Oil Boom Sustainable?," *Europe–Asia Studies*, 60, 6, 1051–1072.

Ryavec, Karl W., 2003. *Russian Bureaucracy: Power and Pathology*. Lanham, MD: Rowman and Littlefield.

Sachs, Jeffrey D. and Pistor, Katharina, eds., 1997. *The Rule of Law and Economic Reform in Russia*. Boulder: Westview Press.

Sakwa, Richard, 1996. *Russian Politics and Society*. London: Routledge, 2nd edn.

2002. *Russian Politics and Society*. London: Routledge, 3rd edn.

2008a. *Putin: Russia's Choice*. London: Routledge, 2nd edn.

2008b. *Russian Politics and Society*. London: Routledge, 4th edn.

Sartori, Giovanni, 1976. *Parties and Party Systems: A Framework for Analysis*. Cambridge: Cambridge University Press.

Schedler, Andreas, ed., 2006. *Electoral Authoritarianism: The Dynamics of Unfree Competition*. Boulder: Lynne Rienner.

2010. "Authoritarianism's Last Line of Defence," *Journal of Democracy*, 21, 1, 69–80.

Schumpeter, Joseph A., 1952. *Capitalism, Socialism and Democracy*. London: George Allen & Unwin, 4th edn.

Scott, James C., 1985. *Weapons of the Weak: Everyday Forms of Peasant Resistance*. New Haven: Yale University Press.

Sen, Amartya, 2006. *Identity and Violence: The Illusion of Destiny*. New York: W. W. Norton.

Shambaugh, David, 2008. *China's Communist Party: Atrophy and Adaptation*. Berkeley: University of California Press.

Shearer, David R., 2009. *Policing Stalin's Socialism: Repression and Social Order in the Soviet Union, 1924–1963*. New Haven: Yale University Press.

Shenfield, Stephen D., 2001. *Russian Fascism: Traditions, Tendencies, Movements*. Armonk, NY: M. E. Sharpe.

Shevchenko, Olga, 2001. "Bread and Circuses: Shifting Frames and Changing References in Ordinary Muscovites' Political Talk," *Communist and Post-Communist Studies*, 34, 1, 77–90.

Shevtsova, Lilia, 2005. *Putin's Russia: Myths and Realities*. Washington, DC: Carnegie Endowment for International Peace, 2nd edn.

Shi, Tianjian, 2008. "China: Democratic Values Supporting an Authoritarian System." In Yun-han Chu, Larry Diamond, Andrew J. Nathan and Doh Chull Shin, eds., *How East Asians View Democracy*. New York: Columbia University Press, 209–237.

Shlapentokh, Vladimir, 1987. *The Politics of Sociology in the Soviet Union*. Boulder: Westview Press.

1989. *Public and Private Life of the Soviet People*. New York: Oxford University Press.

2001. *A Normal Totalitarian Society: How the Soviet Union Functioned and How It Collapsed*. Armonk, NY: M. E. Sharpe.

2006. *Fear in Contemporary Society: Its Negative and Positive Effects*. Basingstoke: Palgrave Macmillan.

Silver, Brian D., 1987. "Political Beliefs of the Soviet Citizen: Sources of Support for Regime Norms." In Millar, 1987, 100–141.

Simon, Janos, 1998. "Popular Conceptions of Democracy in Postcommunist Europe." In S. H. Barnes and J. Simon, eds., *The Postcommunist Citizen*. Budapest: Erasmus Foundation and Institute for Political Science of the Hungarian Academy of Sciences, 79–112.

Smith, Benjamin R., 2005. "Life of the Party: The Origins of Regime Breakdown and Persistence Under Single-Party Rule," *World Politics*, 57, 3, 421–451.

Solnick, Steven L., 1998. *Stealing the State: Control and Collapse in Soviet Institutions*. Cambridge, MA: Harvard University Press.

Steenbergen, Marco and Jones, Bradford, 2002. "Modeling Multilevel Data Structures", *American Journal of Political Science*, 46, 1, 218–237.

Stokes, Susan C., ed., 2001. *Public Support for Market Reforms in New Democracies*. New York: Cambridge University Press.

2007. "Political Clientelism." In Carlos Boix and S. Stokes, eds., *The Oxford Handbook of Comparative Politics*. New York: Oxford University Press, 604–620.

Thornhill, John, 2009. "A Russia United by Anti-Westernism," *Financial Times*, 4 February.

Tompson, William, 2004. "The Russian Economy Under Vladimir Putin." In Cameron Ross, ed., *Russian Politics Under Putin*. Manchester: Manchester University Press, 114–132.

Treisman, Daniel, 2011. "Presidential Popularity in a Hybrid Regime: Russia Under Yeltsin and Putin", *American Journal of Political Science*.

UNICEF (United Nations Children's Fund), 2009. *Innocenti Social Monitor 2009*. Florence: Innocenti Research Centre Monee Project.

Vanhanen, Tatu, 2003. *Democratization: A Comparative Review of 170 Countries*. London: Routledge.

Vu, Tuong, 2010. "Studying the State Through State Formation," *World Politics*, 62, 1, 148–175.

Wädekin, Karl-Eugen, 1994. "Agriculture." In Archie Brown, Michael Kaser and Gerald S. Smith, eds., *The Cambridge Encyclopedia of Russia and the Former Soviet Union*. Cambridge: Cambridge University Press, 399–403.

Watson, Peggy, 1995. "Explaining Rising Mortality Among Men in Eastern Europe," *Social Science and Medicine*, 41, 923–934.

Watson, Roland, 2005. "I'll Be a Democrat – Well, Almost, Putin tells Bush." *The Times* (London), 25 February.

Way, Lucan A., 2005, "Authoritarian State Building and the Sources of Regime Competitiveness in the Fourth Wave," *World Politics*, 57, 2, 231–261.

Weatherford, M. Stephen, 1987. "How Does Government Performance Influence Political Support?," *Political Behavior*, 9, 1, 5–28.

Weber, Max, 1947. *The Theory of Social and Economic Organization*. Glencoe, IL: Free Press. Translated by A. M. Henderson and Talcott Parsons.

Wedel, Janine R., 1986. *The Private Poland*. New York: Facts on File.

Weil, Frederick D., 1987. "Cohorts, Regimes, and the Legitimation of Democracy: West Germany Since 1945," *American Sociological Review*, 52, 308–324.

　　1989. "The Sources and Structure of Legitimation in Western Democracies," *American Sociological Review*, 54, 4, 682–706.

White, Stephen, 1979. *Political Culture and Soviet Politics*. London: Macmillan.

　　1983. "Political Communications in the USSR: Letters to Party, State and Press," *Political Studies*, 31, 1, 43–60.

　　1996. *Russia Goes Dry: Alcohol, State and Society*. Cambridge: Cambridge University Press.

　　2006. "Russia and 'Europe': The Public Dimension." In R. Allison, S. White and M. Light, *Putin's Russia and the Enlarged Europe*. Oxford: Wiley Blackwell and Royal Institute of International Affairs, 130–159.

　　2009. "Is There a Pattern?," *Journal of Communist Studies and Transition Politics*, 25, 2–3, 396–412.

　　2010. "Classifying Russia's Politics." In S. White, R. Sakwa and H. E. Hale, eds., *Developments in Russian Politics 7*. Basingstoke: Palgrave Macmillan, 263–282.

　　2011. *Understanding Russian Politics*. Cambridge: Cambridge University Press.

White, Stephen, Rose, Richard and McAllister, Ian, 1997. *How Russia Votes*. Chatham, NJ: Chatham House.

Whitefield, Stephen, 2009. "Russian Citizens and Russian Democracy," *Post-Soviet Affairs*, 25, 2, 93–117.

Wigell, Mikael, 2008. "Mapping 'Hybrid Regimes': Regime Types and Concepts in Comparative Politics," *Democratization*, 15, 2, 230–250.

Wilson, Kenneth, 2006. "Party-System Development Under Putin," *Post-Soviet Affairs*, 22, 4, 314–348.

2009. "Party-System Reform in Democracy's Grey Zone: A Response to Moraski," *Government and Opposition*, 44, 2, 188–207.

Winiecki, Jan, 1988. *The Distorted World of Soviet-Type Economies.* London: Routledge.

World Bank, 2010a. *Russian Economic Report No. 22.* Washington, DC: World Bank.

2010b. *Russian Economic Report No. 23.* Washington, DC: World Bank.

Yakovlev, Alexander N., 2002. *A Century of Violence in Soviet Russia.* New Haven: Yale University Press.

Young, Peyton, 1998. *Individual Strategy and Social Structure: An Evolutionary Theory of Institutions.* Princeton: Princeton University Press.

Index

L = language (good)
Q = quote
R = reference (to lookup)
F = key fact

1.: R
): F
.: F
): F
1: R; F
-13: R; F
16: F/R
17: F
18: F
19: F; Q
21: F
6: F